# *Anglican Religious Life*

*A Year Book of Religious orders and
communities in the Anglican Communion,
and tertiaries, oblates, associates and
companions*

## *2008-2009*

Published by
**Canterbury Press Norwich**
a publishing imprint of The A & M Group Ltd *(a registered charity)*
9-17 St Albans Place, London N1 0NX
www.scm-canterburypress.co.uk

© Anglican Religious Communities 2007

*ARL 2008-2009* published August 2007

ISBN: 978-1-85311-814-2

*Agents for Canterbury Press outside the UK:*

Rainbow Book Agency Pty Ltd
303 Arthur Street, Fairfield
Victoria 3078
**Australia**
*Tel: 9481 6611 Fax: 9481 2371*

Church Stores
8 Robert Street
Ellerslie, Auckland 1005
**New Zealand**
*Tel: 649 525 1380  Fax: 649 525 1664*

Novalis Books
10 Lower Spadina Avenue
Suite 400
Toronto, ON M5U 2Z2
**Canada**
*Tel: 416 363 3303  Fax: 416 363 9409*

Westminster John Knox
100 Witherspoon Street
Louisville
KY 40202-1396
**USA**
*Tel: 800 227 2872  Fax: 800 227 5113*

Columba Bookstores
55A Spruce Avenue
Stillorgan Industrial Park
Blackrock, Co Dublin
**Republic of Ireland**
*Tel: 1 294 2556*
*Fax: 1 294 2564*
*Email: info@columba.ie*

Pearson South Africa
Pearson Education
PO Box 396
Cape Town 8000
**South Africa**
*Tel: 021 532 6000*

*for continental Europe:*
Durnell Marketing
2 Linden Close
Tunbridge Wells
Kent TN4 8HH
UK
*Tel: 01892 544272*
*Fax: 01892 511152*
*Email: mail@durnell.co.uk*

Hugh Dunphy, PO Box 413, Kingston 10, Jamaica, **West Indies**
*Tel: 926 4645  Fax: 968 1874*

Original line drawings by Sister Sheila CAH
The cover design is by Leigh Hurlock

# Contents

# Foreword
## by
## Most Revd John Sentamu, Archbishop of York

The metaphor of life as a journey is one with which we are all familiar. Whether it be travelling along a "rocky road" or life being just "plain sailing" the metaphor is easily accessible and can be applied to both the moment at hand as well as to our whole life, from birth to death.

So when we speak about life not as a general journey, but as a pilgrimage, then we need to reassess our meaning of what we our saying about life. Seeing life as a pilgrimage means saying something very particular about the journey, in both its meaning and its purpose.

A pilgrimage is a particular type of journey. Its purpose is not simply to get from A to B, although each pilgrimage would begin and end in a particular place. For the pilgrimage the starting place and end point are secondary to the purpose of the journey and the nature of the journey itself. Drawing closer to God through the act of the journey and arriving to pay homage in worship are at the heart of the pilgrim's endeavour. Robert Louis Stevenson's remark that "it is better to travel than arrive" does not apply here. In pilgrimage it is through the travel, through the act of drawing closer to God, that we are enabled to arrive, to offer more deeply our worship and praise

For members of Religious communities, the pilgrimage as a metaphor for life remains a telling analogy. The joys and travails of the journey are reflected in the community, but always there is a higher purpose being served, a drawing nearer to God along the journey of life until the final heavenly destination is reached.

In the spiritual life the pilgrimage can also be difficult. The hard road to Golgotha along our own Via Dolorosa must always be followed by the joys of walking the road to Emmaus with Christ as our companion. Yet in community we learn to travel not alone but as a band of pilgrims, brothers and sisters, united in our desire to reach our goal, sustaining one another along the path. So together we gaze at, and marvel at, the beauty of holiness; we break bread at table and share our common need; and we bear the heavy load of grief as those amongst us move on to that final part of the journey alone, lifted by our prayers.

Whilst much of the world chooses to live their lives as journey, those in Religious communities choose pilgrimage. It is through this journey of the road less travelled, but ever more valued, through these lives lived in Christ, that we re-discover anew the value of pilgrimage. We live no longer to ourselves, but recognise that Christ is the Way to be walked, the Truth to be told and the Life to be lived.

For the God of the Bible is a pilgrimage God who is forever journeying towards us.

# A Prayer for Vocations to the Religious Life

*Setting a particular Sunday each year as a Day of Prayer for Vocations to the Religious Life was begun in 1992. This is currently **The Fifth Sunday after Trinity**. The Collect for this Sunday has been printed in previous editions of the Anglican Religious Communities Year Book. All are also invited to pray each Friday for the life and work of the Religious communities in the Church, using the following prayer, written by a Little Brother of Francis, originally for communities in Australia and New Zealand.*

Lord Jesus Christ
in your great love you draw all people to yourself:
and in your wisdom you call us to your service.
We pray at this time you will kindle in the
hearts of men and women the desire to
follow you in the Religious life.
Give to those whom you call, grace to accept their vocation readily
and thankfully, to make the whole-hearted surrender which
you ask of them, and for love of you, to persevere to the end.
This we ask in your name.
Amen.

## We give thanks for the Religious Life in all its forms

1 Community of All Hallows *in the UK*
All Saints Sisters of the Poor *in the UK & the USA*
Society of the Precious Blood *in Lesotho, South Africa & the UK*
2 Community of the Holy Spirit *in the USA*
Community of St Mary *in Malawi, the Philippines & the USA*
3 Community of the Resurrection *in the UK*
Community of the Resurrection of Our Lord *in South Africa*
4 Community of Saint Francis & Society of Saint Francis *in Australia, Brazil,*
  *New Zealand, Papua New Guinea, the Solomon Islands, the UK & the USA*
Korean Franciscan Brotherhood & Korean Franciscan Sisterhood *in Korea*
Little Brothers of Francis *in Australia*
Society of the Franciscan Servants of Jesus & Mary *in the UK*
Third Order SSF *throughout the world*
5 Community of the Servants of the Will of God *in the UK*
Community of Sisters of the Church *in Australia, Canada, Solomon Islands & UK*
6 Brotherhood & Sisterhood of St Gregory *in the USA*
Christa Sevika Sangha *in Bangladesh*
7 Community of Jesus' Compassion *in South Africa*
Community of the Holy Name *in Lesotho, South Africa, Swaziland & the UK*
8 Society of the Servants of Jesus Christ *in Madagascar*
Order of Julian of Norwich *in the USA*
9 Community of St Denys *in the UK*
Community of the Divine Compassion *in Zimbabwe*
Society of the Sacred Advent *in Australia*
10 Community of St Laurence *in the UK*
Chita che Zita Renoyera (Holy Name Community) *in Zimbabwe; and* Chita che
Zvipo Zve Moto (Community of the Gifts of the Holy Fire) *in Zimbabwe*
11 Order of St Benedict *in independent Abbeys and Priories throughout the world*
Benedictine Community of Christ the King *in Australia*
Benedictine Community of the Holy Cross *in the UK*
Benedictine Community of Our Lady and St John *in the UK*
12 Community of the Holy Transfiguration *in Zimbabwe*
Community of the Transfiguration *in the Dominican Republic & the USA*
Oratory of the Good Shepherd *in Australia, north America, South Africa & the UK*
13 Community of Celebration *in the UK & the USA*
Community of the Glorious Ascension *in France & the UK*
Brotherhood of the Ascended Christ *in India*
14 Community of the Servants of the Cross *in the UK*
Order of the Holy Cross *in Canada, South Africa & the USA*
Society of the Holy Cross *in Korea*
Society of the Sacred Cross *in the UK*
15 Community of St Mary the Virgin *in the UK*
Society of Our Lady St Mary *in Canada*
Society of Our Lady of the Isles *in the UK*

*in the Church, and today we pray especially for:*

16 Order of the Teachers of the Children of God *in the USA*
Community of the Companions of Jesus the Good Shepherd *in the UK*
Community of the Good Shepherd *in Malaysia*
17 Melanesian Brotherhood *throughout the Pacific region*
Community of the Sisters of Melanesia *in the Solomon Islands*
18 Companions of St Luke - Benedictine *in the USA*
Company of Mission Priests *in the UK*
Order of the Community of the Paraclete *in the USA*
19 Order of the Holy Paraclete *in Ghana, South Africa, Swaziland & the UK*
Community of the Holy Name *in Australia*
20 Society of St Margaret *in Haiti, Sri Lanka, the UK & the USA*
Community of Nazareth *in Japan*
21 Community of St Clare *in the UK*
Little Sisters of St Clare *in the USA*
Order of St Helena *in the USA*
22 Community of the Sacred Passion *in the UK*
Community of St Mary of Nazareth and Calvary *in Tanzania & Zambia*
23 Community of Celebration *in the USA*
Community of St John the Evangelist *in the Republic of Ireland*
24 Community of St John Baptist *in the UK & the USA*
Worker Brothers & Sisters of the Holy Spirit
*in Australia, Canada, Haiti & the USA*
25 Community of St Paul *in Mozambique*
Society of St Paul *in the USA*
Sisterhood of the Holy Nativity *in the USA*
26 Order of St Anne *in the USA*
Community of the Sisters of the Love of God *in the UK*
27 Community of St John the Divine *in the UK*
Sisterhood of St John the Divine *in Canada*
Society of St John the Divine *in South Africa*
Society of St John the Evangelist *in the UK & the USA*
Sisters of Charity *in the UK & the USA*
28 Society of the Sacred Mission *in Australia, Lesotho, South Africa & the UK*
Sisters of the Incarnation *in Australia*
29 Community of St Michael & All Angels *in South Africa*
Community of St Peter (Woking) *in the UK*
Community of St Peter, Horbury *in the UK*
Society of the Sisters of Bethany *in the UK*
30 Community of St Andrew *in the UK*
Community of the Sacred Name *in Fiji, New Zealand & Tonga*
31 Congregation of the Sisters of the Visitation of Our Lady *in Papua New Guinea*
Community of the Blessed Lady Mary *in Zimbabwe*
Sisterhood of St Mary *in Bangladesh*

# News
# of
# Anglican
# Religious Life

# Even More Communities

The *Anglican Religious Communities Year Book* has become even bigger. This sixth edition has been re-titled as *Anglican Religious Life* because this issue includes full entries for a broader range of communities. The first section of the Directory still continues to record the traditional celibate communities and orders, but a new section is now included for communities whose members are not required to take a vow of celibacy. The introductory paragraphs to the sections clarify the important distinctions between the different types of community, but all are dedicated to a witness to the Christian Gospel and to promoting the values of love that it proclaims to the world. We hope readers will enjoy discovering the breadth and variety of Anglican Religious Life.

# A bit of a 'do' (or two) in CSC

*Sister Judith writes:*

The year 2007 began with a BANG for us as we celebrated Sister Scholastica's Platinum (yes, 70th) Profession Anniversary on 21 January. 'Schol', as she is affectionately known, was born in Sussex, but moved, aged eleven, with her family to Australia, when her father, Revd Percy Ferris, volunteered for mission work in the outback. Schol joined the community in Melbourne, was professed at Kilburn in 1937, and, apart from the war years, spent over fifty years in Australia. She held many offices including those of Head of School and eventually Provincial. On her 'retirement', she spent some years in the Solomon Islands. More than once, she was seen sitting on a roof on one of the houses in Tetete ni Kolivuti, hammering in nails in the tropical sun. It is significant that the sisters in the Solomons have called a house that we have founded this year, on the island of Isabel, St Scholastica's.

Schol had asked that our Chaplain General, Father Jonathan Ewer SSM, preside and preach on the great day. His excellent sermon was on the call of Religious as prophets and teachers (text on the web at *www.sistersofthechurch.org*), and was masterful in the way in which he said so much, but so discreetly that Schol was not in the

Sister Scholastica CSC

least embarrassed. The music was lovely and Hilda Mary danced with her usual exuberance and grace. Anita, as deacon, and our Ham convent chaplain, Nicholas Roberts, assisted at the altar.

A week or two later we had our quinquennial Visitation. Bishop Peter Price and the team were very impressed with Schol's agility when, on her ninety-fifth birthday, she rose and did an energetic jig in the refectory! Having been an athlete in her youth and champion hurdler, she was known as a novice to hurdle over the dustbins in Melbourne. You can't keep a good girl down!

Sister Sheila Julian's twenty-fifth profession anniversary was on 18 February and, at her request, we joined the congregation of St Richard's, Ham, for a festive liturgy to the obvious delight of priest and people. With long-standing links to that church, Sheila preached a quiet yet powerful homily, which wove the two communities together. She spoke of the multitude of small ways, sometimes judged insignificant, that she had noticed people making a difference to others' lives, and urged us to continue. Formerly a missionary with USPG, Sheila had met the Community in the Solomons, to which she returned for a time after profession.

We give thanks for this wonderful pair and for all that they pour into the Community, the Church and the world. Alleluia!"

# *Love Fulfilled*

In 2006, two communities reached the fulfilment of their earthly work. On 5 January 2006, Esther Mary CRJBS died, aged 96, having been professed 59 years. On 17 July following, Hilda OSEH died aged 98, after 64 years in profession.

The **Community of Reparation to Jesus in the Blessed Sacrament** had been founded in 1869 originally as a group of tertiaries who were to work with the poor in the parish of St Peter's, Vauxhall, in the docks area of London. Soon, however, several members asked to be trained as first order Religious by the Community of St John the Baptist at Clewer. The Vicar who had initiated the order moved to St Alphege's, Southwark, so it was in that parish that the first sisters worked amongst some of the poorest people in the capital, concentrating particularly on education. They shared the people's deprived conditions. With disease rife, typhoid, consumption and smallpox took their toll amongst professed and novices, and the sisterhood remained small, as few could maintain the life. Those who did stay were sustained by an increasingly rich prayer life, including devotions before the Blessed Sacrament, then considered an 'advanced' practice in the Church of England.

Under the third superior, Mother Faith, the community at last began to grow and their parish work took them to several parts of London. By 1945, there were over thirty sisters in profession. After the Second World War, however, with the community's main convent having suffered bomb damage, the sisters moved their mother house to Woking and explored becoming a more contemplative form of community life. In the event, this move did not encourage vocations. By the time they moved back to Southwark in 1957, the last profession had been received. Numbers gradually dwindled, and in 1980 the remaining sisters moved to live alongside CSJB to complete their witness.

The **Order of St Elizabeth of Hungary** had also been founded from a group of tertiaries in 1913. Its inspiration was Franciscan and, once fully established, the sisters were based in Redcliffe Gardens, Kensington. The simplicity of their life was marked by their having no invested funds so that their dependence on donations and what they earned was absolute. They grew quickly and established a branch house in Australia in 1928. Teaching became a primary work as was the provision of retreat facilities. By the late 1930s, there were thirty-six in profession.

As with CRJBS, vocations became fewer after the Second World War and work was eventually concentrated at the retreat house in Heathfield in Sussex. In 1993 the two remaining sisters came under the care of CSP in Woking.

For the witness of these two communities, faithful unto death, thanks be to God.

# *Triple Golden Jubilee*

In the spring of 2006 came a unique event for the Community of the Sacred Passion. Three sisters reached their Golden Jubilee on the same day. Sisters Dorothy, Thelma Mary and Mary Joan were professed together in 1956, and never before in the Community's history had a group all lived to celebrate such an occasion together.

*Mother Philippa writes*, "It is an event which cannot be repeated and so we had an impressive celebration. Our Vicar ensured that we had a very joyful service in our parish church with wonderful music, such as could never have been heard in Africa when the Sisters were originally professed, and in which we were supported by many members of the congregation. We also had the joy of having a retired missionary doctor with whom we worked, sharing the celebrations with us. We managed to accommodate our friends at home for a buffet meal after the service and we were grateful that our new home is so versatile spacewise."

# Developments in CMM

The Community of St Mary of Nazareth and Calvary, the community initiated by the Community of the Sacred Passion continues to grow and develop. They undertake a large variety of work. Some engage in traditional ministries such as teaching and nursing, but the Bishop of Tanga has asked some Sisters in his diocese to learn to drive and maintain tractors. They can thereby improve their own crops and pass on their skills to others. The community have been given a tractor and helping people with ploughing provides an opportunity to earn some money. The Sisters' milling machine also brings in money and it is a great help to local people who can now arrange to have their crops ground locally instead of facing huge transport costs.

In 2006, the Community saw another group of novices clothed, an event which took place in the new (as yet uncompleted) chapel as the old one is now too small for such gatherings. Of the life professions, one was of the first Sister trained by CMM to come from Zambia. She will now lead the CMM house in Zambia, founded there at the request of local Christians. Sister Jacqueline CSP, who attended the ceremony during her official three-week visit to CMM, and who also visited ten of the CMM houses in Tanzania, said that everywhere she went she saw 'new life and expression and great joy in the Gospel'.

*CMM sisters make final profession*

# Edgware celebrates 140 years

The foundation of the Edgware Community was established on 28 August 1866 when Mother Monnica (Hannah Skinner) made her solemn commitment under Life Vows. The 140th anniversary was celebrated on 26 August 2006 at Edgware with friends gathered and many other Communities represented. It was our pleasure to welcome Dr Peta Dunstan, from the Faculty of Divinity in Cambridge, who treated us to a most practical and encouraging homily, lifting the hearts of ourselves and our visiting Brothers and Sisters, confirming our worth and value in

*A photograph taken after the thanksgiving Eucharist for the 140th anniversary of the foundation of the Edgware Abbey community.*

today's society and Church.

During the Eucharist, we followed the custom of reading the letter which our Co-Founder, Father Henry Nihill, wrote to Mother Monnica on the eve of her profession, known as 'The Little Boat Letter'. A letter full of encouragement to a small frail group starting out, it epitomizes the spiritual and Benedictine ethos in which the Community has been grounded from its beginning, firmly rooted in the Love of God, and still ever relevant for life today as it was 140 years ago. A life lived through unconditional love in the joy of the Lord is one in which continuously to seek him, meet him and serve him in those we meet every day: the sick, the poor, the pilgrims; and with much thankfulness in the Lord, we go forward "ourselves your servants for Jesus's sake." (Little Boat letter)

# *In Search of the Lost*

The seven Brothers of the Melanesian Brotherhood killed on Guadalcanal, Solomon Islands, on the orders of the rebel leader, Harold Keke, were commemorated in Rome on 22 November, 2006, at a service led by the Archbishop of Canterbury, Dr Rowan Williams, himself a Companion of the Brotherhood. Assistant Head Brother Robin Lindsay and six brothers (Nathaniel Sado, Francis Tofi, Alfred Hill, Patteson Gatu, Tony Sirihi and Ini Paratabatu) had been murdered in April 2003. Nathaniel was the first to be killed, and the others, when they went to retrieve his body, met the same fate, some being first tortured as well. The Archbishop preached at the service and Father Richard Carter, former chaplain and member of the Brotherhood, told their story and gave testimony of the martyrs' lives.

The commemoration was arranged by the Community of Sant' Egidio, a lay organization of the Roman Catholic church, originally founded in 1968 to work among the poor and homeless in Rome, but now with 50,000 members worldwide dedicated to the wider goals of prayer, communicating the Gospel, solidarity with the poor, ecumenism and dialogue. The service was held at the Basilica of San Bartolomeo on the Isola Tiberina, an island in the river Tiber, a church dedicated in 2000 by Pope John Paul II to the modern martyrs of different denominations. Prominent in the Basilica is the ikon of the New Martyrs, painted by Renata Sciachi of the Sant' Egidio community. On it are portrayed martyrs of the Roman Catholic, Orthodox, Anglican and other Churches, including Archbishop Janani Luwum of Uganda (Anglican) **and** Archbishop Romero of El Salvador (Roman Catholic).

Dr Monica Attias, a member of the Sant' Egidio community, spent three years planning the event, from the time she first heard the story. She said she believed that the story of these martyrs crosses all Christian divides and unites all in love and service, for Christ calls us to be peacemakers.

Father Richard Carter has written a book, based on his own journals, recording the experiences of the Brothers and himself during the 'ethnic tension' in the Solomons at the time of the martyrdoms. Entitled *In Search of the Lost: the Death and Life of the Seven Peacemakers of the Melanesian Brotherhood*, it was launched at St Martin-in-the-Fields, Trafalgar Square, London, on 26 November 2006. Generously illustrated with photographs and maps, it is published by Canterbury Press (ISBN: 1-85311-780-3) and retails at £12.99.

# Holy Cross 150th Celebration

At Southwell Minster, on the 3 May 2007, about 600 people congregated to celebrate the 150th anniversary of the foundation of the Community of the Holy Cross. Fifteen bishops attended, as did about ninety members of Religious communities. The former Archbishop of York, the Rt Revd Dr David Hope, who is the Community's episcopal Visitor, presided at the eucharist which was concelebrated by the priests who regularly celebrate mass for the sisters at Holy Cross Convent, Rempstone. The address was given by the former Warden of the Community, Canon Thomas Christie. The music, which include Parry's 'I was glad', John of Portugal's 'Crux Fidelis' and Haydn's 'Te Deum' was sung by the choir of Southwell Minster, and the girls' choir and men from Lincoln Cathedral, and parts of the eucharist were sung in Latin plainchant. Many were interested to see the range of the sisters' contacts and the breadth of their support. Revd Mother Mary Luke said at the end of the service that the Community was astounded and humbled by the support for its celebration. The bishop of Southwell and Nottingham, the Rt Revd George Cassidy, had very kindly offered the use of his garden to erect two marquees in so that we could feed everyone. Although the weather at the start of the service was cloudy, cold and windy, by the time it had finished the sun had come out, which enabled everyone to enjoy sitting in the garden. Bishop David Hope said, "Today's wonderful celebration is a testimony to the dedication, tenacity and faithful witness of members of the Community through the years, and a clear demonstration of the need for a continuing prayerful attentiveness at the heart of the Church's life."

# RooT Reporting

In 2006 an excellent Conference on the monastic contribution to East/West unity was held in Oxford. Speakers included Father Aidan Nichols OP and Orthodox Sister Nadejda Owing. In 2007 separate day meetings were held on a regional basis. A 2008 conference is planned.

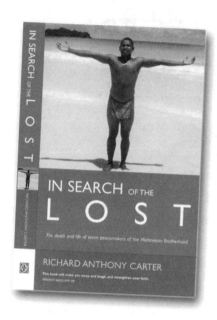

# Articles

# Brotherhood Boys Home
## by Father Monodeep Daniel BAC

The story of the Brotherhood Boys Home began one year ago. The nine boys of the street, who were living in the Brotherhood Night Shelter, had opted to leave the streets of Delhi and live in the Brotherhood House. Initially the House was small, but in 2005 we were able to get land and build a new building with good facilities for the children in Shahidnagar located just in the Delhi/Uttar Pradesh border. On 27 May 2006, Father Ian Weathrall, Chairman of Delhi Brotherhood Society, inaugurated the new building. They shifted into the building and were admitted to the Deenbandhu High School of the Delhi Brotherhood Society.

The Brotherhood Boys Home aims to set a new workable model at a micro level to rehabilitate the street children in Delhi. This model involves four phases: first, is the work at the contact point. Here the street educators contact the street children to build their capacities of awareness, possibilities, options, choice, dangers of street, issues of dignity etc. Second, if a boy on the street opts, he can join the Night Shelter, where he has the advantage of security, protection and facilities for toilets and nutrition. The Night Shelter has the routine programme for literacy, counselling and culture. Living at the Night Shelter also gives the boys the choice to leave the street life and live in the Home.

Those who shift to live in the Home are completely off the streets. This is the third phase. During the day they have to go to Deenbandhu School for formal education and to the St John's Centre for technical training. They also have a Rule to follow each day, which includes prayers, studies, food and games. The fourth phase will comprise of each boy being properly integrated into the mainstream of society, by having a job to earn a living, a family to support and will be able to access the civic provisions of bank, school, police associations etc.

The second thing is to give boys a spiritual formation. It is our hope that the boys will profit out of this formation in building and living a disciplined way of life. It might also challenge a few to embrace the Brotherhood as their vocation to serve God.

This springs out of the Brotherhood's experience over the last thirty-five years

*Some of the boys playing chess*

of ministry. The present growth of membership has been out of the old Children's Home where ten boys were nurtured. Eventually this Home closed down as the boys had grown up, but those who joined the Brotherhood started up this Boys Home once again.

Arjun, Karan, Yogesh Pandey, Usman Khan, Sanjay, Rudal, Mohit and Rohit presently live in the Brotherhood Boys Home. Mr. Anand, who himself was brought up in the previous Children's Home, is their caretaker. He lives with the boys. They rise at 5.30am in the morning and do some physical exercise. They then quickly get ready for the day. They have their prayers in the chapel, followed by breakfast. Then they go to school. Mohit goes to St. John's Centre for Automobile Mechanic training. Arjun has completed his training and has joined Bajaj Auto Company as an apprentice. They also have an English conversation class every day in the afternoon. Evening is engaged with prayers and dinner. They go to bed in time to rise early the next day.

Sunday is a bit different. The boys, along with their warden, go to St Francis Church in the morning. After lunch they all travel ten kilometres by bus and come to the Brotherhood House. They spend time in entertainment, games and join in Evensong with the Brethren. They have supper with the Brethren in the refectory. Thereafter, they return to the Boys Home with their warden by bus.

# What is a Tertiary?
## by Ken Norian TSSF
### Minister Provincial in the Americas of the
### Third Order of the Society of St Francis

What is a Tertiary? This is a question often asked since it is a term not in the vocabulary of most people. Tertiary has a Latin derivation indicating "third". Members of a Third Order are then, called Tertiaries.

So, what is a Third Order and, more specifically, The Third Order of the Society of Saint Francis? Why are people called to this Order? What do Tertiaries value about being Third Order Franciscans? The answer to these questions begins with Francis of Assisi who was called by God to rebuild the Church.

Francesco Bernadone was the son of a wealthy merchant who was born late in the 12th century in Italy. Through a powerful conversion experience Francis came to mirror the love of Christ and the living Gospel so closely that nearly everyone who met him wanted to follow his way of life. He realized that not everyone could or should take up a celibate life of poverty and homelessness, yet he recognized that people unable to do this were still drawn to serve God with deeply committed hearts and lives. Long before Francis was born, groups of men and women or ordinary secular walks of life were living under rule and vows as members of "Third Orders". Francis saw this as appropriate answer for many of his followers and so, over eight hundred years ago, the "Brothers and Sisters of Penance", later known as "Third Order" or "Secular" Franciscans came to be.

The Anglican Franciscan movement began in the United States, England, and India early in the twentieth century and merged into the Society of Saint Francis. The Third Order of the Society of Saint Francis is a fully independent order with its own Provincial and worldwide constitution, Rule, Principles and Statutes.

Tertiaries are no less committed that Friars or Sisters who live in community. Our vocation is lived out in a different and, some would say, more challenging way. We are not "wanna be" nuns or friars, a "pious guild" nor a devotional society. We are lay and clergy, single or in committed relationships, serving God as we are called, in the ordinary occupations of life. Because we are an Order, the shape of our lives is formed in the context of the Order's Principle and Rule.

There are three Aims of the Third Order that summarize our mission. First we seek to make our Lord known and loved everywhere. By word and example, Tertiaries witness to Christ in their daily lives. By prayer and sacrifice, we help forward God's work wherever He has called us.

We seek to spread the spirit of fellowship, love and harmony within the family of God. By working happily with people of different race, color, creed, education and opportunity, Tertiaries seek to break down the divisions in the world. We try to live in the spirit of the prayer written in the spirit of St. Francis: "Lord, make me an instrument of your peace."

We strive to live simply. Acknowledging that everything belongs to God, we seek to use His gifts wisely and to be good stewards of this fragile earth, never destroying or wasting what God has made. We provide the things necessary for ourselves and our families without demanding luxuries. We seek never to forget the needs of others.

Tertiaries seek to serve God through Prayer, Study and active work for the Kingdom. Tertiaries are called to prayerful lives -- of openness to God and to others. The Eucharist is the heart of our prayer. While Tertiaries give first place to the study of the Scriptures, we also seek to widen our understanding of the Church's mission, of our Franciscan vocation, and of God's world. Tertiaries seek to discover what God wants us to do. In our daily work and lives, we try to serve God and work for the good of others. The best service we can offer is to reflect the love of Christ, and to show his joy and peace to others by example.

Tertiaries seek to live their lives in a spirit of humility, love and joy. While most Tertiaries do not physically live together, we are truly a community that is knit together in community and prayer. We are called daily to share in an offering of prayer for each other. We rejoice in all of the marks of a Christian community - a rule, shared prayer, well wrought liturgies, a formation process of several years, shared stories, spiritual friendships and heroic pioneers like Francis and Clare. The mutual support we offer each other in all aspects of life, especially in ministry and prayer is most appreciated by members of the Third Order community. This support stems from the unconditional love and acceptance from others with similar commitments to seeking and serving Christ in all people. Tertiaries make a lifetime commitment to live a Rule of Life in company with the sisters and brothers in their Order.

If you are striving to be a peacemaker; feel called to action and contemplation; are yearning for a deeper relationship with God; passionate about social justice;

concerned about ecology, the poor and the marginalized then the Third Order may be a place where you can find a spiritual home. There are several thousand Anglican Tertiaries in many countries organized around five areas: the African Province; the Australian Province and Hong Kong; the European Province; the New Zealand Province and Solomon Islands; and the Province of the Americas.

As St. Francis of Assisi said at the time of his death: "God has shown me what was mine to do; may God show you what is yours to do."

# Two hundred years of monastic life: two communities celebrate centenaries
## by Sister Avis Mary SLG
## & Sister Mary David OSB

For two communities, the Benedictine Community at St Mary's Abbey at West Malling, Kent, and the Community of the Sisters of the Love of God at Fairacres, Oxford, September 2006 saw the culmination of celebrations of a centenary of monastic life.

### Foundation and early years

On 12 September 1906, ten sisters from what was to become the Malling community renewed their Religious profession, taking simple Benedictine vows and beginning the enclosed life at Baltonsborough in Somerset. The community had previously been a flourishing active sisterhood, founded in 1891 in North London, inspired in 1903 by the preaching of Abbot Aelred Carlyle to begin to adopt the Rule of St. Benedict. The life at Baltonsborough was poor, austere and hidden. Abbot Carlyle was Visitor until his conversion to Rome in 1913, but the real instructor in Benedictine life and worship was the chaplain, Father Frederick P. Vasey, until his death in 1931. The sisters moved to Malling in 1916, and as there had been Benedictine nuns at Malling from 1090 to 1538, this move set a seal upon their confidence in their Benedictine identity.

On the Feast of the Holy Cross 1906, two days after the Baltonborough sisters took Benedictine vows, three women began the Religious life in a small house in East Oxford, thus founding the Sisters of the Love of God, a community envisioned and brought together by the 'Cowley Fathers' (the Society of St. John the Evangelist, or SSJE), and in particular by Fr Hollings. SLG began in the Cowley district of Oxford, accommodated in first one, then in another, small house, until in 1911 they found their eventual home nearby, at what became the Convent of the Incarnation, Fairacres. Fr Hollings died suddenly in 1914, whereupon Fr Cary SSJE began to direct the community, remaining in post until his death in 1950. From the beginning, the community took its inspiration from Carmel. The sisters lived in poverty and simplicity, whitewashing the windows of their first little house as a sign of their 'enclosure'. Matins said corporately in the night at 2 a.m. was an important element in the sisters' vocation for most of their first century, until this eventually became too difficult to sustain. Life and prayer in the cell has always been central.

## The first half century

For the first five decades, Malling took its model of Benedictine life from the Roman Catholic Church. Abbot Aelred had insisted upon the Latin Office (with Matins at 2 a.m.), the Roman rite Mass and papal enclosure; furthermore, Roman devotional practice, ceremonial and austerities were adopted. Seen as marginal and even suspect, the community faced indifference and hostility from Anglican bishops and others, and so kept a low profile. SSJE was influential for Malling as well as for SLG, as trustees of the fund administering the Abbey and later as confessors and spiritual directors. Fr William O'Brien SSJE, who became warden of SLG after Fr Cary's death, also guided Malling through difficult times.

## Renewal and growth as the second half-century began

SLG's numbers rose constantly and steadily from the early beginnings, additional houses being founded in Hertfordshire in 1928 and East Sussex in 1935. SLG flourished in the 1960s and early 1970s, following some difficult years in the 1950s. Mother Mary Clare, in partnership with Father Gilbert Shaw (Warden 1964-1967), put her stamp upon the community's life, and her influence extended into the wider Church. SLG Press was begun in 1967, ecumenical contacts and contacts with other Religious communities were established, and the number of Sisters reached an all-time high. The solitary life was encouraged, and Bede House, intended at first as a lavra, opened at Staplehurst in Kent in 1967.

At Malling, too, these were years of renewal and growth and also of increasing confidence in the community's Anglican identity. Creative talents flowed into a new English liturgy, a new Abbey church, cloister and domestic wing, simplification of lifestyle, arts and crafts, organic gardening, new ecumenical contacts and a stream of new guests. The community had begun to feel more in control of its own affairs. The presence of Anglican Cistercian monks on the Abbey estate in Ewell Monastery meant that a chaplain was no longer needed. Local clergy began to celebrate on a rota, as was also now the case for SLG, and for Malling a happier relationship with the diocese was established through Bishop David Say.

## Spirituality and tradition

SLG draws its inspiration, if not its Rule (which is relatively modern), from Carmel, but is also open to many other influences, absorbing much of the Benedictine tradition of the centrality of the Divine Office as the opus Dei or work of God. SLG was unusual for a contemplative community in founding other smaller houses which were not autonomous-in addition to the properties already mentioned, which have now closed, SLG ran a community house for over ten years at a property offered for the purpose in New Zealand. The practice of "rotating" sisters fairly regularly between houses was a successful adjunct to SLG's tradition of enclosure, the strictness of which has been modified over time.

Malling's emphasis has been on Benedictine life taken as a whole-seeking God through corporate worship, lectio divina, prayer, work and a strong common life-with stability and perseverance in these being the chief source of nourishment for the sisters' personal prayer lives. The community differed slightly from the Benedictine norm, in that no foundation was made and scholarship was not seen as a priority: the sisters' historical, musical and artistic talents were poured into liturgical renewal or eclipsed by work demands.

### Outside contacts

For both SLG and Malling, the initial strict enclosure and commitment to the 'hidden life' meant that for decades there were, for example, few local or diocesan contacts, and even fewer with other Anglican Religious. This began to change for SLG in the 1950s, when a small house was bought on the edge of the property to accommodate guests, particularly associates. Mother Mary Clare went to Malling on a journey of discovery, coming back with an ideal for SLG's Divine Office drawn from the Benedictine choir Office. For Malling, the strict enclosure changed somewhat later. Towards the end of the 1980s, sisters began to attend meetings, conferences and other events, and local contacts began in earnest in 1990, with celebrations and open days for the Abbey's ninth centenary.

### Celebrations in 2006, and looking to the future

2006 was a year of blessing for both communities. Each held a variety of celebratory days for friends, neighbours, Religious, local clergy, oblates, associates, and sisters' families. For SLG, the culmination was on 14 September; for Malling, two days earlier. Dr Rowan Williams, Archbishop of Canterbury, spent time with each community on its respective day. In this centenary year, each community experienced a certain fragility through reduced numbers and increased age, yet this did not detract from a general sense of thanksgiving, and each reaffirmed the commitment to the priorities of worship, prayer and the common life, and the importance of perseverance, stability, gospel values and the virtue of hope.

*Abbess Mary John of Malling Abbey & Mother Rosemary SLG*

# Ministering to Pilgrims
## by Sister Joan Michael SSM

The year 2006 saw the seventy-fifth anniversary of the Translation of Our Lady of Walsingham from the parish church to the newly-built Holy House. For nine years, Father Alfred Hope Patten had worked long and hard to create a place for pilgrims from Britain and abroad to visit 'England's Nazareth'. Father Hope Patten knew that there was a ministry there for Religious Sisters. Several attempts were made to establish this, from an attempt at a brand new community to groups from well-established Orders. For various reasons they all had to withdraw and Walsingham was, in 1947, without Sisters.

The Sisters of the Society of St. Margaret, with their maxim 'the impossible must be done', responded to the priest's urgent request and a branch house of St. Saviour's Priory was set up. The first three Sisters originally lived in part of the old Pilgrim Hospice. Their ministry was twofold: there was work in the village, in the church and local homes, especially teaching the children. Then there was the pilgrim work: taking bookings, allocating and cleaning rooms, laundry, preparing and serving meals; and all with the number of pilgrims steadily growing. As such a task was impossible for just three Sisters, many villagers came to work at the Hospice. Some had pilgrims to stay in their own homes when accommodation ran out, and some took on tasks such as of laundry. It was hard work and much organising - but it brought close contact between the Sisters and the local people. The Sisters were also responsible for the sacristy work at the Shrine (as they were for the parish church too), preparing for Masses (no concelebrations in those days) and doing all the Shrine laundry.

In 1955 the Sisters were sufficiently part of the pilgrimage scene for the branch house to become an autonomous house of the Society, and the Bishop of Norwich installed the first Superior. Now the community could receive and train its own novices and the Society received a centenary gift of a house in England's Nazareth, where the truth of the Incarnation could be proclaimed.

However, as Sisters increased so did the number the pilgrims, and perhaps inevitably the ministry of the Sisters changed. The pilgrim's Hospice and other added buildings could now accommodate over two hundred pilgrims in residence, so the work multiplied beyond our capacity. The bookings, the housework, the laundry, the kitchen and refectory, all of which now have their own office and staff, no longer involve any Sisters, although the Sisters still do the main sacristy laundry. Until recently they have been responsible for all the sacristy work, but now there is a secular Sacristan, with four Sisters helping on a rota basis. This is very important as the pilgrimage programme depends on an efficiently run sacristy. As the Shrine has more than fifteen altars, one for each mystery of the Rosary, there can be a good number of Masses going on at any one time, or a quick change over at half-hourly intervals. The Pilgrim Masses - when all the parish groups in at any one time worship together, an essential element of pilgrimage - can have twenty or so concelebrants, all with matching vestments.

Another 'must' at a pilgrimage is Sprinkling at the Well. Several other Sisters, beside the sacristans, are involved in this and are available should a pilgrim wish to talk or be in need of any spiritual help, or simply just want a practical enquiry answered. Our ministry is mainly to be there, to be available and to listen. Every pilgrim has a different story to tell, but then so did Chaucer's pilgrims. Every pilgrim, it seems, comes with different expectation or sometimes none. Some are full of faith, gratitude and hope; some are sceptical; some are just open for God to act. All, or so it seems, are given something; companionship, relaxation, refreshment, healing or renewal. In my experience, the vast majority of pilgrims intend to come back and they feel that they never have long enough. They would not because God's love and generosity is as abundant as the flowing water from the Well.

Just over ten years ago, the Shrine opened an Education Department, and now, as 'pilgrimage' is on the school curriculum, school groups come to experience it for themselves and Sisters are often involved in this, having a "Sister slot" in the crowded day.  There is now a Youth Pilgrimage in August, the Children's Pilgrimage in Lent and more recently the Young Adults' and the Family Pilgrimages. Sisters are involved in different ways in all of these, so covering all age groups. As is clear from this, we do come into contact with thousands of pilgrims each year but we may only speak to a person once. This is a very difficult ministry in that you cannot easily go back and sort out any mistakes you might make. Of course, sometimes a pilgrim may ask to keep in touch or seek out the same Sister on another visit, but we cannot depend on it.

All this may have left the reader breathless. It does have that effect, but we have our Priory next door to the Shrine, where the full Divine Office, daily Mass and prayer go on and these undergird our own ministry. But in addition, we are able to welcome pilgrims to our own chapel, a haven of peace, after the bustle of the Shrine, to share in our Office or Mass - or simply to be in the silent Presence of Our Lord in the Blessed Sacrament.

*Making contact*

# The Lightness of the Little Boat

## by Petà Dunstan (a Companion SSF)

### Adapted from a sermon preached at Edgware Abbey on 26 August 2006

I have always had a bit of difficulty with the saying, "My yoke is easy and my burden light." [Matthew 11:30]   For life is very often not easy - we have to contend with disappointments and frustrations, and sometimes the terrible pain of bereavement and suffering, not just for ourselves but also for those we love.  Being a Christian in an age of secularism and materialism does not feel very easy.  There's much at first sight over which to be anxious in our society and our world, from war and terrorism to poverty to devastation from natural catastrophes.  In our own lives, we have to face challenges and worries that are a burden to us.

Yet we know the Bible has treasure for us for all times - and this phrase about the yoke and the burden must mean more than the surface piety.  So how can we find its relevance for us today?   I want to explore this by considering two things: community and smallness.

There was a stimulating exchange of views on the BBC's website recently.   In response to the suggestion that crime rates might have dropped in London and so one could now leave the front door unlocked, many strongly disagreed.   But one person added that her parents were able to leave their door unlocked when going out.  The reason?  'They live in an area where everyone knows each other and looks out for one another.'  Yet such areas are fewer today.

The comment was a reminder of how isolated we have all become from our neighbours: this lack of contact impoverishes our lives.  The model for relationship today is very much the object and the onlooker.  You are either looked at or you are an observer.  We read about celebrities in magazines and think we know them.  We feel part of their lives even though we have never met them.  But of course it's a mirage: they don't know us and we don't know them.  We do the same with soap operas, where the drama engages us so much that it is difficult to remember that it is not true, but a fiction.  Then there is Big Brother: so addictive because we see a group of people and get to know their thoughts, their weaknesses, their humour, their eccentricities - all without revealing a single thing about ourselves.

All this is the *faux*-intimacy model presented by our society.  You are either the person observed, who never knows anything about those looking on; or you are the onlooker, anonymous, in the shadows, never having to reveal any vulnerability.

These relationships are hollow constructions.  The stars of Big Brother, however well we know their foibles, will not be there when we are in trouble or needing a helping hand.  These are not real relationships.  Yet it is these very models that lure our society into a superficial and false view of community.

Christianity offers us a different vision: a difficult one to put into practice as we have to make ourselves vulnerable.   Nevertheless, it is a real model for relationship.  We have a mutual interaction with the other person.  We are there for them in good times and also in bad.  Sometimes it is painful, as we quarrel and get annoyed;

sometimes we are let down. But our vulnerability brings us the reward of a solid connection and real love, and this type of relationship is the building block of community. Our society needs to rediscover this sense of true community if we are to face the problems of the future: climate change, the exhaustion of oil reserves, inter-religious conflict, and so on.

That is why community matters today - and it is one of the significant reasons that Religious Life matters. For Religious are beacons of this truth about relationship and community: they are a living sign and a reminder that we can all achieve more if we work together than we can acting individually. We may not all be called to the Religious Life, but Religious remind us of how important this dimension of our Christian commitment is. If we put this into practice, then the yoke can truly become easier and the burden lighter, because it is shared in love.

But if this is the way forward, there is another question that follows: in this case, why does God leave us so small and fragile? This is where it would be relevant to turn to a letter of the founder of the Edgware community, Father Nihill, written to Mother Monnica. One phrase stands out for me: "Yet the little boat has sometimes lived when the mighty ship has gone down ..." It is easy when we are in pessimistic mood to assume that smallness means weakness and probable failure. We live in a culture where size does seem to matter and it is easy to be discouraged if we feel we are part of something small. So we judge ourselves as not being of consequence or of influence and we resign ourselves to being able to achieve very little. Yet all things that are of influence begin small. The Christian church was tiny in apostolic times. The adherents of the faith were few: but we can now see that, far from fragile, they had enormous strength. When Father Nihill and Mother Monnica founded the Edgware community in 1866, it was insecure, untried, seemingly weak. The times were difficult with suspicion and opposition and the few sisters had little means to counteract hostile propaganda. Yet, 140 years later, the Community of St Mary of the Cross still has life and a future.

It could be argued that numbers would be of great assistance in some ways: the more sisters, the more work could be done, the more impact could be made. Yet this can also bring remoteness and lack of cohesion. Think of an office: it is much easier to work in a small friendly group than in an anonymous large organization where you see faces but do not know who they are. And maybe, just maybe, what our culture needs now is not large groups transforming social problems but small ones working quietly to revolutionise the way we relate. The little boat may indeed reach its destination while the big ship will go aground. Social cohesion will not come with national government initiatives, but by people talking and relating to their neighbours. Small steps can spread a new consciousness where big campaigns meet cynicism. These days, a one-to-one conversation will be more effective than a mass movement because we are all rightly suspicious of the manipulation of advertising and spin. Whether Religious or parish, communities today have mobility, flexibility, an intimacy that can be a force for good. Instead of seeing ourselves then as weak and insignificant, we should recapture a sense of hope: never let us believe there is no potential for the future. Whether we are many or few, we can still strive for the Kingdom and be channels of God's grace in the world. In the knowledge of that trust, the yoke really can be easier and the burden lighter.

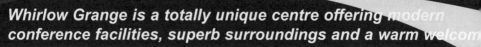

# Directory of traditional celibate Religious Orders and Communities

# Section 1

**R**eligious communities in this section are those whose members take the traditional vows, including celibacy. For many, these are the 'evangelical counsels' of chastity, poverty and obedience. In the Benedictine tradition, the three vows are stability, obedience and conversion of life, celibacy being an integral part of the third vow.

These celibate communities may be involved in apostolic works or be primarily enclosed and contemplative. They may wear traditional habits or modern dress. However, their members all take the traditional Religious vows. In the Episcopal Church of the USA, these communities are referred to in the canons as 'Religious Orders'.

There are an estimated 2,395 celibate Religious in the Anglican Communion, (1,075 men and 1,320 women).

The approximate regional totals are:

Africa: 365   (Men 40, Women 325)

Asia: 80   (Men 15, Women 65)

Australasia & Pacific: 1005   (Men 780, Women 225)

Europe: 605   (Men 135, Women 470)

North & South America & Caribbean: 340   (Men 105, Women 235)

### International telephoning

Telephone numbers in this directory are listed as used within the country concerned. To use them internationally, first dial the international code (usually 00) followed by the country code (see list below).

| | | | | | |
|---|---|---|---|---|---|
| Australia | + 61 | Haiti | + 509 | Solomon Islands | + 677 |
| Bangladesh | + 880 | India | + 91 | South Africa | + 27 |
| Belgium | + 32 | Republic of Ireland | + 353 | Swaziland | + 268 |
| Brazil | + 55 | Japan | + 81 | Tanzania | + 255 |
| Canada | + 1 | Korea | + 82 | UK | + 44 |
| Fiji | + 679 | Lesotho | + 266 | USA | + 1 |
| France | + 33 | New Zealand | + 64 | | |
| Ghana | + 233 | PNG | + 675 | | |

# Society of All Saints Sisters of the Poor

## ASSP

*Founded 1851*

All Saints Convent
St Mary's Road
Oxford
OX4 1RU
UK
Tel: 01865 249127
Fax: 01865 726547
Email:
admin@socallss.co.uk

**Mattins**  6.30 am

**Terce or Eucharist**
9.00 am

**Eucharist**
12.00 noon
or **Midday Office**
12.15pm

**Vespers**  5.30 pm

**Compline**  8.00 pm

Variations on Sundays,
Saturdays
& major festivals

**Office book**
ASSP Office, based on
Anglican Office Book 1980

We believe we are called to be alongside the homeless and unemployed, the sick, the dying, the bereaved, the old and lonely - any who welcome the friendship we offer as companions journeying together.

In Oxford the community has the oversight of St John's Home, a residential home for elderly women and men. It has pioneered Helen and Douglas House, offering respite and end-of-life care for children with life-shortening conditions and support for their families. The Porch Steppin' Stone Centre for homeless and vulnerably-housed people provides support and an opportunity for change. These are both independent charities associated with All Saints. Hospitality, lay and ordained ministry and interfaith relations are some of the ways we live out our calling. At the centre of this activity, and undergirding it, is the daily round of celebrating the liturgy together, with time to set aside for prayer, reading, and waiting upon God. We also give time for one another, respecting and cherishing each other. It is only in being with God and with one another, amidst all our activity, that we come to know the true purpose of our lives.

Sister Helen Mary ASSP
*(Community Leader, assumed office 9 March 2006)*
Sister Frances Dominica ASSP *(Assistant)*

| | |
|---|---|
| Sister Margaret | Sister Ann Frances |
| Sister Helen | Sister Margaret Anne |
| Sister Jean Margaret | *(Novice Guardian, priest)* |
| Sister Mary Julian | Novices: 2 |

**Obituaries**
13 Oct 2006         Sister Elisabeth May, aged 90,
                                        professed 63 years

**Associates**
Those in sympathy with the aims of the community are invited to become Associates or Priest Friends.

**Community Publication**
*New Venture*, published annually in November.   Order from the Society of All Saints.

**Community Wares**
The Embroiderers make, repair and remount vestments, frontals etc.

**Bishop Visitor:** Rt Revd John Bone

**Registered Charity:** No. 228383

**Other Addresses**
All Saints, 19 Mulready Walk, Apsley, Hemel Hempstead, HP3 9FS, UK
*Tel & fax: 01442 243447*

St John's Home *(for the elderly)*, St Mary's Road, Oxford OX4 1QE, UK
*Tel: 01865 247725     Fax: 01865 247920     Email: admin@st_johns_home.org*

All Saints Embroidery, All Saints Convent, St Mary's Road, Oxford OX4 1RU, UK,
*Tel: 01865 248627*

**Associated Houses**
Helen and Douglas House, 14a Magdalen Road, Oxford OX4 1RW, UK
*Tel: 01865 794749     Fax: 01865 202702*
*Email: admin@helenanddouglas.org.uk     Website: www.helenanddouglas.org.uk*
Registered Charity No: 1085951

The Porch, All Saints Convent, St Mary's Road, Oxford OX4 1RU, UK
*Tel: 01865 728545     Fax: 01865 792231*
*Email: info@theporch.fsbusiness.co.uk     Website: www.theporch.org.uk*
Registered Charity No: 1089612

**Community History & Books**
Peter Mayhew, *All Saints: Birth & Growth of a Community*, ASSP, Oxford, 1987.

Kay Syrad, *A Breath of Heaven: All Saints Convalescent Hospital, Eastbourne, 1869-1959*,
Rosewell Publishing, St Leonard's on Sea, 2002.
   [This is the history of All Saints Convalescent Hospital, Eastbourne, started by our
Mother Foundress in 1869 and run by the community until 1959.]

Sister Frances Dominica ASSP, *Just My Reflection: Helping families to do things their
own way when their child dies*, Darton, Longman & Todd, London, 2nd ed 2007, £6.50.

*Behind the big red door: the story of Helen House*, Golden Cup Printing Co, Oxford,
2006, £12.00

**Guest and Retreat Facilities**
New guest house with six en-suite rooms, including one double and one twin, and
meeting room for up to fifteen people, both with self-catering facilities.

*ASSP sisters with their Bishop Visitor, Rt Revd John Bone.*

# The Society of All Saints Sisters of the Poor

Founded 1851

All Saints Convent
PO Box 3127
Catonsville
MD 21228-0127
USA

Tel: 410 747 4104
Fax: 410 747 3321

**Website:** www.
ASSPconvent.org

**Meditation** *6.00 am*

**Lauds** *6.30 am*

**Eucharist** *7.00 am*

**Terce** *9.30 am*

**Sext** *12.00 noon*

**None** *3.00 pm*

**Vespers** *5.00 pm*

**Compline** *8.30 pm*

**Office Book**
*The Monastic Diurnal
adapted to our use*

All Saints is a traditional Community desiring to uphold orthodox Christian faith and morality, and to support the Apostolic tradition in ministry and practice. We are united by our common commitment to the Lord Jesus Christ, and by our desire to live for Him. Within that unity there is great diversity both in our personalities and our talents. In giving these as an offering to the Lord, our communal life is enhanced.

Founded in London, three Sisters came to Baltimore, Maryland, in 1872, at the request of the Rector of Mount Calvary Church. The American sisterhood became an independent House in 1890.

The daily Eucharist is the center of our life. The six-fold Divine Office and our times of personal prayer enable us to pour forth Christ's love to others, in all of our works. Hospitality is an important aspect of our various houses. We also give retreats and missions of various types both at the Convent and elsewhere. Training for a vocation to the sisterhood begins with a month's Observership, then Postulancy and Novitiate. Three years under Junior Vows precede Life Profession.

THE REVEREND MOTHER CHRISTINA OF ALL SAINTS
*(Mother Superior, assumed office 2005)*
THE SISTER EMILY ANN OF ALL SAINTS *(Assistant Superior)*

| | |
|---|---|
| Sister Virginia | Sister Julia Mary |
| *(sometime Mother)* | Sister Mary Joan |
| Sister Hannah | Sister Jane Teresa |
| Sister Barbara Ann | Sister Mary Charles |
| Sister Elaine | Sister Margaret |
| Sister Catherine Grace | Sister Monica |
| *(sometime Mother)* | Novices: 1 |
| Sister Elizabeth | |

EDITOR'S NOTE: *The Community uses no abbreviations of the title of the Society. Sisters put 'of All Saints' after their names.*

### Associates and Fellowship
The All Saints Sisters offer two forms of association. These are *The Associates* and *The Fellowship of All Saints*. Both groups follow a Rule of Life.

### Community Publications
*New Every Morning* - a photographic journal featuring pictures of the Convent and Sisters.
*Beakless Bluebirds and Featherless Penguins* - a nature/non-fiction book.

*All Saints Convent Scriptorium* - a catalog featuring greeting cars for sale and other items.

*The Illuminating Tale of Three Old Monks and a Very Bad Boy* - a story to illuminate, more suitable for adults.

For these, contact *The Scriptorium* at All Saints Convent.

### Community Wares

*The Scriptorium* produces holy cards and greetings cards, notes and occasional creations by the Sisters.

### Addresses

St Gabriel's Retreat House, PO Box 3106, Catonsville, MD 21228-0106, USA
        *Tel: 410 747 6767*
St Anna's House, 115 North Van Pelt Street, Philadelphia, PA 19103-1195, USA
        *Tel: 215 665 8889*
The Joseph Richey Hospice, 838 North Eutaw Street, Baltimore, MD 21201, USA
        *Tel: 410 523 2150*

### Guest and Retreat Facilities

While no fees are set, the primary source of income is derived from the donations of those guests who are able to pay.

ST GABRIEL'S RETREAT HOUSE - address above.

THE GUEST WING, ALL SAINTS CONVENT - address above.

This is located inside the Convent itself. It is a designated area for female visitors offering nine private bedrooms and shared bathrooms. Meals are in a guest dining room and visitors are encouraged to attend the Eucharist and the Divine Office and enter into the stillness of the Sisters' life.

### Most convenient time to telephone

The telephone is usually answered daily between:
        10.00 am - 11.45 am, 2.00 pm - 2.45 pm, 3.30 pm - 4.45 pm EST/EDT

**Bishop Visitor:** The Rt Revd Donald J Parsons

*The Sister Barbara Ann of All Saints at illustration.*

# Brotherhood of the Ascended Christ

## BAC

*Founded 1877*

*Brotherhood House*
*7 Court Lane*
*Delhi* 11054
*INDIA*
Tel: 11 2396 8515
or  11 2393 1432
Fax: 11 2398 1025
Email: mono@
del2.vsnl.net.in

*Morning Worship &*
*Eucharist*
*6.30 am*

*Forenoon Prayer (Terce)*
*8.30 am*

*Midday Prayer (Sext)*
*12.45 pm*

*Afternoon Prayer (None)*
*3.50 pm*

*Evening Worship*
*7.30 pm*

*Night Prayer (Compline)*
*9.10 pm*

Today, the Brotherhood has one bishop, four presbyters, one lay-brother and one lay-probationer who belong to the Church of North India. Since the earliest days, the Brotherhood has had a concern for serving the poor and underprivileged. In 1975, the Delhi Brotherhood Society was set up to organise social development projects in the poorer parts of Delhi. The work and social outreach of the Brotherhood is with and not for the poor of Delhi. The Brotherhood has initiated programmes of community health, education, vocational training and programmes for street and working children.

IAN WEATHRALL BAC
*(Head, assumed office 27 March 2004)*
COLLIN THEODORE BAC *(Assistant Head)*

Monodeep Daniel
Solomon George         *Novices:* 1
Raju George              *Postulants:* 2

### Associates and Companions
There are twenty-six Presbyter Associates and eight Lay Companions who follow a simple Rule of Life adapted to their individual conditions.

### Community Publication
Annual Newsletter and Report (free of charge).

### Community History
Constance M Millington, *"Whether we be many or few": A History of the Cambridge/Delhi Brotherhood*, Asian Trading Corporation, Bangalore, 1999
*Available from:* SPCK, Partnership House, 167 Waterloo Road, London SE1 8XA

### Guest and Retreat Facilities
The Brotherhood House at Court Lane has a large garden and well-stocked library. It is used as a centre for retreats, quiet days and conferences. The small Guest Wing receives visitors from all over the world.

*Most convenient time to telephone:*
 7.30 am - 8.30 am, 4 pm - 5 pm   (Indian Standard Time)

### Office Book
The Church of North India Book of Worship & Lesser Hours & Night Prayer (BAC)

*Bishop Visitor:* Rt Revd E W Talibuddin

# Chama cha Mariamu Mtakatifu

## (Community of St Mary of Nazareth and Calvary)

# CMM

*Founded 1946*

*The Convent Kilimani*
*PO Box 502*
*Masasi, Mtwara Region*
*TANZANIA*

Tel: 023 251 0126

**Morning Prayer**
*5.30 am*

**Mass**
*6.30 am*

**Midday Prayer**
*12.30 pm*

**Evening Prayer**
*3.00 pm*

**Compline**
*8.30 pm*

**Office Book**
*Zanzibar Prayer Book*
*(Swahili) &*
*The Daily Office SSF*

The Community was founded by the former Bishop of Masasi, Rt Revd William Vincent Lucas, in 1946 and was brought up by the Sisters of the Community of the Sacred Passion until 1968, when we had our first Reverend Mother.

We are seeking to serve God by living the three vows of Poverty, Chastity and Obedience in the community in the spirit of the Blessed Virgin Mary. The daily life of the community is centred around the daily Office and the Eucharist. We are an international Community; we accept girls and women from any diocese and any country. Because of the large number of novices, the novitiate is in two places for training, Sayuni and Masasi.

The Sisters work in primary schools and hospitals, and teach Religious Education in Sunday schools. We have Kindergarten schools and run development groups for girls and women. Some Sisters serve the needy, visit the sick and prisoners. Through this daily work, we serve God and try to bring people to know him.

SISTER GLORIA PRISCA CMM
*Revd Mother Superior, assumed office 22 May 2004)*
SISTER HELEN CMM (*Sister Superior, Mother House*)
SISTER MARTHA BRIJITA CMM
*(Sister Superior, Northern Zone)*

| | |
|---|---|
| Sister May Elizabeth | Sister Berita |
| Sister Magdalene | Sister Mercy |
| Sister Rehema | Sister Lidia |
| Sister Cesilia | Sister Stella |
| Sister Ethel Mary | Sister Agnes Margaret |
| Sister Neema | Sister Marina Felistas |
| Sister Ester | Sister Jane |
| Sister Christina | Sister Rabeca |
| Sister Tabitha | Sister Dorothy |
| Sister Eunice Mary | Sister Perpetua |
| Sister Joy | Sister Jenifer |
| Sister Franciska | Sister Anjelina |
| Sister Anjela | Sister Julia Rehema |
| Sister Anna | Sister Joceline Florence |
| Sister Priska | Sister Jane Rose |
| Sister Nesta | Sister Susana Skolastika |
| Sister Bertha Martha | Sister Anna Beatrice |
| Sister Aneth | Sister Mariamu Upendo |
| Sister Mary | Sister Josephine Joyce |
| Sister Agatha | Sister Skolastika Mercy |
| Sister Lucy | Sister Mary Priska |

Sister Paulina Anna
Sister Janet Margaret
Sister Thekla Elizabeth
Sister Janet Elizabeth
Sister Edna Joana
Sister Josephine Brijita
Sister Daines Charity
Sister Agnes Edna
Sister Jane Felistas
Sister Asnath Isabela
Sister Ethy Nyambeku
Sister Vumilia Imelda
Sister Anna Mariamu
Sister Debora Skolastika
Sister Foibe Edina
Sister Veronika Modesta
Sister Hariet Helena

Sister Hongera Mariamu
Sister Lulu Lois
Sister Martha Anjelina
Sister Lucy Lois
Sister Penina Skolastika
Sister Anet Olivia
Sister Roda Rahel
Sister Edith Natalia
Sister Hariet
Sister Victoria
Sister Violet Jacqueline
Sister Debora Dorothy
Sister Joyce
Sister Nesta Sophia
Sister Lea Felicia
Sister Dokas Paulina
Sister Hongera Elizabeth

Sister Edith Grace
Sister Elizabet Getrude
Sister Bernadine Jane
Sister Philippa Sapelo
Sister Joana Patricia
Sister Jessie Mary
Sister Veronika
Sister Imani
Sister Antonia Tereza

*Novices:* 29
*Postulants:* 6

## Obituaries

20 Feb 2006    Sister Jessie, aged 78, professed 57 years,
one of the founding sisters, and Novice Mistress 1968-72

## Community Wares

Vestments, altar breads, agriculture products, cattle products, crafts, candles.

## Bishop Visitor

Rt Revd Patrick P Mwachiko, Bishop of Masasi

## Other addresses

PO Box 116, Newala,
Mtwara Region,
TANZANIA
*Tel: 023 2410222*

PO Box 162, Mtwara,
TANZANIA
*Tel: 023 2333587*

PO Box 45, Tanga,
TANZANIA
*Tel: 027 2643205*

PO Box 195, Korogwe,
Tanga Region,
TANZANIA
*Tel: 027 2640643*

The Convent, PO Kwa
Mkono, Handeni, Tanga
Region, TANZANIA

Ilala, PO Box 25068, Dar
es Salaam, TANZANIA
*Tel: 022 2863797*

PO Box 150, Njombe,
Iringa Region,
TANZANIA
*Tel: 026 2782753*

Sayuni, PO Box 150,
Njombe, Iringa Region,
TANZANIA
*Tel: 026 2782753*

PO Box 6, Liuli,
Mbinga-Ruvuma Region,
TANZANIA

Fiwila Mission, PO Box
840112 Mkushi, ZAMBIA

# Chita Che Zita Rinoyera

## (Holy Name Community)

## CZR

*Founded 1935*

*St Augustine's Mission*
*PO Penhalonga*
*Mutare*
*ZIMBABWE*

Tel:
Penhalonga 22217

*Mattins or Morning*
*Prayer*

*Mass*

*Midday Office*

*Evensong*

*Compline*

*Bishop Visitor*
*Rt Revd Sebastian*
*Bakare, Bishop of*
*Manicaland*

Our Community was started by Father Baker of the CR Fathers at Penhalonga, with Mother Isabella as the founder. The CZR Sisters were helped by CR Sisters (Liz and Lois), and later by OHP Sisters (especially Lila, Mary Francis, Joyce and Hannah). When they left, Sister Isabella was elected Mother.

Today the CZR Sisters work at the clinic and at the primary and secondary schools. Some do visiting and help teach the catechism. We make wafers for several dioceses, including Harare. Some of the Sisters look after the church, seeing to cleaning and mending of the church linen. We have an orphanage that cares for sixty-six children, with an age range of eighteen months to eighteen years.

In 1982, half the Sisters and the novices left CZR and created another community at Bonda. Six months later, some of those Sisters in turn went to found Religious Life at Harare. In 1989, some of the Bonda community left to go to Gokwe and begin Religious Life there. So CZR has been the forerunner of three other communities in Zimbabwe.

Please pray that God may bless us.

MOTHER ANNA MARIA CZR
*(assumed office 2005)*

Sister Stella Mary
Sister Hilda Raphael
Sister Felicity
Sister Elizabeth
Sister Betty
Sister Emelia
Sister Annamore
Sister Allegria

*Novices: 1*
*Postulants: 3*

**Obituaries**
6 Oct 2005    Mother Isabella, aged 103, foundress 1936

**Community Wares**
We sell chickens, eggs, milk, cattle (two or three a year) and wafers.

# Chita che Zvipo Zve Moto

## (Community of the Gifts of the Holy Fire)

## CZM

*Founded 1977*

*Convent of Chita che Zvipo Zve Moto*
*PO Box 138*
*Gokwe South*
*ZIMBABWE*
Telefax: 263 059 2566

**House Prayer**
*5.00 am*

**Mattins** *followed by meditation  5.45 am*

**Holy Communion**
*6.00 am*

**Midday prayers**
*12 noon*

**Evensong**
*followed by meditation*
*5.00 pm*

**Compline**  *8.30 pm*

**Office Book**
*Book of Common Prayer*
*& CZM Office Book 2002*

The Community is a mixed community of nuns and friars, founded by the Revd Canon Lazarus Tashaya Muyambi in 1977. On a visit to St Augustine's Mission, Penhalonga, he was attracted by the life of the CR fathers and the CZR sisters. With the inspiration of the Spirit of the Lord, he believed it was of great value to start a Religious community. The first three sisters were attached to St Augustine's for three months, Sister Gladys being the first admission on 14 May 1978. The first convent was officially opened in 1979 and the initial work was caring for orphans at St Agnes Children's Home.

In January 2000, Canon Muyambi stepped down from leadership, believing the Community was mature enough to elect its own leaders, which it did in March 2000. The Community have a Rule, Constitution and are governed by a Chapter. They take vows of Love, Compassion and Spiritual Poverty. The Community is progressing well with young people joining every year. Each member is qualified or skilled in one trade or another.

SISTER GLADYS CZM
*(Archsister in charge, assumed office 10 March 2000)*
FRIAR JOSHUA CZM *(Deputy Archfriar)*

| | |
|---|---|
| Sister Eugenia | Sister Martha |
| Sister Elizabeth | Sister Alice |
| Sister Lydia | Friar Shane |
| Sister Eustina | Sister Itai |
| Sister Phoebe | Sister Juliet |
| Sister Anna | Sister Constance |
| Sister Patricia | Sister Tirivatsva |
| Sister Gladys B | |
| Sister Teresah | *Novices:* 4 |
| | *Postulants:* 3 |

*Other addresses*
St Patrick's Mission Branch House,
P. Bag 9030, Gweru, ZIMBABWE
Nyamuroro Kubatana Secondary School,
P. Bag 002, Gokwe North, ZIMBABWE

*Community Wares*
Sewing church vestments, school uniforms, wedding gowns; knitting jerseys; garden produce; poultry keeping.

*Bishop Visitor*
Rt Revd Ishmael Mukuwanda,
Bishop of Central Zimbabwe

# Christa Sevika Sangha (Handmaids of Christ)

## CSS

*Founded 1970*

*Jobarpar*
*Barisal Division*
*Uz Agailjhara* 8240
*BANGLADESH*

*Oxford Mission,*
*Bogra Road, PO Box* 21
*Barisal* 8200
*BANGLADESH*
*TEL:* 0431 54481

*Morning Prayer*
*Holy Communion*
*Midday Prayer*
*Quiet Prayer together*
*Evening Prayer*
*Compline*

*Office Book*
*Church of Bangladesh*
*Book of Common Prayer*
*&*
*Community Office Book*
*(all Offices are in Bengali)*

*Bishop Visitor*
*Rt Revd Michael S. Baroi*

The Community was founded in 1970 and was under the care of the Sisterhood of the Epiphany *(see separate entry)* until 1986, when its own Constitution was passed and Sister Susila SE was elected as Superior.

The Sevikas supervise girls' hostels and a play-centre for small children. They also help in St Gabriel's School and supervise St Mary's Asroi (Home) at Barisal. The Community also produces for sale a wide variety of goods and produce.

### MOTHER SUSILA CSS
*(Mother Foundress, 25 January 1970;*
*elected Reverend Mother CSS in July 1986)*

| | |
|---|---|
| Sister Ruth | Sister Kalyani |
| Sister Jharna | Sister Shefali |
| (House Sister, Jobarpar) | Sister Shalomi |
| Sister Sobha | Sister Shikha |
| Sister Agnes | Sister Shipra |
| Sister Dorothy | |
| (House Sister, Barisal) | Novices: 1    Postulants: 1 |
| Sister Margaret | |

### Community Wares
Vestments, children's clothes, embroidery work, wine, wafers, candles. Farm produce: milk, poultry, fish. Land produce: rice, fruit, coconuts & vegetables. Twenty-four books translated into Bengali are for sale.

### Community Publication
*The Oxford Mission News,* twice a year. Write to Oxford Mission, PO Box 86, Romsey, Hampshire SO51 8YD.
*Tel:* 01794 515004    Annual subscription: £4.00, post free.

### Community History
Brethren of the Epiphany, *A Hundred Years in Bengal,*
   ISPCK, Delhi, 1979
Mother Susila CSS, *A Well Watered Garden,*
   (editor: M Pickering), Oxford Mission, Romsey, 2000
   available from O. M. address above, £5 including p & p.

### Guest and Retreat Facilities
Two rooms for men outside the Community campus. One house (three beds) for women. Donations received.

### Fellowship of the Epiphany
The Oxford Mission Fellowship of the Epiphany was founded in 1921 for friends of the Mission in India, Bangladesh, the British Isles and elsewhere.

There is also a Prayer Fellowship group, which so far has ten members with their families.

# Community of All Hallows

## CAH

Founded 1855

All Hallows Convent
Belsey Bridge Road
Ditchingham
Bungay, Suffolk
NR35 2DT
UK
Tel: 01986 892749
(office)
01986 894607
(Sisters)
Fax: 01986 895838
Email:
allhallowsconvent
@btinternet.com

**Lauds** 7.30 am

**Eucharist**
8.00 am (9.30 am Sat,
10.00 am Sun)

**Sext** 12.15 pm

**Evening Prayer** 5.30 pm

**Compline** 8.00 pm

**Office Book**
Daily Prayer;
we also use BCP & CW
on a regular basis on
Sundays.

A Registered Charity.

There is no typical All Hallows sister: we are as diverse in gifts and personality as are the Saints under whose patronage we try to live out the life to which God has called us. Central to the life of the Community is the daily Eucharist, the Divine Office and time for private prayer, meditation and spiritual reading.

The desire 'to serve Christ in one another and love as He loves us' overflows into the active life of the Community; into the welcome given to the many visitors to our three Guest Houses and our Retreat and Conference Centre where Sisters are involved in the ministries of hospitality, spiritual direction and retreat giving.

The Community also cares for those with other needs – the very young at our day nursery and the elderly at our nursing/residential home. Our hospital is a special place for those needing to convalesce or having respite care, for distinctive long-term care, for day care, those needing physiotherapy and also for those nearing the end of their earthly pilgrimage. There is also a very loving concern and care for those who suffer from AIDS.

The ministry of hospitality and prayer continues to flourish at our house in Rouen Road, Norwich, with the work and witness being shaped according to demands and resources.

All enquiries about the life and work of CAH should be directed in the first place to the Revd Mother CAH at the Convent.

MOTHER ELIZABETH CAH
*(Revd Mother, assumed office 8 July 2004)*
SISTER PAMELA CAH *(Assistant Superior)*

| | |
|---|---|
| Sister Sheila | Sister Edith Margaret |
| Sister Violet | Sister Mary |
| Sister Winifred | Sister Rachel |
| Sister Jean | Sister Anne |
| Sister Margaret | |
| Sister Winifred Mary | *Novices: 1* |

Mother Winifred SE

### Oblates and Associates
OBLATES, ASSOCIATES and CONTACT MEMBERS offer themselves to God within the community context in a varying degree of 'hands-on' commitment. Apply to the Convent for details.

### Bishop Visitor
Rt Revd Graham James, Bishop of Norwich

*Other addresses and telephone numbers*
The following all share the same address as All Hallows Convent:

St Gabriel's Conference and Retreat House
*Tel: 01986 892133 (staff & bookings)*       *01986 895765 (residents)*

Holy Cross Guest House                       All Hallows Guest House
*Tel: 01986 894092*                          *Tel: 01986 892840*

St Mary's Lodge *(House of silence & retreat)*    *Tel: 01986 892731*

| All Hallows Hospital | All Hallows Nursing | All Hallows House |
| Station Road | Home | St Julian's Alley |
| Ditchingham | Adèle House | Rouen Road |
| Bungay | St John's Road | Norwich |
| Suffolk NR35 2QW | Bungay, Suffolk | NR1 1QT |
| UK | NR35 1DL | UK |
| *Tel: 01986 892728* | UK | *Tel: 01603 624738* |
| | *Tel: 01986 892643* | |

*Community Publication*
A newsletter is circulated yearly at All Saints tide. To be included on the mailing list, please write to All Hallows Convent at the address above.

*Community History and books*
Sister Violet CAH, *All Hallows, Ditchingham*, Becket Publications, Oxford, 1983.

Mother Mary CAH, *Memories*, privately published 1998.
    (A collection of memories and reflections primarily intended for friends and associates but available to all.)

*Community Wares*
A wide selection of photography cards, as well as some others.

*Guest and Retreat Facilities*
Enquiries about booking for the Retreat/Conference Centres should be addressed to the Convent Secretary at the Convent. Enquiries about staying at one of our guest houses should be addressed to the sister-in-charge of the relevant house.

*Most convenient time to telephone:*
9.00 am - 12 noon, 2.15 pm - 4.30 pm (Monday to Friday)
7.00 pm - 7.55 pm (any day)

THE
ULTIMATE
BACK-UP

# Benedictine Community of Christ the King

## CCK

Founded 1993

344 Taminick Gap Road
South Wangaratta
Victoria 3678
AUSTRALIA
Tel/Fax: 3 57257343

**Monastic Mattins
& Prayer Time**
4.30 am

**Lauds** 6.00 am

**Eucharist & Terce**
8.00 am

**Sext** 12 noon

**None** 1.15 pm

**Vespers & Prayer Time**
5.00 pm

**Compline** 7.45 pm

**Office Book**
The Divine Office is based
on the Sarum Rite, using
AAPB for the Psalms.
Whenever the Office is
sung, it is in Plainsong
using BCP Psalms.

The Community of Christ the King is a Traditional Anglican Benedictine order, enclosed and contemplative. Its members endeavour to glorify God in a life of prayer under the threefold vow of Stability, Conversion of Life and Obedience. They follow a rhythm of life centred on the worship of God in the Daily Eucharist and sevenfold Office.

The convent nestles at the foot of the Warby Ranges in Victoria, Australia. It is surrounded by attractive flower gardens, a citrus orchard and a kitchen garden. The fruit and vegetables ensure a certain amount of self-sufficiency, and afford the opportunity and privilege of manual labour, essential to the contemplative life.

Hospitality aimed at helping visitors deepen their spiritual lives through prayer is a feature of the life. The property, with its extensive views, bush walks and seclusion, is ideally suited to relaxation, quiet reflection and retreat. It is ringed by fourteen large crosses providing opportunity for meditation on the way of the cross, and for prayer in solitude. We hold silent retreats and hope to develop this outreach.

MOTHER RITA MARY CCK
*(Revd Mother, assumed office 31 July 1997)*
SISTER PATIENCE CCK *(Assistant)*
Sister Clare

*Obituaries*
3 Sep 2006     Sister Margery, aged 95, professed 53 years

*Oblates*
An Order of Benedictine Oblates has been established, open to women and men, clerical and lay.

*Community Publication*
The Community publishes a letter twice a year, sent free of charge to all interested in CCK (approximately 300 copies).

*Guest and Retreat Facilities*
We cater for those who want to deepen their life in Christ. There is a guest house which can accommodate three people (women or men): a self-contained cottage. There is no charge. A flat is attached to the chapel. A large fellowship room provides for parish quiet days and study groups. The original farmhouse is being renovated for additional accommodation.

*Most convenient time to telephone:*
10 am - 12 noon, 2 pm - 4 pm, 6.45 pm - 7.40 pm.

*Bishop Visitor:* Rt Revd R D Farrer, Bishop of Wangaratta

*Chaplain:* Father Richard Seabrook SSC

# Community of the Companions of Jesus the Good Shepherd

## CJGS

*Founded 1920*

The Priory
2 *Spring Hill Road*
*Begbroke*
Kidlington
*Oxford* OX5 1RX
UK

Tel: 01865 855326
or
01865 855320
Fax: 01865 855336

Email:
cjgs@csjb.org.uk

*Lauds* 7.30 am

*Tierce* 9.00 am

*Eucharist* 9.10 am

*Midday Office*
12.00 noon

*Vespers* 5.00 pm

*Compline* 8.30 pm

When the Community was founded, the first Sisters were all teachers living alone or in small groups but coming together during the school holidays. In 1943, West Ogwell House in South Devon became the Mother House and the more usual form of conventual life was established as well. The work of Christian education has always been of primary concern to the Community, whether in England or overseas, although not all the Sisters have been teachers.

In 1996, the Community moved to Windsor to live and work alongside the Community of St John Baptist, while retaining its own ethos. The Community aims 'to express in service for others, Christ's loving care for his flock.' At present, this service includes involvement in lay and ordained local ministry training; offering companionship to those seeking to grow in the spiritual life through spiritual direction, quiet days and retreats; and especially the befriending of the elderly, lonely, deaf and those in need.

In 2001, the Community moved with the Community of St John Baptist to The Priory, Begbroke.

MOTHER ANN VERENA CJGS
*(Mother Superior, assumed office 20 March 1996)*
SISTER FLORENCE CJGS *(Assistant Superior)*
Sister Evelyn Theresa
Sister Kathleen Frideswide

### Associates
Associates of the Community are members of the Fellowship of St Augustine. They follow a rule of life drawn up with the help of one of the Sisters. They give support to the Community through their prayer, interest and alms, and are remembered in prayer by the Community. They and the Community say the 'Common Devotion' daily. They are truly our extended family.

### Community Publication
*CJGS News.* Contact the Mother Superior.

### Guest and Retreat Facilities
See under the entry for the Community of St John Baptist.

**Office Book:** Common Worship with additions from the old CSJB Office

**Bishop Visitor:** Rt Revd Dominic Walker OGS,
Bishop of Monmouth
**Registered Charity:** No. 270317

# Community of the Glorious Ascension

## CGA

*Founded 1960*

**Brothers:**

The Priory
Lamacraft Farm
Start Point
Kingsbridge
Devon
TQ7 2NG
UK

Tel & Fax:
01548 511474

Email:
cga@fish.co.uk

**Registered Charity:**
*No. 254524*

**Sisters:**

Prasada
Quartier Subrane
Montauroux
83440 *Fayenne*
Var
FRANCE

Tel & Fax:
04 94 47 74 26

## BROTHERS

The life of the Community is shaped through a patterned living of prayer, worship and work. The mission of the Community is to be with and amongst people in daily living.

BROTHER SIMON CGA
*(Prior, assumed office 20 May 1993)*
Brother David
Brother John
Brother Wilfrid

**Obituaries**
18 Oct 2005          Brother Edwin, aged 77,
                              professed 40 years

**Community Publication**
*CGA Newsletter*, published annually. Write to the Prior.

**Guest and Retreat Facilities**
The Priory in Devon is not simply a retreat facility, but aims to offer opportunity for relaxation, reflection or holiday by groups, individuals and families. The Community welcomes groups by day and has two rooms in the main house which comfortably accommodate ten people for gatherings and meetings. Self-catering accommodation is also available in cottages set in a converted barn adjacent to the main house.

## SISTERS

Prasada is set on the edge of a Provençal hill village, where guests are welcome for a time of rest and refreshment. Many join the Community in their chapel for the Eucharist and Divine Office.

The Sisters are also involved in various activities with the local English-speaking and French communities.

SISTER JEAN CGA *(Prioress)*
Revd Sister Cécile

# Community of the Good Shepherd

## CGS

Founded 1978

Christ Church Likas
PO Box 519
88856 Likas
Sabah
MALAYSIA
Tel: 088 383211

Morning Prayer
&
Evening Prayer
daily

Compline
7.45 pm

Holy Communion
8.00 am (Wed)

Office Book
ASB and the
Service Book of the
Province of the Anglican
Church
in South East Asia

The CGS Sisters in Malaysia were formerly a part of the Community of the Companions of Jesus the Good Shepherd in the UK *(see separate entry)*. They became an autonomous community in 1978. Their Rule is based on that of St Augustine and their ministry is mainly parish work.

Since October 2000, the Sisters have moved to Kota Kinabalu, the capital of Sabah, and have settled in at Likas, just opposite to Christ Church. On 25 April 2006, the Venerable Albert Vun Cheong Fui was consecrated and installed as the fifth Diocesan Bishop of Sabah. He has appointed John Yeo, the new Rector of Christ Church, Likas, to be our chaplain. The Bishop has decided to build a new house for the Community. It is expected that it will completed by October 2007. It will be in the vicinity of Christ Church, Likas.

In Kota Kinabalu, the Community, with the help of the associates, see the need to supply wafers to the Diocese and to gather the associates to pray for the Diocese.

SISTER MARGARET LIN-DIN CGS
*(Sister-in-charge, assumed office 1978)*
Sister Oi Chin CGS

**Associates**
In Kotu Kinabalu, some committed Christian women from the three Anglican Churches join in fellowship with the Community and have become associate members. They follow a simple rule of life to support the Community through prayer and to share in the life and work of the Community. Whenever they can, they come to join the annual retreat.

**Community Wares**
Stoles and wafers (to supply the Sabah diocese at present).

**Bishop Visitor**
Rt Revd Albert Vun Cheong Fui,
Bishop of Sabah

# Benedictine Community of the Holy Cross, Rempstone

## CHC

Founded 1857

Holy Cross Convent
Ashby Road
Rempstone
near Loughborough
LE12 6RG
UK

Tel: 01509 880336
Fax: 01509 881812
*(Southwell Diocese)*

**Matins**
6.15 am

**Lauds** 7.30 am

**Terce**
9.15 am

**Sext** 12.15 am
*(subject to change)*

**None**
1.30 pm

**Vespers** 4.30 pm
*(4.00 pm Thu & Fri)*

**Compline**
8.00 pm

**Mass** 9.30 am
*(subject to change)*

The Community of the Holy Cross was founded in 1857 by Elizabeth Neale (sister of John Mason Neale, the hymnographer), at the invitation of Father Charles Fuge Lowder. The foundation was intended for Mission work in Father Lowder's parish of London Docks, but succeeding generations felt that the Community was being called to a life of greater withdrawal, and in the twentieth century the Benedictine Office, and later the Rule of St Benedict, were adopted.

The Community aims to achieve the Benedictine balance of prayer, study and work. All the work, whether manual, artistic or intellectual, is done within the Enclosure. The daily celebrations of the Eucharist and the Divine Office are the centre and inspiration of all activity.

Apart from worship, prayer and intercession, and the work of maintaining the house, garden and grounds, the Community's works are: the publications and greetings cards described below; providing retreats and quiet days; and dealing with a large postal apostolate.

SISTER MARY LUKE WISE CHC
*(Mother Superior, elected 8 November 1991)*
SISTER MARY JULIAN GOUGH CHC *(Assistant Superior)*
Sister Mary Michael Titherington
Sister Mary Bernadette Priddin
Sister Mary Joseph Thorpe
Sister Mary Cuthbert Aldridge

*Novices:* 1

**Obituaries**

| | |
|---|---|
| 12 Mar 2006 | Sister Mary Sylvia Driscall, aged 82, professed 29 years |
| 31 Mar 2006 | Sister Mary Laurence Bagshaw, aged 78, professed 35 years, Reverend Mother 1974-78 |

**Oblates and Associates**
The Community has women Oblates who are attached to it in a union of mutual prayers. Each has a rule of life adapted to her particular circumstances. Oblates are not Religious but they seek to live their life in the world according to the spirit of the Rule of St Benedict.
There are also Associates who have a much simpler rule.

**Office Book:** CHC Office

**Bishop Visitor:** Rt Revd Dr David Hope

### Community Publications
A *Newsletter* published in the Spring. Available free from the Publications Secretary.

### Community History
Alan Russell, *The Community of the Holy Cross Haywards Heath 1857 - 1957: A Short History of its Life and Work*, 1957.

A leaflet: *A short history of the Community of the Holy Cross.*
Available from the Publications Secretary.

### Community Wares
A great variety of prayer and greeting cards are available for sale. Some are produced by the sisters and others are from a number of different sources.

### Guest and Retreat Facilities
There is limited accommodation for residential, private retreats: main meals are taken at the Convent. The Community also provides for Quiet Days for individuals or groups up to twenty. The Guest House is closed at Christmas.

*Registered Charity:* No 223807

*CHC sisters on a visit to the SSF brothers at Alnmouth Friary*

# Community of the Holy Name

## CHN

*Founded 1888*

*Community House*
40 *Cavanagh Street*
*Cheltenham*
*Victoria* 3192
AUSTRALIA

Tel: 03 9583 2087
Fax: 03 9585 2932
Email: chnmelb@
bigpond.com

*Eucharist*
7.30 am

*Mattins*
9.00 am

*Midday Office*
12.45 pm

*Vespers*
5.30 pm

*Compline*
8.00 pm

*Office Book*
*CHN adaptation of the*
*Anglican Office Book*

The Community of the Holy Name was founded in 1888 within the Diocese of Melbourne by Emma Caroline Silcock (Sister Esther). The work of the Community was initially amongst the poor and disadvantaged in the slum areas of inner-city Melbourne. Over the years, the Sisters have sought to maintain a balance between a ministry to those in need and a commitment to the Divine Office, personal prayer and a daily Eucharist.

For many years, CHN was involved in institutions, like children's homes and a Mission house. There were many and varied types of outreach. The Holy Name Girls' High School was established in Papua New Guinea, and the indigenous Community of the Visitation of Our Lady fostered there.

Today, Sisters are engaged in parish work in ordained and lay capacities, and in a great variety of other ministries, including hospital chaplaincies, both general and psychiatric, spiritual direction and leading of Quiet Days and retreats. The offering of hospitality to people seeking spiritual refreshment or a place away from their normal strains and stresses has become an important part of our life and ministry. In 2007, we will open a small new Retreat and Spirituality centre, St Julians, where affordable, comfortable facilities will be available.

JOSEPHINE MARGARET CHN
*(Mother Superior, assumed office 11 April 2005)*

AVRILL CHN,
CAROL CHN
& PAMELA CHN
*(Leadership Team)*

| | | |
|---|---|---|
| Andrea Clare | Jean | Ruth |
| Betty | Jenny | Sheila |
| Elizabeth Gwen | Lyn | Sheila Anne |
| Felicity | Maree | Shirley |
| Francine | Margaret Anne | Valmai |
| Gwendoline | Margot | Winifred Muriel |
| Hilary | Philippa | |
| Hilda | Penelope | |

## Obituaries

| | |
|---|---|
| 13 Nov 2005 | Sister Jennifer, aged 64, professed 38 years |
| 28 May 2006 | Sister Aileen, aged 95, professed 70 years |
| 26 Apr 2007 | Sister Lois, aged 81, professed 53 years |

*Oblates and Associates*
The Order of Oblates is for women and men who desire to lead lives of prayer and dedication in close association with the Community. The Oblates have a personal Rule of Life based on the Evangelical Counsels of Poverty, Chastity and Obedience and renew their dedication annually.

The Associates and Priests Associate support and pray for the Community. In some areas they have regular meetings for fellowship. Priests Associate offer the Eucharist with special intention for the Community and seek to promote the Religious Life.

*Other Australian Addresses*

St Julians, 33 Lorna Street, Cheltenham, VIC 3192
68 Pickett Street, Footscray, VIC 3011
48 Charles Street, Lorne, VIC 3232
15 Gisborne Street, East Melbourne, VIC 3002
5 Coronation Street, Sunshine North, VIC 3020
2/7 James Street, Brighton, VIC 3186
8/7 James Street, Brighton, VIC 3186

*Community Publication*
An *Associates Letter* is published four times a year. Write to Sister Avrill, the Associates Sister, for a subscription, which is by donation.

*Community History*
Sister Elizabeth CHN, *Esther, Mother Foundress,* 1948.
Lynn Strahan, *Out of the Silence,* OUP, Melbourne, 1988.

*Community Wares*
Cards are sold at the Community House.

*Guest and Retreat Facilities*
There is accommodation for eight guests at the Community House. A Sister is available for help and guidance if requested. The new St Julian's will accommodate ten people, and a variety of programmes will be available there.

*Most convenient time for guests to telephone*
10.00 am - 12.30 pm, 2.00 pm - 5.00 pm

*Bishop Visitor:* Most Revd Dr Philip Freier, Archbishop of Melbourne

EDITORS' NOTE: *The Community of the Holy Name in the UK and Africa, which forms several of the subsequent entries in this directory, is a community entirely distinct from CHN in Australia. Although sharing the same name, the two communities were founded independently of each other.*

# Community of the Holy Name

## (UK Province)

## CHN

*Founded 1865*

*Convent of the Holy Name*
*Morley Road*
*Oakwood*
*Derby*
DE21 4QZ
*UK*

Tel: 01332 671716
Fax: 01332 669712
Email: bursarsoffice
@tiscali.co.uk

**Website:**
www.chnderby.org

*Prime   7.45 am*

*Eucharist   8.00 am*
*(12.20 pm Tue & Thu)*

*Mattins   9.15 am*
*(8.45 am Tue & Thu)*

*Midday Office   12.45 pm*
*(12.05 pm Tue & Thu)*

*Vespers   5.00 pm*

*Compline   9.15 pm*
*(8.45 pm Sat)*

*Office Book*
*Daily Office CHN*

The Sisters combine the life of prayer with service to others in their evangelistic and pastoral outreach and by maintaining their houses as centres of prayer where they can be available to others. They run a small guest house in Derby, and are able to take one or two guests in the house at Keswick. In our houses, and from the Convent in Derby, the Sisters are involved in parish work, prison and hospital visiting, retreat-giving and work among the wider community, and with those who come for spiritual guidance.

The members of the Fellowship of the Holy Name are an extension of its life and witness in the world. We encourage those who wish to live alongside for a period of time.

MOTHER MONICA JANE CHN
*(Provincial Superior, assumed office 10 January 2004)*
SISTER EDITH MARGARET CHN *(Assistant Superior)*

| | |
|---|---|
| Sister Michael | Sister Vivienne Joy |
| Sister Christian | Sister Charity |
| Sister Penelope | Sister Elizabeth Clare |
| Sister Judith | Sister Diana |
| Sister Ruth | Sister Dorothy |
| Sister Francesca Mary | Sister Pauline Margaret |
| Sister Marjorie Jean | Sister Carol |
| Sister Barbara | Sister Pippa |
| Sister Joy | Sister Rosemary |
| Sister Brenda | Sister Irene |
| Sister Verena | Sister Lynfa |
| Sister Jean Mary | Sister Elaine Mary |
| Sister Constance | Sister Julie Elizabeth |
| Sister Lilias | Sister Linda Frances |
| Sister Theresa Margaret | Sister Gillian Paul |
| Sister Mary Patricia | Sister Christine |
| Sister Beryl | |
| Sister Lisbeth | *Novices:* 1 |

**Obituaries**

| | |
|---|---|
| 12 Oct 2005 | Sister Jessica Mary, aged 86, professed 51 years |
| 17 Dec 2005 | Sister Mary Alison, aged 82, professed 52 years |
| 3 Feb 2006 | Sister Marjorie Eileen, aged 90, professed 43 years |
| 18 Jul 2006 | Sister Renate, aged 83, professed 40 years |
| 31 Oct 2006 | Sister Vivienne, aged 90, professed 39 years |

*Other UK houses*

*Holy Name House*
*Ambleside Road*
**Keswick**
*Cumbria*
CA12 4DD
Tel: 017687 72998
Email:
holynamehouse
@yahoo.co.uk


*Cottage* 5
**Lambeth Palace**
*London*
SE1 7JU
Tel: 020 7898 5407


*St Peter's Vicarage*
*177 Hartley Road*
**Radford**
*Nottingham*
NG7 3DW
Tel: 0115 9785101


*64 Allexton Gardens*
*Welland Estate*
**Peterborough**
PE1 4UW
Tel: 01733 352077


*Registered Charity:*
*No. 250256*

### Fellowship of the Holy Name

The Fellowship is comprised of ecumenically-minded Christians who feel called to share with the Community in their life of prayer and service.

Members have a personal Rule of Life, which they have drawn up in consultation with a particular Sister. She will keep in contact and help with a regular review. This rule will include daily private prayer, regular prayer and worship with the local Christian community, as well as time and space for their own well-being and creativity. Each rule varies with the individual. A six-month probation living the rule is required before formal admission to the Fellowship. This usually takes place at the Convent in the context of the Eucharist. There are regional meetings for members living in the same area, and the Community distributes a magazine comprised of articles submitted by members.

### Community History

*History of the Community of the Holy Name, 1865 to 1950,*
        published by CHN, 1950.
Una C. Hannam, *Portrait of a Community,*
        printed by the Church Army Press, 1972.

### Community Wares

Hand-painted cards, as well as painted prayer stones, are all for sale at the Convent (but not through the post).

Booklet of Stations of the Cross, from original paintings by Sister Theresa Margaret CHN, with biblical texts. Can be ordered from the Convent: £5.00 each, or for orders of ten or more £4.50 each. Icons are also available.

### Guest and Retreat Facilities

There are opportunities for up to seven individuals to make a private retreat at the guest house, and Sisters would be prepared to give help and guidance if requested. We do not organise group retreats. The guest cottage is closed from Sunday afternoon to Tuesday morning.

### Most convenient time to telephone:
10.00 am - 12.30 pm, 2.00 pm - 5.00 pm, 5.30 pm - 9.00 pm

### Bishop Visitor : Rt Revd John Inge

# Community of the Holy Name
## (Lesotho Province)

## CHN

*Founded 1865 (in UK)*
*1962 (in Lesotho)*

*Convent of the Holy Name*
*PO Box 22*
*Ficksburg 9730*
SOUTH AFRICA
Tel: 22400249
Email:
cahona@data.co.ls

**Morning Prayer** *6.30 am*
*(6.45 am Sun)*

**Terce**
*7.45 am (Sun only)*

**Eucharist**
*7.00 am (8.00 am Sun;*
*12 noon Wed)*

**Midday Office** *12.15 pm*
*(12.30 pm Sun,*
*11.45 am Wed)*

**Evening Prayer** *5.00 pm*

**Compline** *8.15 pm*

**Office Book**
*South African Prayer Book,*
*supplemented by the CHN*
*Office Book (using both*
*Sesotho & English)*

**Bishop Visitor**
*Rt Revd Philip Mokuk*

The Basotho Community of St Mary at the Cross was founded in Leribe, Lesotho, in 1923, under the Community of St Michael & All Angels, Bloemfontein. In 1959, CHN Sisters were invited to take over this work and started at Leribe in 1962. They had invited the Sisters of S. Mary at the Cross to become members of CHN and the full amalgamation of the two communities was completed in 1964. As a multi-racial community, the witness against racism at a time when apartheid was in the ascendant in South Africa was an important strand of the Community's vocation. New members have joined the Community in succeeding years, and they have continued the evangelistic and pastoral work which is also an important part of the CHN vocation. Sisters are involved in children's work, prison visiting, as well as other outreach in both Lesotho and South Africa. The Sisters in Leribe run a hostel for secondary school students who live too far from home to travel daily. Some Sisters are 'Volunteers of Love' for families where there is HIV/AIDS. This work is enabled and strengthened by the daily round of prayer, both corporate and private, which is at the heart of the Community's Rule. A daily Eucharist at the centre of this life of prayer is the aim, but in some houses this is not always possible owing to a shortage of priests.

SISTER JULIA CHN
*(Provincial Superior, assumed office April 2007)*
SISTER MPOLOKENG CHN *(Assistant Superior)*

| | |
|---|---|
| Sister Angelina | Sister Lerato Maria |
| Sister Lucia | Sister Gertrude |
| Sister Calista | Sister Ryneth |
| Sister Alphonsina | Sister Lineo |
| Sister Hilda Tsepiso | Sister Exinia Tsoakae |
| Sister Maria | Sister Lebohang |
| Sister Mary Selina | Sister Malineo |
| Sister Josetta | *Novices: 3* |

**Obituaries**
Apr 2007          Sister Elizabetha, professed 53 years

**Other houses**
For other houses, please contact the main house.

**Community Wares**
Church sewing (including cassocks, albs & stoles); communion wafers; Mothers Union uniforms; mohair and woven goods from the Leribe Craft Centre and the disabled workshop, started by the Community.

# Community of the Holy Name

## (Zulu Province)

## CHN

*Founded 1865 (in UK)*
*1969 (in Zululand)*

*Convent of the Holy Name*
*Pt. Bag 806*
*Melmoth 3835, Zululand*
SOUTH AFRICA
Tel: 3545 02892
Email: bursarchn
@mweb.co.za

**Mattins**   *6.30 am*

**Eucharist**   *7.00 am*
*(Tues, Wed, Thurs;*
*12 noon Fri)*

**Terce**   *8.30 am*

**Midday Office**
*12.30 pm (11.45 am Fri)*

**Evening Prayer**   *5.00 pm*

**Compline**   *7.45 pm*

**Office Book**
*Offices are mainly in Zulu,*
*based on the South African*
*Prayer Book & the CHN*
*Office Book.*

**Bishop Visitor**
*Bishop of Zululand*

The Community of the Holy Name in Zululand was founded by three Zulu Sisters who began their Religious Life with the Community in Leribe. All three Provinces of CHN have the same Rule of life, but there are differences of customary and constitutions to fit in with cultural differences. The daily life of the Community centres around the daily Office, and the Eucharist whenever the presence of a priest makes this possible.

The Sisters are involved extensively in mission, pastoral and evangelistic work. The Zulu Sisters have evangelistic gifts which are used in parishes throughout the diocese at the invitation of parish priests. Several Sisters have trained as teachers or nurses. They work in schools or hospitals, where possible within reach of one of the Community houses. Their salaries, and the handicrafts on sale at the Convent at Kwa Magwaza, help to keep the Community solvent.

MOTHER BONAKELE CHN
*(Provincial Superior, assumed office January 2002)*
SISTER NOKUBONGWA CHN *(Assistant Superior)*

| | |
|---|---|
| Sister Gertrude Jabulisiwe | Sister Grace |
| Sister Claudia | Sister Nqobile |
| Sister Olpha | Sister Dumsile |
| Sister Nesta Gugu | Sister Makhosazana |
| Sister Victoria Nokuthula | Sister Cynthia |
| Sister Sibongile | Sister Sibekezelo |
| Sister Zodwa | Sister Xolisile |
| Sister Mantombi | Sister Philisiwe |
| Sister Nonhlahla | Sister Ntsoaki |
| Sister Jabu | Sister Nomphumelelo |
| Sister Sibusisiwe | Sister Nozibusiso |
| Sister Thulisiwe | Sister Beauty |
| Sister Lindiwe | Sister Thandukwazi |
| Sister Gloria | Sister Nomathemba |
| Sister Sebenzile | Sister Zamandla |
| Sister Thembelihle | Sister Sindisiwe |
| Sister Benzile | Sister Agnetta |
| Sister Samkelisiwe | Sister Bongile |
| Sister Thandazile | Sister Maureen |
| Sister Thandiwe | Sister Xoliswa |
| Sister Nondumiso | Sister Nosekethe |
| Sister Thokozile | Sister Noyolo |
| Sister Duduzile | |
| Sister Patricia | *Novices: 5* |
| Sister Phindile | |

*Other Houses*
Usuthu Mission, PO Luyengo, SWAZILAND
For other houses, please contact the main
house.

*Community Wares*
Vestments, cassocks, albs and other forms of
dressmaking to order.

---

# Community of the Holy Transfiguration

## CHT

*Founded 1982*

St David's Bonda Mission
P Bag T 7904
Mutare
ZIMBABWE

**House Prayer**
*5.00 am*

**Meditation**
*5.10 am*

**Mattins**  *5.45 am*

**Mid-day Office**
*12.00 noon*

**Vespers**
*6.00 pm*

**Compline**
*8.00 pm*

The Community started in 1982 with eight members who broke away from the Community of the Holy Name (Chita Che Zita Renoyera). The Community is stationed at St David's Bonda Mission and it is an open community. We assist the Church in the evangelistic work and other ministerial duties. Some members are employed by the diocese as priests and some as Evangelists. We run an orphanage with a maximum number of twenty-five children aged 0-6. As of now, the age-group is going beyond this age range because of the HIV/AIDS pandemic. We are also a self-reliant community through land tilling and poultry. We look forward to opening branch houses in the near future, and at present we have one in the town where several members live.

SISTER WINNIE CHT
*(Mother, assumed office 29 December 2000)*
SISTER GLORIA CHT *(Sister Assistant)*

| | |
|---|---|
| Sister Francesca | Sister Letwin |
| Sister Lucy | Rev Friar |
| Sister Mildah | Fungayi Leonard |
| Sister Merina | Evangelist Friar Henry |
| Sister Gloria B | |
| Sister Violet | *Novices:* 1 |
| Sister Dorothy | *Postulants:* 1 |
| Sister Felicity | |

**Other Address**
85 - 2nd Street, Mutare, ZIMBABWE

**Bishop Visitor**
Rt Revd Sebastian Bakare, Bishop of Manicaland

**Office Book:** Book of Common Prayer

# Community of the Holy Spirit

## CHS

*Founded 1952*

621 *West* 113th *Street*
*New York*
*NY* 10025-7916
*USA*
Tel: 212 666 8249
Fax: 801 655 8249
Email:chssisters
@chssisters.org

**Website:**
www.chssisters.org

*Morning Prayer* 6.30 am
*(Sun 7.20 am)*

*Eucharist* 7.00 am
*(Sun 8.00 am)*

*Noon Office* 12 noon
*(Sun 12.45 pm)*

*Evening Prayer*
*(Sun Vespers/Compline)*
5.30 pm

*Compline* 7.15 pm

*Note: the daily schedule
varies with the season.*

*Monday is a Sabbath Day
on which there is no
corporate worship.*

Each person is given an invitation to follow Christ. The Sisters of our monastic community respond to that invitation by an intentional living out of the vows of poverty, chastity, and obedience within the structure of a modified Augustinian Rule. Through the vow of poverty, we profess our trusting dependence upon God by embracing voluntary simplicity and responsible stewardship of creation. Through chastity, we profess the sanctity of all creation as the primary revelation of God. Through obedience, we profess our desire to be dependent on God's direction and to live and minister in ways that respect all creation, both now and for generations to come.

Compassionate, respectful love is God's gift to life. Prayer and the worship of God are the lifeblood and heart of our Community and the source of inspiration for all that we undertake. Through our prayer, worship, and creative talents we encourage others to seek God. Through our ministries of hospitality, retreat work, spiritual direction, and education through simple, sustainable, spiritual living, we seek to grow in love and communion with all whose lives touch us and are touched by us. We also provide spiritual support for women and men who wish to be linked with our Community as Associates. By adopting a personal rule of life, they extend the Community's ministry through prayer, worship and service.

SISTER HELÉNA MARIE CHS *(June 2001)*
SISTER FAITH MARGARET CHS *(June 2001)*
SISTER CATHERINE GRACE CHS *(June 2001)*
SISTER LESLIE CHS *(June 2007)*
*(Community Council)*

| | |
|---|---|
| Sister Élise | Sister Emmanuel |
| Sister Mary Christabel | Sister Maria Felicitas |
| Sister Mary Elizabeth | Sister Donna Martha |
| Sister Jerolynn Mary | Sister Lilli Ana |
| Sister Madeleine Mary | |
| Sister Dominica | *Candidates: 4* |

### Associates

From the Community's early days, Christian women and men have sought an active association with the Sisters, wishing to live out their baptismal commitments by means of a rule of life.

The Community provides four rules: Fellowship, St Augustine, Confraternity and Priest Associate. Each consists of prayer, reading, self-denial and stewardship.  Each provides an opportunity for growth toward God and daily renewal of life in Christ.  Each calls for a commitment to pray daily for the Sisters and all others in their life, worship and ministry, using the collect for Pentecost and the Lord's Prayer.

In consultation with the Sister for Associates, they may formulate their own rule if the ones provided cannot be fulfilled as they stand, or if they need to be expanded.  As far as is possible Associates support the Community through gifts of time, talents and financial resources.  There is an annual fee of $50, if possible.

***Other Address***
118 Federal Hill Road, Brewster, NY 10509-5307, USA
*Tel: 845 278 9777   Fax: 425 944 1085*

***Community Wares:*** Anglican rosaries, prayer beads, books, maple syrup.

***Community Publications***
Contact Cheryl Helm, administrator.
*Tel: 212 666 8249 extension 312*
*Email: cheryl@chssisters.org*

*The Associates' Newsletter.*
Contact the Sister for Associates.
*Tel: 212 666 8249 extension 302*
*Email: associates@chssisters.org*

***Community History***
The Revd Mother Ruth CHS,
*"In Wisdom Thou Hast Made Them",*
Adams, Bannister, Cox, New York, 1986

***Guest and Retreat Facilities***
St Hilda's House, New York, NY: fourteen rooms with a capacity for seventeen guests; closed 21-28 August & 24 December-2 January;
for reservations, call *212 932 8098* or email *outpourings@chssisters.org*
St Aidan's House, Brewster, NY: capacity for ten guests; closed periodically.
For information, call *845 278 9777 x 12   or*   email *melrose@chssisters.org*

***Most convenient time to telephone:***
Tue-Sat: 9.00 am - 12 noon, 2.00 pm - 5.00 pm  Please leave a message if there is no answer.

***Bishops Visitor:***
Rt Revd Bruce Caldwell, Bishop of Wyoming
Rt Revd Mark Andrus, Suffragan Bishop of Alabama
A third Bishop Visitor to be selected

***Office Book:*** CHS Office book, modified from SSJE

# Community of Jesus' Compassion

## CJC

Founded
1993

PO Box 153
New Hanover
3230
SOUTH AFRICA
Tel: 033 502 0010

Tel: 033 502 0200
*(for second CJC house
in the same vicinity)*

*Morning Prayer,
followed by Terce*
5.30 am

*Midday Prayer*
12.30 pm

*Evening Prayer*
4.30 pm

*Compline*
8.15 pm

Founded in the Diocese of Natal by a sister from the Community of the Holy Name in Zululand, CJC have been based in Newcastle and Ixopo. However, the sisters have now settled at New Hanover, which is half an hour's drive from the cathedral city of Pietermaritzburg.

The main work of the sisters is evangelising in the local parish and children's ministry. The Sisters care for around thirty-five children, which is demanding, but good progress is being made.

On the 19th December 1998, the first professions within the community were received. The Community's formal recognition by the Church of the Province of South Africa followed in 2000 with the first life professions.

In 2006, Sister Thandi became the first nun in the diocese to be ordained to the stipendiary ministry, and she now serves in a parish in Durban. Her priesting followed in June 2007.

MOTHER LONDIWE CJC
*(Mother Superior, assumed office 8 January 2000)*
SISTER THANDI CJC *(Assistant Superior)*

Sister Yeki
Sister Nontombi
Sister Zandile
Sister Jabulile
Sister Nontokozo
Sister Thokozile
Sister Nqobile
Sister Nonhlanhla
Sister Celiwe
Sister Ncebakazi
Sister Mbali

*Novices: 4*

**Community Wares**
Girdles, Prayer Book and Bible covers, vegetables.

**Bishop Visitor**
Rt Revd Rubin Phillip, Bishop of Natal

**Office Book**
Anglican Prayer Book 1989 of the Church of the Province of Southern Africa
Midday Office book & Celebrating Night Prayer

# Community of Nazareth

## CN

Under the guidance of the Sisters of the Community of the Epiphany (England), the Community of Nazareth was born and has grown. The Community is dedicated to the Incarnate Lord Jesus Christ, especially in devotion to the hidden life which he lived in Nazareth.

In addition to the Holy Eucharist, which is the centre and focus of our community life, the Sisters recite a sixfold Divine Office.

We run a Retreat house and make wafers and vestments. We welcome enquirers and aspirants.

*Founded 1936*

SISTER DORCAS MIYOSHI CN
(*Revd Mother, assumed office 4 March 2004*)
SISTER NOBU CN (*Assistant Mother*)

4-22-30 *Mure*
*Mitaka*
*Tokyo* 181-0002
*JAPAN*

Tel: 0422 48 4560
Fax: 0422 48 4601

Sister Yachiyo
Sister Chiyo
Sister Haroko
Sister Kayoko
Sister Chizuko
Sister Asako
Sister Setsuko
Sister Yukie
Sister Junko
Sister Sachiko

**Morning Prayer**
6.25 am

*Associates*
Clergy and laity may be associates.

**Eucharist**
7.00 am

*Other Address*
81 Shima Bukuro, Naka Gusuku Son, Naka Gami Gun, Okinawa Ken 901-2301, JAPAN

**Terce**
8.15 am

*Community Wares*
Wafers, vestments, postcards.

**Sext**
12 noon

*Guest and Retreat Facilities*
There are twenty rooms available, for men or women, but not children. The suggested donation is ¥6,000 per night, including three meals.

**None**
after lunch

**Evening Prayer**
5.00 pm

*Bishop Visitor*
Rt Revd Jintarō Ueda, Bishop of Tokyō

**Night Prayer**
8.15 pm

*Office Book*
BCP of Nippon Seiko Kai Office Book

# Benedictine Community of Our Lady & Saint John

## Alton Abbey

## OSB

*Founded 1884*

*Alton Abbey*
*Abbey Road*
*Beech, Alton*
*Hampshire*
*GU34 4AP*
*UK*

Tel: 01420 562145
& 01460 563575
Fax: 01420 561691

**Morning Prayer**
*6.30 am*

**Conventual Mass**
*9.00 am*
*(10 am Sun)*

**Midday Office**
*12.00 noon*

**Evening Prayer**
*5.00 pm*

**Night Prayer**
*8.30 pm   (7.30 pm Sun)*

The monks follow the Rule with its balance of prayer, work and study, supported by the vows of stability, conversion of life and obedience. A wide ministry of hospitality is offered, and visitors are welcome at the daily Mass and Divine Office. The purpose built monastery is built around two cloister garths; the Abbey Church dates from the beginning of the twentieth century. Set in extensive grounds, with contrast between areas that are cultivated and others that are a haven for wildlife, the Abbey is situated about four miles from Alton.

RT REVD DOM GILES HILL OSB
*(Abbot, elected 12 September 1990)*
VERY REVD DOM WILLIAM HUGHES OSB
*(Prior and Novice Master)*
Dom Andrew Johnson
Revd Dom Nicholas Seymour *(Guest Master)*
Dom Anselm Shobrook
Rt Revd Dom Timothy Bavin

**Oblates**
For details of the Oblates of St Benedict, please contact the Oblate Master.

**Community Publication**
*The Messenger*, occasional, write to the Abbey.

**Community Wares**
Altar bread and incense: contact the brother in charge of the bakery.

**Guest and Retreat Facilities**
Guest house facilities for up to eighteen persons, for both group and individual retreats. There is a programme of retreats each year, available from the Guestmaster.
No smoking in the house.

**Most convenient time to telephone:** 4.00 pm - 4.30 pm.

**Bishop Visitor:** Rt Revd Michael Scott-Joynt,
Bishop of Winchester

**Website:** www.btinternet.com/~nbchAbbey.html

**Office Book:** Alton Abbey Office Book

**Registered Charity:** No. 229216

# Community of the Resurrection

# CR

*Founded 1892*

*House of the Resurrection*
*Mirfield*
*West Yorkshire*
WF14 0BN
*UK*

Tel: 01924 494318
Fax: 01924 490489
Email:
community
@mirfield.org.uk

**Mattins**
*6.45 am (7.30 am Sun)*

**Midday Office**
*12.00 noon*

**Mass**
*12.15 pm*
*On festivals on week days,*
*the time of Mass may*
*change.*

**Evensong**
*6.30 pm*

**Compline**
*9.15 pm*

**Office Book**
*CR Office*

The Community consists of priests and laymen li' life of worship, work and study within the monastic life. They undertake a wide range of pastoral ministry including retreats, teaching and counselling.

GEORGE GUIVER CR
*(assumed office 29 December 2002)*
PETER ALLAN CR *(Prior)*

| | |
|---|---|
| Dominic Whitnall | Crispin Harrison |
| Anselm Genders *(bishop)* | Antony Grant |
| Roy France | Nicolas Stebbing |
| Timothy Stanton | John Gribben |
| Vincent Girling | Andrew Norton |
| Zachary Brammer | Philip Nichols |
| Benedict Green | Thomas Seville |
| Eric Simmons | Steven Haws |
| Aidan Mayoss | Oswin Gartside |
| Robert Mercer *(bishop)* | *Novices: 1* |
| Simon Holden | |

### Obituaries

16 Jul 05    Kingston Erson, aged 76, professed 46 years
30 Jan 06    Harry Williams, aged 86, professed 33 years
13 May 06    Jonathan Critchley,
                  aged 76, professed 36 years

### Oblates

OBLATES, clergy and lay, are those who desire to make a special and permanent offering of themselves to God in association with the Community of the Resurrection.

### The Companions of the Community

COMPANIONS seek to live the baptismal vocation of all Christians through a commitment to each community to which they belong and also to the Community of the Resurrection; a commitment to Eucharistic worship, corporate and private prayer and the use of the sacrament of reconciliation; a commitment of time, talents and money. Those who wish to be Companions keep their commitments for at least a year before being admitted, and thereafter, with all Companions, renew their commitment each year. All Companions have a spiritual director or soul friend with whom their commitments are discussed and who undertakes to support them on their journey.

ASSOCIATES have a less demanding relationship with the Community for whatever reason, but do have an obligation of prayer and worship. For more information please contact the Chaplain to the Companions at Mirfield.

### Community Publication
*CR Quarterly*. Write to the Editor. Many subscribe to this who are not Oblates, Companions or Associates. The minimum annual subscription is £10.00.

### Community History
Alan Wilkinson, *The Community of the Resurrection: A centenary history*, SCM Press, London, 1992.

### Community Wares
Postcards of the buildings, theological and spiritual books, leaflets on prayer, CDs of Community's music, clothes with logo: apply to Mirfield Publications at the House of the Resurrection.

### Guest and Retreat Facilities
Retreats are listed on the website.
HOUSE OF THE RESURRECTION
Twenty-four single rooms, two double rooms, nine en-suite rooms, one small flat.

*Most convenient time to telephone*: 9.00 am - 12 noon, 2.00 pm - 6.30 pm

A further retreat house, owned but not staffed by CR, is:
ST FRANCIS' HOUSE, Hemingford Grey, Huntingdon, Cambs., PE18 9BJ, UK
     *Tel: 01480 462185            Email: hemingford@mirfield.org.uk*
Seventeen single rooms, three twin rooms. Apply to the Warden.

MIRFIELD CENTRE
The Centre offers a meeting place at the College for about fifty people. Small residential conferences are possible in the summer vacation. Day and evening events are arranged throughout the year to stimulate Christian life and witness.

The Mirfield Centre (College of the Resurrection), Mirfield, West Yorkshire
WF14 0BW, UK
*Tel: 01924 481920        Fax: 01924 418921        Email: centre@mirfield.org.uk*

COLLEGE OF THE RESURRECTION        *Principal: to be appointed September 2007*
The College, founded in 1902 and run by its own independent Council, trains men and women and also provides opportunities for others to study for degrees.

College of the Resurrection, Mirfield, West Yorkshire WF14 0BW, UK
     *Tel: 01924 481900      Fax: 01924 481921      Email: registrar@mirfield.org.uk*

*Registered Charity:* No. 232670

*Bishop Visitor:* Rt Revd Graham James, Bishop of Norwich

# Community of the Resurrection of Our Lord CR

*Founded 1884*

*St Peter's*
*PO Box 72*
*Grahamstown* 6140
SOUTH AFRICA

Tel & Fax: 046 622 4210
Email: comres
@imaginet.co.za

**Morning Office**
*6.30 am*

**Eucharist** *7.00 am*
*(Sun, Tue, Thu & Fri)*
*(at the Cathedral*
*Mon & Wed)*

**Midday Office**
*followed by silent intercession*
*12.30 pm*

**Evening Office**
*followed by silent intercession*
*5.30 pm*

**Compline**
*7.30 pm*

**Office Book**
*Anglican Prayer Book 1989,*
*CPSA; Traditional Midday*
*Office & Compline*

This Community was founded in 1884 by Bishop Allan Becher Webb and Cecile Isherwood to undertake pastoral and educational work in Grahamstown. These two types of work, and later Social Welfare work, have predominated in the Community's undertakings throughout its history. The regular life of monastic Offices and personal prayer and intercession has always been maintained, both in the Mother House (Grahamstown) and all branch houses, wherever situated. It is still maintained in Grahamstown, the only centre where the Community life continues, our numbers being now much reduced.

The Sisters are involved in various ministries: at the Cathedral and other churches as needed; in the Raphael Centre for people suffering from HIV/Aids etc; in visiting at Old Age Homes and the hospital; soup kitchens; and needlework/banners.

MOTHER ZELMA CR *(priest)*
*(Mother Superior, assumed office 24 November 2005)*
SISTER KEKELETSO CR *(Assistant Superior)*
Sister Dorianne
Sister Nonie *(priest)*
Sister Joyce Mary
Sister Carol *(priest)*
Sister Makhosazana

**Obituaries**

| 27 Oct 2005 | Sister Heloise, aged 93, professed 64 years |
| 22 Nov 2005 | Sister Jean Mary, aged 91, professed 52 years |

**Oblates and Associates**

OBLATES OF THE RISEN CHRIST live under a Rule drawn up for each individual according to circumstances, on their observance of which they must report monthly to the Oblate Sister.

ASSOCIATES undertake a simple Rule, including regular prayer for the Community. Priest Associates undertake to give an address or preach on Religious Vocation at least once a year.

FRIENDS are interested in the Community and pray for it, and keep in touch with it.
There is a Fellowship Meeting twice a year, after Easter and near the Foundress's birthday on 14 November.

Also there is a Festival gathering of UK Associates at St Peter's Bourne, Whetstone, north London, on the Saturday nearest to St Peter's Day, 29 June, each year, at which two Sisters from South Africa are always present to preserve our links with the UK.

### Community Publication
A Newsletter is sent out three times a year to all bishops and Religious communities of CPSA, and also to all the Oblates and Associates of the Community.

*Community Wares:* Cards, banners and girdles.

### Guest and Retreat Facilities
Ten or more guests can be accommodated; though prior consultation is needed. The charge is negotiable. There is also a guest flatlet for two.

### Community History and Books
A pictorial record of the Community's history, with commentary, was published in its centenary year, 1984. It was a collaborative work.

Lives of Mother Cecile and her successor, Mother Florence, have been published, in each case written by 'a Sister':

A Sister of the Community (compiler), *Mother Cecile in South Africa 1883-1906: Foundress of the Community of the Resurrection of Our Lord,* SPCK, London, 1930

A Sister of the Community, *The Story of a Vocation: A Brief Memoir of Mother Florence, Second Superior of the Community of the Resurrection of Our Lord,* The Church Book Shop, Grahamstown, no date.

Guy Butler, *The Prophetic Nun,* Random House, 2000. (Life and art works, with colour illustrations, of Sisters Margaret and Pauline CR, and Sister Dorothy Raphael CSMV.) This is a coffee-table type book available in South Africa and the UK.

### Bishop Visitor
Rt Revd Thabo Makgoba, Bishop of Grahamstown

*CR sisters*

# Community of the Sacred Name

## CSN

*Founded 1893*

181 *Barbadoes Street*
*Christchurch* 8011
NEW ZEALAND
Tel: 03 366 8245
Fax: 03 366 8755

Email: comsacnm
@xtra.co.nz

*Morning Prayer*
*6.40 am*

*Mass*
*7.30 am*

*Terce*
*9.00 am*

*Midday Office*
*12 noon*

*Vespers*
*5.15 pm*

*Compline*
*7.30 pm*

*Office Book*
*Communities Consultative*
*Council*

The Community of the Sacred Name was founded in Christchurch in 1893 by Sister Edith (Deaconess). She was released from the Community of St Andrew in London to establish an indigenous community to respond to the needs of the colonial Church. A wide variety of teaching, childcare and parish work has been undertaken over the years. Today there are three houses. Since 1966, the Sisters have run a large children's home in Fiji. In 1997, the Sisters undertook work in Tonga, helping in the Church in various ways. The mother house in Christchurch has a small retreat house. The major work is ecclesiastical embroidery. Underpinning all the work is a life of worship.

MOTHER KELENI CSN
*(Mother Superior, assumed office 16 November 2006)*
SISTER ANNE CSN *(Assistant)*

| | |
|---|---|
| Sister Leona | Sister Malaea |
| Sister Annette | Sister Manu |
| Sister Brigid | Sister Alena |
| Sister Rose Ana | Sister Fehoko |
| Sister Lu'isa | Sister Vutulongo |
| Sister Litia | Sister Kalolaine |
| Sister Mele | Sister Sandra |
| Sister Judith | |

### Obituaries

16 Mar 2006    Sister Zoe, aged 82, professed 55 years, Mother Superior 1961-71, 1976-81, 1986-91

### Oblates and Associates

The Community has Oblates, men and women called by God to live the contemplative life in the world.
We also have Companions, Associates, Friends of Polynesia and the Guild of Help. These may be women or men, priests or lay.

### Other Addresses

St Christopher's Home, PO Box 8232, Nakasi, Suva, FIJI
*Tel: 679 341 0458*

PO Box 1824, Nuku'alofa, TONGA    *Tel: 27998*

### Bishops Visitor

Rt Revd Dr David Coles. Bishop of Christchurch
Rt Revd Jabez Bryce, Bishop of Polynesia

### Community History

Ruth Fry, *The Community of the Sacred Name - a Centennial History*, PPP Printers, PO Box 22.785, Christchurch, New Zealand, 1993

*Guest and Retreat Facilities*
There is a separate guest/
retreat house with fourteen
single rooms and one
double for private or group
retreats, available to both
men and women. NZ$25
per person per night for
bed and breakfast.
Write to Reverend Mother
re bookings.

*Community Publication*
Community    *Newsletter,*
published at Easter, Holy
Name    and    Christmas.
Write   to   the   Reverend
Mother at the Christchurch
address.

*Community Wares:*
Embroidery, cards,
vestments.

*Mother Keleni CSN*

# Community
# of the Sacred
# Passion

# CSP

*Founded 1911*

*Convent of the Sacred Passion*
*22 Buckingham Road*
*Shoreham-by-Sea*
*West Sussex* BN43 5UB
*UK*
Tel: 01273 453807

The Community was founded to serve Africa by a life of prayer and missionary work, but withdrew from active work in Tanzania in 1991, leaving behind the Tanzanian Community of St Mary of Nazareth and Calvary (CMM) *(see separate entry).*

Although not actively engaged in Africa, the Sisters hold that continent particularly in their prayers and continue to support in many small ways the Tanzanians who are continuing the gospel work.

Goods and money given for overseas work are collected and sent out.

A Sister lives in south London where, being a member of the World Community for Christian Meditation, she communicates and nurtures meditation in the spirit of serving the unity of all.

MOTHER PHILIPPA CSP
*(Revd Mother, assumed office 30 August 1999)*
SISTER JACQUELINE CSP *(Deputy Superior)*

| | |
|---|---|
| Sister Etheldreda | Sister Gillian Mary |
| Sister Jean Margaret | Sister Rhoda |
| Sister Dorothy | Sister Angela |
| Sister Thelma Mary | Sister Lucia |
| Sister Mary Joan | Sister Mary Kathleen |
| Sister Joan Thérèse | Sister Phoebe |

## Obituaries

| | |
|---|---|
| 26 Jul 2005 | Sister Greta, aged 92, professed 64 years |
| 10 Jan 2006 | Sister Olive Marian, aged 92, professed 57 years |
| 11 Nov 2006 | Sister Felicitas, aged 90, professed 63 years |
| 7 Jun 2007 | Sister Mary Margaret, aged 79, professed 55 years |

## Oblates
These are men and women who feel called to associate themselves with the aims of the community, by prayer and service, and by a life under a Rule. They have their own Rule of Life which will vary according to their particular circumstances. The Oblates are helped and advised by the Oblates' Sister.

## Associates
These are men and women who share in the work of the community by prayer, almsgiving and service of some kind. They pray regularly for the community.

## Priest Associates
They pray regularly for the community and offer Mass for it three times a year, of which one is Passion Sunday (the Sunday before Palm Sunday).

## Friends
They pray regularly for the community and help it in any way they can.

All those connected with the community are prayed for daily by the Sisters and remembered by name on their birthdays. They receive the four monthly intercession paper.

## Other Address
725 Wandsworth Road, London, SW8 3JF, UK

## Community History
Sister Mary Stella CSP, *She Won't Say 'No': The History of the Community of the Sacred Passion,* privately published, 1984.

**Bishop Visitor:** Rt Revd Ian Brackley, Bishop of Dorking

# Community of St Andrew

## CSA

Founded 1861

8/9 Verona Court
Chiswick Lane
London W4 2JD
UK
Tel: 020 8987 2799
Fax: 020 8987 0377
Email:
MrrsL2@aol.com

*Morning Prayer* 7.30 am
*followed by the*
**Eucharist** on Tuesday

*Midday Prayer* 12.45 pm
1.15 pm (Sun)

*Evening Prayer*
6.00 pm

*Compline*
8.30 pm

*Office Book*
Common Worship

*Bishop Visitor*
Rt Revd & Rt Hon
Richard Chartres,
Bishop of Lonodon

Full membership of the Community consists of Professed Sisters who are ordained, or who, though not seeking ordination, serve in other forms of diaconal ministry, such as the caring professions. The fundamental ministry is the offering of prayer and worship, evangelism, pastoral work and hospitality. This is carried out through parish and specialised ministry.

REVD MOTHER LILLIAN CSA *(deacon)*
*(Mother Superior, assumed office 6 November 2000)*
Revd Sister Denzil *(priest)*
Revd Sister Patricia *(deacon)*
Revd Sister Donella *(deacon)*

Sister Dorothy *(deaconess)*
*St Mary's Convent & Nursing Home, Burlington Lane, Chiswick, London W4 2QE*

Sister Pamela *(deaconess)*
*17 War Memorial Place, Harpsden Way, Henley on Thames, Oxon RG9 1EP    Tel: 01491 572224*

Revd Sister Teresa *(priest)*
*St Andrew's House, 16 Tavistock Crescent, London W11 1AP*
*Tel & Fax: 020 7221 4604*
*Email: sister.teresa@london.anglican.org*

## Obituaries
19 May 2006      Revd Sister Joan *(deacon)*
aged 99, professed 69 years

## Associates
Our Associates may be men, women, clergy or lay, and follow a simple Rule of Life, which includes praying for the Sisters and their work. Friends are also part of our fellowship of prayer and support the Sisters in many ways. The Sisters pray for the Associates and Friends every day. Meetings are also arranged for them. The Sisters are available to give help or guidance if required.

## Community Publications
*St Andrew's Review & St Andrew's Newsletter.* Write to the Revd Mother CSA.
*Distinctive Diaconate News & Distinctive News of Women in Ministry,* both edited by Revd Sister Teresa CSA.

**Registered Charity:** No 244321

# Community of St Clare

# OSC

Founded 1950

St Mary's Convent
178 Wroslyn Road
Freeland, Witney
OX29 8AJ
UK

Tel: 01993 881225
Fax: 01993 886912
Email: community
@oscfreeland.co.uk

**Office of Readings**
6.30 am

**Morning Prayer** 8.00 am

**Eucharist** 8.30 am

**Midday Prayer** 12.30 pm

**Evening Prayer** 5.30 pm

**Night Prayer** 8.00 pm

**Office Book**
The Daily Office SSF

**Community History**
P Dunstan, This Poor
Sort, DLT, London 1997,
pp157-167

**Bishop Protector:**
Rt Revd Michael Perham,
Bishop of Gloucester

The Community of St Clare is part of the Society of St Francis. We are a group of women who live together needing each other's help to give our whole lives to the worship of God. Our service to the world is by our prayer, in which we are united with all people everywhere. We have a guest house so that others may join in our worship, and share the quiet and beauty with which we are surrounded. We try to provide for our own needs by growing much of our own food, and by our work of printing, wafer baking, writing and various crafts. This also helps us to have something material to share with those in greater need.

SISTER PAULA FORDHAM OSC
*(Abbess, elected 30 January 2007)*
SISTER ALISON FRANCIS HAMILTON OSC *(Assistant)*

Sister Damian Davies     Sister Mary Margaret
Sister Elizabeth Farley               Broomfield
Sister Kate Sneade     Sister Michaela Davis
Sister Kathleen Marie Staggs Sister Susan Elisabeth Leslie
Sister Mary Kathleen Kearns     *Novices: 1*

## Obituaries
7 Sep 2006   Sister Elsie Felicity Watts, aged 89
           professed 56 years, Revd Mother 1971-83
8 Nov 2006   Sister Gillian Clare Amies, aged 72,
           professed 41 years
13 Nov 2006   Sister Patricia Wighton, aged 77,   professed
           51 years, Revd Mother 1989-97, Abbess 2003-06

## Community Wares
Printing: *Tel & Fax to Print Shop: 01993 882434*
Cards, crafts, altar breads:
           *Tel: 01993 881225    Fax: 01993 886912*

## Guest and Retreat Facilities
Men, women and children are welcome at the guest house. It is not a 'silent house' but people can make private retreats if they wish. Eleven rooms (some twin-bedded). Donations, no fixed charge. Closed for two weeks mid-May and two weeks mid-September, and 16 Dec-8 Jan.
Please write to the Guest Sister at the Convent address.

## Most convenient time to telephone:
6.00 pm - 7.00 pm - on Convent telephone: *01993 881225*

*Address of the Guest House (for guests arriving)*
The Old Parsonage, 168 Wroslyn Road, Freeland, Witney
      OX29 8AQ, UK     *Tel: 01993 881227*

# Community of St Francis

## CSF

*Founded 1905*

**UK Houses**

43 Endymion Road
**Brixton**
London SW2 2BU
UK
Tel: 020 8671 9401
Email: brixtoncsf@
franciscans.org.uk

**Minister General**
Email:
ministergeneralcsf
@franciscans.org.uk

*St Francis Convent*
**Compton Durville**
*South Petherton*
*Somerset TA13 5ES*
Tel: 01460 240473
or 241248
Fax: 01460 242360
Email:
comptondurvillecsf
@franciscans.org.uk

**Minister Provincial**
Email: ministercsf@
franciscans.org.uk

**Website:** www.
franciscans.org.uk

As Franciscan sisters, an autonomous part of the Society of St Francis, our primary vocation is to live the gospel in our time and in the places to which we are called. The setting for this is our life in community, under vows. Our wide range of backgrounds, abilities and gifts contributes to many ways of expressing the three elements of prayer, study and work. Prayer together and alone, with the Eucharist having a central place, is the heart of each house and each sister's life. Five of our sisters are priests; and three live the solitary life. Study nurtures our spiritual life and enables and enriches our ministries. Work includes the practical running of our houses and a wide range of ministries; currently these include hospitality, spiritual direction, prison chaplaincy, parish work and missions, preaching, leading quiet days and retreats, writing, being a presence in poor urban areas, nursing, and work with deaf blind people. Some of this work is salaried, much is voluntary. Each new sister brings her unique gifts, adding a new dimension to our life. As we begin our second century, we are excited by the challenge of living the Franciscan life in the twenty-first century.

JOYCE CSF
*(Minister General, assumed office 8 February 2002)*

### EUROPEAN PROVINCE

HELEN JULIAN CSF
*(Minister Provincial, assumed office 8 February 2002)*

| | |
|---|---|
| Angela Helen | Jennifer Chan |
| Beverley | Judith Ann |
| Catherine Joy | Liz |
| Chris | Maureen |
| Christine James | Moyra |
| Elizabeth | Nan |
| Gina | Patricia Clare |
| Gwenfryd Mary | Phyllis |
| Hilary | Sue |
| Jannafer | Teresa |
| Jennie | |

*Novices: 2*

*Companions & Third Order*
Companions are individual Christians who wish to associate themselves with the Society through prayer, friendship and in seeking to live the spirit of the Gospel in the way of St Francis. For more information about becoming a Companion contact the Secretary for

St Francis House
113 *Gillott Road*
**Birmingham** B16 0ET
*UK*
Tel: 0121 454 8302
Email: birminghamcsf
@franciscans.org.uk

St Matthew's House,
25 *Kamloops Crescent,*
**Leicester** LE1 2HX
Tel: 0116 253 9158
Email: leicestercsf
@franciscans.org.uk

10 *Halcrow Street*
**Stepney**
*London* E1 2EP
*UK*
Tel: 020 7247 6233
Email: stepneycssf
@franciscans.org.uk

*Office Book: Daily Office SSF*

**Bishop Protector**
*Rt Revd Michael Perham,*
*Bishop of Gloucester*

**US house**
St Francis House
3743 *Cesar Chavez Street*
**San Francisco**
*California* 94110
*USA*
Tel: 415 824 0288
Fax: 415 826 7569
Email: csfsfo@aol.com

**Website:** www.
communitystfrancis
.org

**Office Book**
*CSF Office Book*

Companions, Hilfield Friary, Dorchester, Dorset DT2 7BE, UK. For the Third Order SSF, see page 173.

## Community Publication

*franciscan*, three times a year. Subscription: £6.00 per year (£7.00 from January 2008). Write to the Editor of *franciscan*, The Friary of St Francis, Hilfield, Dorchester, Dorset DT2 7BE, UK.

## Community History

Elizabeth CSF, *Corn of Wheat*,
Becket Publications, Oxford, 1981.

## Guest and Retreat Facilities

COMPTON DURVILLE

Guests are welcome, both men and women, in groups or as individuals. There are fourteen single rooms and two twin-bedded. A self-catering cottage, sleeping up to six, and a hermitage for one are also available. Day guests, as individuals or in groups of up to fifty, can also be accommodated. Further information and a programme of events led by sisters are available on request from the Guest Sister. It is also possible to make a longer stay, working alongside the community, as a working guest or Sojourner, for periods from a few days up to six months. For further information, please contact the Guardian.

## AMERICAN PROVINCE

The Sisters came to the United States in 1974, and for over thirty years we have engaged in many types of ministry, but with special concern for the poor, the marginalized, and the sick. We can be found in hospitals and nursing homes; among the homeless, immigrants, and people with AIDS; teaching student deacons and serving on diocesan commissions; providing spiritual direction and directing retreats in parishes. In all things we strive to be instruments of God's love.

JEAN CSF
(*Minister Provincial, assumed office June 2004,*
*re-elected 2007*)

| | |
|---|---|
| Cecilia | Pamela Clare |
| Lynne | Ruth |
| Maggie | *Novices: 1* |

*Associates:* Contact:Yvonne Koyzis Hook TSSF, Secretary for Associates, 37 North Main Street, Stewartstown, PA 17363, USA.

*Community Wares*
We sell the *CSF Office Book,* home retreat booklets and Franciscan prayer cards.

*Community Publication: The Canticle.*
Contact St Francis House to subscribe - $5 for two years.

*Guest and Retreat Facilities*
At the San Francisco house, there is a guest apartment, which has one bedroom (two beds) and a small kitchen. It has its own entrance. The suggested cost is $40 per night.

*Most convenient time to telephone:* 9.00 am - 5.00 pm, 7.45 pm - 9.00 pm.

*Bishop Protector:* [Awaiting election]

---

# Community of St John Baptist
## (UK)
## CSJB

*Founded 1852*

The Priory
2 *Spring Hill Road*
*Begbroke, Kidlington*
*Oxford*
OX5 1RX
*UK*

Tel: 01865 855320
Fax: 01865 855336
Email: csjbteam@
csjb.org.uk

Website:
www.csjb.org.uk

Founded by Harriet Monsell and Thomas Thelluson Carter to help women rejected by the rest of society, we are now a Community of women who seek to offer our gifts to God in various ways. These include parish and retreat work, spiritual direction, and ministry to the elderly. Two sisters are ordained to the priesthood: one is serving her title in a nearby benefice; the other is chaplain to the homeless community in the centre of Oxford. Both preside regularly at the Community Eucharist. We have links with the Justice and Peace Movement and are specially committed to prayer for peace. There are close links with the sisters of our affiliated community at Mendham, New Jersey, USA *(see separate entry).*

Daily life centres on the Eucharist and the Divine Office, and we live under the threefold vows of poverty, chastity and obedience. Following the Rule of St Augustine, we are encouraged to grow into 'an ever-deepening commitment of love for God and for each other as we strive to show forth the attractiveness of Christ to the world'.

SISTER MARY STEPHEN CSJB
SISTER ANNE CSJB
SISTER ANN VERENA CJGS *(co-opted)*
*(Leadership Team, service of blessing 22 July 2004)*

Sister Sheila
Sister Doreen
Sister Jane Olive
Sister Edna Frances

Sister Monica
Sister Elizabeth Jane
Sister Zoe

| Morning Prayer | Obituaries | |
|---|---|---|
| *7.30 am* | 5 Jan 2006 | Sister Esther Mary CRJBS, aged 96, professed 59 years |
| *Tierce* | 28 Feb 2006 | Sister Moira, aged 94, professed 59 years |
| *9.00 am* | | |

**Eucharist**
*9.10 am*

**Midday Office**
*12 noon*

**Evening Prayer**
*5.00 pm*

**Compline**
*8.30 pm (8.15 pm Sun)*

**Registered Charity:**
*No 236939*

### Oblates & Associates

CSJB has women oblates. Men and women may become Associates or members of the Friends of Clewer - these answer to a call to prayer and service while remaining at home and work. This call includes a commitment to their own spiritual life development and to active church membership. Oblates, Associates and Friends support the sisters by prayer and in other ways, and are likewise supported by the Community, and are part of the extended family of CSJB.

### Office Book
*Common Worship Daily Prayer*, with our own plainsong hymns and antiphons.

## Community Wares
Cards, books, ribbon markers, Anglican prayer beads, holding crosses.

## Community Publication
*Associates' Letter*, three times a year. Contact the Leadership team - payment by donation.

## Community History
Books by Valerie Bonham, all published by CSJB:
*A Joyous Service: The Clewer Sisters and their Work* (1989),
*A Place in Life: The House of Mercy 1849-1883* (1992),
*The Sisters of the Raj: The Clewer Sisters in India* (1997).

## Guest and Retreat Facilities
Ten single rooms (two ground floor). Non-resident groups up to fifteen. Payment by donation - suggestions: £35 for the first 24 hours, and £30 subsequently, for resident visitors. Private Quiet Days and groups: £7-£14, depending on requirements. Most of the guest facilities have wheelchair access. Disabled guests are welcome if accompanied by a carer.

*Most convenient time to telephone*: 10.00 am - 4.30 pm, Monday to Saturday.

*Bishop Visitor*: Rt Revd John Pritchard, Bishop of Oxford

# Community of St John Baptist
## (USA)
## CSJB

*Founded 1852 (in UK)*
*1874 (in USA)*

PO Box 240 -
82 W. Main Street
Mendham
NJ 07945
USA
Tel: 973 543 4641
Fax: 973 543 0327
Email:
csjb@csjb.org

**Website:**
www.csjb.org

*Lauds 8.30 am*

*Eucharist 8..00 am*

*Terce 9.30 am*

*Noonday Office 12 noon*

*Vespers 5.45 pm*

*Compline 8.30 pm*

**Office Book**
*Our own book based upon
the Book of Common
Prayer of the Episcopal
Church of the USA*

The Community of St John Baptist was founded in England in 1852. The spirit of the Community is to "prepare the way of the Lord and make straight in the desert a highway for our God." We follow the call of our patron through a life of worship, community, and service.

Our Community is made up of monastic women, who share life together under the traditional vows of poverty, chastity and obedience. Our life includes daily participation in the Eucharist and the Divine Office, prayer, and ministry to those in need. We also have married or single Oblates, who commit themselves to a Rule of life and service in the Church, and Associates, who make up the wider family of CSJB.

We live by an Augustinian Rule, which emphasizes community spirit. Those who live with us include Oblates and friends, as well as our pony, dog, and cat. Our Retreat House and guest wing are often full of persons seeking spiritual direction and sacred space. Our buildings are set in a beautiful wooded area.

Our work includes spiritual direction, retreats, hospitality, youth ministry and chaplaincy. The Community participates in a mission in Africa, helps the homeless, and works in parishes.

SISTER BARBARA JEAN CSJB
(*Sister Superior, assumed office 2 October 1997*)
SISTER ELEANOR FRANCIS CSJB (*Assistant Superior*)
SISTER LAURA KATHARINE CSJB (*Novice Director*)

| | |
|---|---|
| Sister Suzanne Elizabeth | Sister Shane Margaret |
| Sister Pamela | Sister Linda Clare |
| Sister Mary Lynne | Sister Lura Grace |
| Sister Margo Elizabeth | |
| Sister Deborah Francis | *Novices: 1* |

### Oblates & Associates
Oblates make promises which are renewed annually. The Rule of Life includes prayer, study, service, spiritual direction, retreats. Associates keep a simple Rule. Membership is ecumenical.

### Address of other house
St Mary's Mission House, 145 W. 46th Street, New York, NY 10036, USA.
*Tel: 212 869 5830*

### Community Publication
Michaelmas, Christmas & Easter Newsletters.

*Community Wares*
Tote bags, mugs, cards, jewelery, candles, ornaments, tapes, prayer beads.

*Community History & Books*
James Simpson & Edward Story, *Stars in His Crown*, Ploughshare Press, Sea Bright, NJ, 1976.

Books by Valerie Bonham, all published by CSJB:
  *A Joyous Service: The Clewer Sisters and their Work* (1989),
  *A Place in Life: The House of Mercy 1849-1883* (1992),
  *The Sisters of the Raj: The Clewer Sisters in India* (1997).

P Allan, M Berry, D Hiley, Pamela CSJB & E Warrell, *An English Kyriale*.

*Guest and Retreat Facilities*
ST MARGUERITE'S RETREAT HOUSE
This has twenty-five rooms. The address is the same as for the Convent but the telephone number is: *973 543 4582*

CONVENT GUEST WING
This has six rooms (for women only). The cost is $75.00 for an overnight stay with three meals. Closed Mon and Tue.

*Most convenient time for guests to telephone*
Please telephone between 10 am and 4.45 pm.

*Bishop Visitor:* Rt Revd Herbert A Donovan, retired Bishop of Arkansas

*CSJB sisters*

# Community of St John the Divine

## CSJD

*Founded 1848*

*St John's House*
*652 Alum Rock Road*
*Birmingham*
*B8 3NS*
*UK*

Tel: 0121 327 4174

Email:
csjd@onetel.net

**Office Book**
*Celebrating Common Prayer*

**Acting Bishop Visitor**
*Rt Revd Gordon Mursell,*
*Bishop of Stafford*

**Registered Charity:**
*No. MAR 210 254*

The last twenty-five years have been a time of enormous evolutionary change within our Community, as we have prayed and sought the vision to work towards a new expression of the Religious Life for the future. In the last two years, we have been studying in greater depth the essence of the Religious Life, so that we have wisdom and courage to go on further developing new patterns for living our life and sharing it with others. In 2006, we have been working on a new model, currently in draft form, of the structure we hope to use in a pilot study, one that fits the culture of our time.

Those coming to test their vocation in CSJD need to be women and men not afraid of joining in the Community's exploration. Whilst the essence of Religious Life is safeguarded and its intrinsic values remain the same, our lifestyle is changing significantly. We are praying there will be those who feel God calling them to a possible vocation in the Religious Life, who would be interested and challenged and like to know more. We would be delighted to meet you.

The new model in some ways reflects older examples of living the Religious Life from earlier centuries, when Religious Houses were generous in sharing their life. We are a small Community at the heart of a multicultural city here in Birmingham. The core Community forms the welcoming centre for a growing number of Associates, Alongsiders and others who share much of our life. Our Associates have a very close relationship with the Community. The programme for Alongsiders has now been running for some five years and continues to be valued by those seriously wanting to deepen their spiritual life, or by those who for a variety of reasons need time and space to consider significant issues in their life.

Together our vision is to be: a growing centre of prayer within the Diocese; to exercise a ministry of hospitality to the many who come, either as individuals or as groups; to offer spiritual accompaniment; and to be more open to new ways in which God might use us here. New ministries are opening up, such as building friendships with our Muslim neighbours and in complementary therapies such as reflexology. All of our ministries seek to reflect something of the ethos of our community which has broadened to cover all aspects of health, healing, reconciliation and pastoral care in its widest context, ministries that all seek in helping people find wholeness.

The underpinning of our life and work is a spirituality

based on St John, the Apostle of love.

SISTER CHRISTINE CSJD
SISTER MARGARET ANGELA CSJD
*(Leaders of the Community, assumed office April 2007)*

| Sister Teresa | Sister Elaine | Sister Helen Alison |
| Sister Dorien | Sister Ivy | |
| Sister Marie-Clare | Sister Shirley | |

## Obituaries
14 Jan 2007    Sister Audrey, aged 93, professed 61 years

## Associates
Associates are men and women from all walks of life who desire to have a close link with the life and work of the Community. They make a simple Commitment to God, to the Community and to one another. Together with the Sisters, they form a network of love, prayer and service. (Guidelines available.)

## Alongsiders
Alongsiders come to the Community for varying lengths of time, usually six months to one year. The aim is to provide an opportunity of sharing in the worship and life of the Community, and could be useful for a sabbatical, a time of spiritual renewal, study, to respond to a specific need, or to allow time and space to consider the way ahead. (Guidelines available.)

## Guest and Retreat Facilities
Quiet Days for individuals and groups. Facilities for residential individual private retreats. Openness to be used as a resource.

## Most convenient time to telephone
9 am, 2.30 pm, 6 pm

## Community History
The brochure written for the 150th anniversary contains a short history.

## Community Publication
Annual Report.

## Community Wares
Various hand-crafted cards for different occasions.

## Community of St John the Evangelist

## CSJE

*Founded 1912*

St Mary's Home
Pembroke Park
Ballsbridge, Dublin 4
IRISH REPUBLIC

Tel: 1 660 2904

Founded in Dublin in 1912, CSJE was an attempt to establish Religious Life in the Church of Ireland, although it did not receive official recognition. The founder believed that a group of sisters living hidden lives of prayer and service would exercise a powerful influence.

From the 1930s, the Community had a branch house in Wales, which became the Mother House in 1967. In 1996, however, the Sisters returned to Dublin. The remaining Sisters of CSJE continue to live the Religious Life to the best of their ability and leave the future in the hands of God.

SISTER ANN DORA CSJE
*(Sister Superior, assumed office February 2000)*
*Professed sisters*: 5

**Associates and Companions**
Associates have a simple Rule, Companions a fuller and stricter Rule. Both groups are now much reduced in number.

**Office Book:**   Hours of Prayer with the Revised Psalter

**Bp Visitor:** Most Revd John Neill, Archbishop of Dublin

---

## Community of St Laurence

## CSL

*Founded 1874*

Convent of St Laurence
4 West Gate
Southwell, Notts
NG25 0JH
UK
Tel: 01636 814800

**Registered Charity:**
No. 220282

The Community was founded in 1874. The Sisters cared for the 'Treasures' of the Church - those in need of love and care, including elderly ladies. In the 1990s, more time was given to Retreat Work after the Residential House was closed, and in 2001 the Community moved to a new purpose-built convent in Southwell, adjacent to Sacrista Prebend Retreat House and the Cathedral.

Sister Brenda
Sister Dorothea
Sister Margareta Mary

**Associates**
Associates pray regularly for the community, and include priests and lay people. There are days organised at the Convent for the associates, at which new members may be admitted, and also retreats. We have over one hundred associates.

**Community Publication**
*Gridiron*, which is free of charge, on request.

**Bp Visitor:** Rt Revd George Cassidy,Bishop of Southwell

**Office Book:** CSL Office & Common Worship

# Community of St Mary
## (Eastern Province)

# CSM

*Founded 1865*

*St Mary's Convent*
*242 Cloister Way*
*Greenwich*
*NY 12834-7922*
*USA*

Tel: 518 692 3028
Fax: 518 692 3029
Email: compunun@
stmaryseast.org

**Website:**
www.stmaryseast
.org

*Matins* 6.30 am
*(7.30 am Sat & Sun)*

*Mass* 7.00 am
*(8.00 am Sat & Sun)*

*Terce* 9.30 am

*Sext* 12 noon

*Vespers* 5.30 pm

*Compline* 7.30 pm

*Bishop Visitor:*
*Rt Revd William Love,*
*Bishop of Albany*

The Sisters of St Mary live a vowed life in community, centered around the daily Eucharist and a five-fold Divine Office. Each sister has time daily for private prayer and study. Our way of life is a modern expression of traditional monastic practice including silent meals in common, plainchant in English for much of our corporate worship, a distinctive habit, and a measure of enclosure.

Our ministry is an outward expression of our vowed life of poverty, chastity and obedience. The specific nature of our work has changed over the years since Mother Harriet and our first sisters were asked to take charge of the House of Mercy in New York City in 1865. Being "mindful of the needs of others," as our table blessing says, we have been led in many ways to care for the lost, forgotten and underprivileged. Today our work is primarily hospitality, retreats, pastoral counselling and exploration of outreach through the Internet. Sisters also go out from time to time to speak in parishes, lead quiet days and provide a praying community within the Diocese of Albany's Spiritual Life Center and the Diocese of Northern Malawi.

MOTHER MIRIAM CSM
*(Mother Superior, assumed office 31 August 1996)*
SISTER MARY JEAN CSM *(Assistant Superior)*

| | |
|---|---|
| Sister Anastasia | Sister Monica |
| Sister Mary Basil | Sister Maria Nema |
| Sister Mary Helen | |
| Sister Mary Francis | *Juniors:* |
| Sister Mary Angela | Sister Esther Ernestina |
| Sister Catherine Clare | Sister Mary Chimwemwe |
| Sister Mary Elizabeth | Sister Maryeva |
| Sister Martha | *Novices: 3    Postulants: 2* |

### Associates

Associates of the Community of St Mary are Christian men and women who undertake a Rule of life under the direction of the Community, and share in the support and fellowship of the Sisters, and of one another, whilst living dedicated and disciplined lives in the world. Any baptized, practising Christian who feels called to share in the life and prayer of the Community of St Mary as part of our extended family is welcome to inquire about becoming an Associate. Each prospective Associate plans his or her own Rule with the advice of a Sister. An outline is provided covering one's share in the Eucharist and the Divine Office; a rule of private prayer; abstinence and fasting; and charity and witness. Individual vocations and circumstances vary so widely in today's world that a 'one size fits all' Rule is no longer appropriate. We do ask Associates to pray specifically for the Community, as we do for them, and, because the Divine Office is central to our way of life, to undertake some form of Daily Office. An Associate is also expected to keep in touch with us, and to seek to bring others to know the Community.

*Address of other house:* Sisters of St Mary, St Mary's Convent, PO Box 20280, Luwinga, Mzuzu 2, MALAWI, South Central Africa

*Office Book: The Monastic Diurnal Revised,* (The Community of St Mary, New York, 1989): a modern English version of the *Monastic Diurnal* by Canon Winfred Douglas with supplemental texts based upon the American 1979 Book of Common Prayer. Copies are for sale.

*Community Publication*
*St Mary's Messenger.* Contact the subscriptions editor. Cost to subscribers in the USA is $5, to those outside the USA $10.

*Community History*
Sister Mary Hilary CSM, *Ten Decades of Praise,* DeKoven Foundation, Racine, WI, 1965. *(out of print).*

*Community Wares:* Assorted illuminated greeting cards., convent-raised honey.

*Guest and Retreat Facilities:* Accommodations for seven in the Convent Guest wing and a further twenty-two accommodations on first-come, first-serve basis at adjacent Spiritual Life Center, in Greenwich, NY.

*Most convenient time to telephone:* 10 am - 7 pm Eastern time

---

# Community
# of St Mary
## (Western Province)

# CSM

*Founded 1865*

*Mary's Margin*
S83 W27815 *BeaverTrail,*
*Mukwonago*
*WI* 53149
*USA*

Tel: 262 363 8489

The Western Province of the Community of St Mary was set apart as a separate branch of the community in 1904. We share a common Rule, but have separate administration. Our basic orientation is toward a life of prayer, corporate and personal, reaching out to the Church and the world according to the leading of the Holy Spirit. We live singly or in small groups, each sister using her gifts for ministry as she feels led with the support of the whole group. Mary's Margin is the main house of the Western Province. We offer hospitality to individuals for private retreats and to small groups for meetings and quiet days. The sisters are available as spiritual companions on request. Other Margin offerings include Transformation Game workshops, quarterly drum circles, and a unique outdoor labyrinth winding through woods and meadows. On many Saturday evenings our chaplain celebrates a Vigil/Eucharist with us. The liturgy of the Word includes two periods of timed meditation followed by danced chants and a dialogue "sermon". Danced hymns frame the Eucharistic Liturgy, which is followed by a simple home-cooked supper.

Email:
srstmary@
marysmargin.com
or
CSM@
marysmargin.com

**Website:** www.
marysmargin.com

*The Farm*
S82 W27570 *Johnson Ave*
*Mukwonago, WI* 53149
*USA*
Tel: 262 363 5856

*Meditation*
*6.30 am*

*Morning Prayer*
*7.00 am*

*Meditation*
*5.00 pm*

*Evening Prayer*
*8.00 pm*

*Vigil/Eucharist*
*4.00 pm (Sat)*

*Office Book*
*Book of Common Prayer*
*of the ECUSA*

SISTER LETITIA PRENTICE CSM
*(President, assumed office January 1992)*
SISTER DORCAS BAKER CSM *(Vice President)*
Sister Mary Faith Burgess
Sister Jean Hodgkins
Sister Mary Paula Bush
Sister Mary Grace Rom

*Associates*
Associates (both men and women) are part of the community family. They follow a Rule of Life and assist the sisters as they are able.

Inner-peace Corps is a program for students or people in transition for whom a year or two of manual labor interwoven with prayer and labyrinthine contemplation would help to go back into the world with more focus and joy. At present we have space for only one candidate at a time (woman or man). (S)he works with the sisters and shares in the life and ministry of the house.

*Community Publication*
*St Mary's Messenger.* This is sent out once a year. There is no charge. Write to the community address.

*Community History and books*
Morgan Dix, *Harriet Starr Cannon,* Longmans, Green & Co, New York, 1896.
Sister Mary Hilary CSM, *Ten Decades of Praise*, DeKoven Foundation, Racine, WI, 1965.
Robert Boak Slocum & Travis Talmadge DuPriest (eds), "*To Hear Celestial Harmonies*", Forward Movement Pubs., Cincinnati, OH, 2002.
All three of these books, and other historical resources, may be accessed via the 'About Us' button on the community's website.

**Bishop Visitor:** Rt Revd Steven Miller

*Guest and Retreat Facilities*
We welcome both men and women guests. There are 3 single spaces in the main house for overnight guests plus 2 hermitages (with heat, no plumbing). There are also 2 double rooms in the farm house which is a 7-minute walk from Mary's Margin. The cost is $60 per day (3 meals and 1 overnight). Day groups up to 12 can be accommodated at Mary's Margin. The cost is $15 per person. A deposit of $10 per person must accompany group reservations. Day groups up to 20 can be accommodated at the Club House on the farm. No meal service is provided, but there is a full kitchen available or people may bring bag lunches. The cost is $10 per person.

# Community of St Mary the Virgin

## CSMV

*Founded 1848*

*St Mary's Convent
Challow Road, Wantage
Oxfordshire* OX12 9DJ
UK
Tel: 01235 763141

Email: conventsisters
@csmv.co.uk

Website:
www.csmv.co.uk

**Lauds**   *6.30 am
(7.00 am Sun
& principal feasts)*

**Terce**   *9.45 am
(9.15 am Sun
& principal feasts)*

**Eucharist**   *10.00 am
(9.30 am Sun
& principal feasts)*

**Sext**   *12.30 pm*

**Vespers**   *5.00 pm*

**Compline**   *8.30 pm*

**Office Book**
*CSMV Office*

The Community of St Mary the Virgin was founded in 1848 by William John Butler, then Vicar of Wantage. As Sisters, we are called to respond to our vocation in the spirit of the Blessed Virgin Mary: "Behold, I am the handmaid of the Lord. Let it be to me according to your word." Our common life is centred in the worship of God through the Eucharist, the daily Office and in personal prayer. From this all else flows. For some it will be expressed in outgoing ministry in neighbourhood and parish, or in living alongside those in inner city areas. For others, it will be expressed in spiritual direction, preaching and retreat giving, in creative work in studio and press, or in other forms of ministry. Sisters also live and work among the elderly at St Katharine's House, our Care Home in Wantage.

The Community has had a share in the nurturing and training of a small indigenous community in Madagascar *(see entry for FMJK)*. It was also in India and South Africa for many years. Involvement with these countries remains through 'Wantage Overseas'. Our links with South Africa are maintained by the groups of Oblates and Associates living there.

*Other Addresses*
St Katharine's House, Ormond Road, Wantage,
Oxfordshire OX12 8EA, UK          *Tel: 01235 767380*

366 High Street, Smethwick, B66 3PD, UK
                                              *Tel: 0121 558 0094*

116 Seymour Road, Harringay, London N8 0BG
                                    *Tel & fax: 020 8348 3477*

*Community History*
*A Hundred Years of Blessing*, SPCK, London, 1946.

*Community Wares*
The Printing Press offers a variety of cards and plainchant music. Catalogues are available from the Sister in charge of the Press at St Mary's Convent.
                    *Email: press@csmv.co.uk*
A variety of other items made by sisters is for sale in the Reception Area.

*Bishop Visitor:* Rt Revd John Pritchard, Bishop of Oxford

*Registered Charity:* No 240513

MOTHER WINSOME CSMV
*(The Reverend Mother, assumed office 8 December 2006)*
SISTER JEAN FRANCES CSMV *(The Assistant)*

Sister Cecily Clare
Sister Hilda Kathleen
Sister Margaret Jean
Sister Joan Elizabeth
Sister Margaret Julian
Sister Christiana
Sister Barbara Noreen
Sister Yvonne Mary
Sister Louise
Sister Margaret Verity
Sister Hilary
Sister Anne Mary
Sister Anne Julian
Sister Ethne Ancilla
Sister Catherine Naomi
Sister Honor Margaret
Sister Deirdre Michael
Sister Enid Mary
Sister Helen Philippa
Sister Valeria

Sister Phoebe Margaret
Sister Margaret Elizabeth
Sister Mary Jennifer
Sister Jean Mary
Sister Christine Ann
Sister Rosemary
Sister Bridget Mary
Sister Eileen
Sister Betty
Sister Rosemary Clare
Sister Sheila Mary
Sister Lorna
Sister Valerie
Sister Barbara Thomas
Sister Barbara Claire
Sister Mary Clare
Sister Margaret Magdalen
Sister Stella
Sister Francis Honor
Sister Patricia Ann

Sister Lynne
Sister Rozalja
Sister Anna
Sister Barbara Anne
Sister Gillian
Sister Althea
Sister Trudy
Sister Jan
Sister Elizabeth Anne
Sister Rachel
Sister Elizabeth Jane
Sister Pauline
Sister Samantha
Sister Alison Joy *(received under promise 2004)*
Sister Jean *(received under promise 2004)*

*Novice Sisters:* 1

## Obituaries

| | |
|---|---|
| 17 Nov 2005 | Sister Sara Maureen, aged 80, professed 39 years |
| 19 Sep 2006 | Sister Millicent Olga, aged 88, professed 61 years |
| 17 Nov 2006 | Sister Grace Mary, aged 90, professed 58 years (7 in CSD, 51 in CSMV) |

## Oblates

The Oblates of the Community respond to their vocation in the same spirit as Mary: "Behold, I am the handmaid of the Lord. Let it be to me according to your word." Oblates may be married or single women or men, ordained or lay. Most are Anglicans, but members of other denominations are also welcomed. There is a common Rule, based on Scripture and the Rule of St Augustine, and each Oblate also draws up a personal Rule of Life in consultation with the Oblates' Sister. There is a two-year period of testing as a Novice Oblate; the Promise made at Oblation is renewed annually. In addition to a close personal link with the Community, Oblates meet in regional groups and support each other in prayer and fellowship.

## Associates

Associates are men and women, ordained and lay, who wish to be united in prayer and fellowship with the Community, sharing in the spirit of Mary's 'Fiat' in their daily lives. Each Associate keeps a personal Rule of Life, undertakes regular prayer for the Community, is expected to keep in touch with the Associates' Sister, and to make an annual retreat. The Community sends out a quarterly letter with an intercession leaflet. Every two years an Associates' Day is held at the Convent.

**Guest and Retreat Facilities**
Guest Wing:  *Tel: 01235 760170    Email: guestwing@csmv.co.uk*

**St Mary's Convent**
The Sisters welcome to the Guest Wing those who wish to spend time in rest, retreat and silence within the setting of a Religious community.  Our particular emphasis is on hospitality to individuals, and where requested we try to arrange individual guidance with a Sister.  We are able to accommodate a small number of groups for Retreats and Quiet Days.

*Most convenient time to telephone*: 11.00 am - 12.15 pm, & 5.30 pm - 6.30 pm

# Community of the Servants of the Cross

## CSC

*Founded 1877*

*St Katharine's House*
*Ormond Road*
*Wantage*
*Oxfordshire*
OX12 8EA

The Community has an Augustinian Rule and for much of its history cared for elderly and infirm women.  In 1997, because of decreasing numbers, the convent at Lindfield (Sussex) was sold and the Mother House moved to the former theological college at Chichester, which had by then become a retirement home.  There they continued their pastoral work and used the former college chapel for Mass and Offices.  In July 2004, there were only two members of the community left and it was decided that they should move for the last time to be with their 'home community', St Mary the Virgin at Wantage, where they live at St Katharine's House.

MOTHER ANGELA CSC
*(Mother Superior, assumed office October 1995)*
Sister Jane

**Bishop Visitor**
Rt Revd John Hind, Lord Bishop of Chichester

**Warden**
Father John Lyon, The Vicarage, 33 Vicarage Lane, East Preston, Littlehampton, BN16 2SP    *Tel: 01903 783318*

# Community of St Michael & All Angels

## CSM&AA

Founded 1874

St Michael's House
PO Box 79
9300 Bloemfontein
SOUTH AFRICA

Tel: 051 401 5721

Mass is celebrated
five days a week.

**Office Book**
Anglican Prayer Book
1989, of the Church of the
Province of Southern
Africa

**Bishop Visitor**
Rt Revd E P Glover,
Bishop of Bloemfontein

**Warden**
Rt Revd T S Stanage,
retired Bishop of
Bloemfontein

The Community of St Michael and All Angels was founded by the second Bishop of Bloemfontein, Allan Becher Webb, for pioneer work in his vast diocese, which included the Orange Free State, Basutoland, Griqualand West and into the Transvaal. The sisters were active in mission, nursing and education. Sister Henrietta Stockdale became the founder of professional nursing in South Africa. The South African Synod of Bishops has placed her on the *CPSA Calendar* for yearly commemoration on 6 October. In 1874, the sisters established St Michael's School for Girls in Bloemfontein, which still exists today as one of the leading schools in South Africa.

CSM&AA continues with St Michael's Relief work in the Bloemfontein informal settlements, meeting with the workers, and supporting it with regular financial help.

Today, there is one sister remaining, living at the School although the postal address is the same.

Sister Joan Marsh

**Obituaries**

21 Jun 2005   Sister Thirza Dorey, aged 103,
professed 51 years
10 Aug 2006   Sister Mary Ruth Brewster, aged 101,
professed 70 years,
Revd Mother 1965-87; sister-in-charge 2002-06

**Associates**

The Associates of CSM&AA in South Africa meet four or five times a year. They keep a simple Rule and have an annual residential retreat in the country at a Roman Catholic religious house and farm in the Eastern Free State.

**Community History**

Margaret Leith, *One the Faith*, 1971.
Mary Brewster, *One the Earnest Looking Forward*, 1991.
Obtainable from St Michael's School, PO Box 12110, Brandhof 9324, SOUTH AFRICA.
Booklets by Sister Mary Ruth on work in Kimberley (*Dust & Diamonds*), on work at Modderpoort Mission (*Cave, Cows & Contemplation*) and on work in Basutoland/Lesotho (*Uphill all the Way*).
Obtainable from PO Box 79, 9300 Bloemfontein, South Africa

**Community Wares**

Handmade notelets and greeting cards.

# Community of St Peter

## CSP

*Founded 1861*

St Peter's Convent
c/o St Columba's House
Maybury Hill
Woking, Surrey
GU22 8AB
UK

Tel: 01483 750739
*(9.30 am - 5 pm
Mon-Thu)*

Fax: 01483 766208

Email:
reverendmother@
stpetersconvent.co.uk

**Office Book**
*Celebrating Common Prayer*

**Bishop Visitor:**
*Rt Revd David Walker,
Bishop of Dudley*

**Community History**
*Elizabeth Cuthbert,
In St Peter's Shadow,
CSP, Woking, 1994*

**Registered Charity:**
*No. 240675*

The Community was founded by Benjamin Lancaster, a Governor of St George's Hospital, Hyde Park, London. He wished his poorer patients to have convalescent care before returning to their homes. The Sisters also nursed cholera and TB patients, and opened orphanages and homes for children and the elderly. They were asked by priests to help in the parish and they were asked to go to Korea in 1892. They have close links with the Society of the Holy Cross in Korea, which was founded by the Community *(see separate entry)*.

Since the closure of their Nursing/Care Home, new work is undertaken outside the Community in the way of continued care, using Sisters' abilities, talents and qualifications in nursing, counselling and social work. The Sisters live in houses located where they can carry out their various works and ministry. They recite their fourfold daily Office either together in their houses or individually within their work place.

REVD MOTHER LUCY CLARE CSP
*(Mother Superior, assumed office 29 June 2006)*
*(St Columba's House address)*

Sister Caroline Jane *(Assistant Superior)*
*(Flat 5, Heriot Court, 1 Barker Road, Chertsey, Surrey KT16 9GZ)*

*St Mary's Convent & Nursing Home, Burlington Lane, Chiswick, London W4 2QE:*
Sister Constance Margaret      Sister Margaret Paul
Sister Rosamond

*41 Sandy Lane, Woking, Surrey, GU22 8BA:*
Sister Angela      Sister Georgina Ruth

**Obituaries**
17 Jul 2006      Sister Hilda OSEH, aged 98,
professed 64 years

**Associates and Companions**
The associates' fellowship meets at St Columba's at Petertide. The associates support the community in prayer and with practical help, as they are able. They have a simple rule and attend the Eucharist in their own Church as their individual commitments permit. Companions have a stricter rule and say the daily Office.

**Community Publication**
Associates' newsletter at Petertide and Christmas.

**Guest and Retreat Facilities**
St Columba's House *(Retreat & Conference Centre)*, Maybury Hill, Woking, Surrey
  GU22 8AB, UK        Director:  Revd Owen Murphy
  *Tel: 01483 766498    Fax: 01483 740441    Email: director@stcolumbashouse.org.uk*
*Most convenient time to telephone*: 9.30 am - 5.00 pm.
  Twenty-two single bedrooms, four twin bedrooms and a disabled suite.  A
programme of individual and group Retreats. Also a Conference centre for
residential and day use.  Refurbished in 1998 for retreatants, parish groups, and
day/overnight consultations.  An outstanding liturgical space with a pastoral, and
liturgical programme.  A place to retreat and reflect on life's journey.

---

# Community of St Peter, Horbury

## CSPH

*Founded 1858*

St Peter's Convent
Dovecote Lane
Horbury, Wakefield
West Yorkshire
WF4 6BD
UK
Tel: 01924 272181

Email:
stpetersconvent@
btconnect.com

The Community seeks to glorify God by a life of loving dedication to him, by worship and by serving him in others. A variety of pastoral work is undertaken including retreat and mission work, social work and ministry to individuals in need. The spirit of the community is Benedictine and the recitation of the Divine Office central to the life.

MOTHER ROBINA CSPH
*(Revd Mother, assumed office 14 Apr 1993)*
SISTER ELIZABETH CSPH *(Assistant Superior)*

| | |
|---|---|
| Sister Gwynneth Mary | Sister Phyllis |
| Sister Margaret | Sister Jean Clare |
| Sister Mary Clare *(priest)* | Sister Monica |

Sister Margaret Ann,
2 Main Street, Bossall, York YO2 7NT, UK
*Tel: 01904 468253*

**Oblates and Associates**
The Community has both oblates and associates.

**Community Publication**
Annual Review: *Keynotes*

**Guest and Retreat Facilities**
A separate guest wing has four single rooms, with shower room and utility room.

**Bishop Visitor:**  Rt Revd Stephen Platten,
                          Bishop of Wakefield

| **Lauds** | **Midday Office** | |
|---|---|---|
| 7.30 am | 12.00 noon | **Compline** |
| | | 8.30 pm |
| **Mass** | **Vespers** | |
| 8.00 am | 6.00 pm | |

# _mmunity of the Servants of the Will of God

## CSWG

Founded 1953

The Monastery of the Holy Trinity
Crawley Down
Crawley
West Sussex
RH10 4LH
UK

Tel: 01342 712074

Email:
(for guests bookings & enquiries)
brother.andrew@
cswg.org.uk

Vigils    5.00 am

Lauds    7.00 am

Terce    9.30 am

Sext    12.00 noon

None    1.45 pm

Vespers    6.30 pm

Mass
7.00 pm Mon – Fri
11.00 am Sat & Sun

This monastery is set in woodland with a small farm attached. The Community lives a contemplative life, uniting silence, work and prayer in a simple life style based on the Rule of St Benedict. The Community is especially concerned with uniting the traditions of East and West, and has developed the Liturgy, Divine Office and use of the Jesus Prayer accordingly. It now includes women living under the same monastic Rule.

FATHER GREGORY CSWG
*(Father Superior, assumed office 14 September 1973)*
FATHER BRIAN CSWG

Father Colin *(Prior)*            Brother Christopher Mark
Brother Martin                   Brother John of the Cross
Sister Mary Angela               Brother Andrew
Father Peter

**Obituaries**
5 Dec 2006    Brother Mark, aged 92, professed 57 years

**Associates**
The associates keep a rule of life in the spirit of the monastery.

**Community Publication**
CSWG Journal: *Come to the Father*, issued Pentecost and All Saints. Write to the Monastery of the Holy Trinity.

**Community History**
Father Colin CSWG, *A History of the Community of the Servants of the Will of God*, 2002. Available from Crawley Down.

**Guest and Retreat Facilities**
Six individual guest rooms; meals in community refectory; Divine Office and Eucharist, all with modal chant; donations c.£15 per day.

*Most convenient time to telephone*: 9.30 am - 6.00 pm.

**Community Wares**
Mounted icon prints, Jesus Prayer ropes, candles and vigil lights, booklets on monastic and spiritual life.

**Office Book**
CSWG Divine Office and Liturgy

**Bishop Visitor:** Rt Revd John Hind, Bishop of Chichester

# Community of the Sisters of the Church

## CSC

*Founded 1870*

*for the whole people of God*

**Worldwide Community Website:**
www. sistersofthechurch .org

*ENGLAND*
*Registered Charity No. for CSC:*
*271790*
*Registered Charity No. for CEA:*
*200240*

*CANADA*
*Registered Charity No. 130673262RR0001*

*AUSTRALIA*
*Tax Exempt - NPO*

Founded by Emily Ayckbowm in 1870, the Community of the Sisters of the Church is an international body of lay and ordained women within the Anglican Communion. We are seeking to be faithful to the gospel values of Poverty, Chastity and Obedience, and to the traditions of Religious Life while exploring new ways of expressing them and of living community life and ministry today. By our worship, ministry and life in community, we desire to be channels of the reconciling love and acceptance of Christ, to acknowledge the dignity of every person, and to enable others to encounter the living God whom we seek.

The Community's patrons, St Michael and the Angels, point us to a life both of worship and active ministry, of mingled adoration and action. Our name, Sisters of the Church, reminds us that our particular dedication is to the mystery of the Church as the Body of Christ in the world.

Each house has its own timetable of corporate worship. The Eucharist and Divine Office (usually fourfold) are the heart of our Community life.

The current houses in England provide different expressions of our life and ministry in inner city, suburban, coastal town and village setting.

ANITA COOK CSC
*(Mother Superior & UK Provincial, assumed office 1 March 1998)*
*Email: anitacsc@mac.com*

## ENGLAND

SUSAN HIRD CSC *(Assistant UK Provincial)*
*Email: susancsc@sistersofthechurch.org.uk*

| | |
|---|---|
| Aileen Taylor | Mary Josephine Thomas |
| Ann Mechtilde Baldwin | Robin Elizabeth Heald |
| Annaliese Brogden | Rosina Taylor |
| Beryl Hammond | Ruth Morris |
| Catherine Heybourn | Ruth White |
| Dorothea Roden | Scholastica Ferris |
| Elspeth Rennells | Sheila Julian Merryweather |
| Hilda Mary Baumberg | Sue McCarten |
| Jennifer Cook | Teresa Mary Wright |
| Judith Gray | Vivien Atkinson |
| Lydia Corby | |
| Marguerite Gillham | *Novices:* 1 |

**Obituaries**

17 May 2007   Marietta Moon, aged 96, professed 66 years
16 Jun 2007   Gillian Broadley, aged 93, professed 53 years

*Addresses in the UK*
St Michael's Convent, 56 Ham Common, Richmond, Surrey TW10 7JH
    *Tel: 020 8940 8711 & 020 8948 2502*          *Fax: 020 8332 2927*
    *Email: infouk@sistersofthechurch.org*

82 Ashley Road,
Bristol BS6 5NT
*Tel: 01179 413268*
*Fax: 01179 086620*

10 Furness Road ,
West Harrow,
Middlesex HA2 0RL
*Tel & Fax:*
    *020 8423 3780*

112 St Andrew's
    Road North,
St Anne's-on-Sea,
Lancashire FY8 2JQ
*Tel & Fax:*
    *01253 728016*

Well Cottage,
Upper Street,
Kingsdown,
near Deal,
Kent CT14 8BH
*Tel: 01304 361601*

*Carrying the cross*

# CANADA
*Arrived in Canada 1890.    Established as a separate Province 1965.*

MARGUERITE MAE EAMON CSC
*(Provincial, assumed office September 2003)*
*Email: margueritecsc@sympatico.ca*

Elizabeth Nicklin          Margaret Hayward          Michael Trott
        (Benedetta)        Mary Adela Carthew        Rita Dugger
Heather Broadwell

*Addresses in Canada*
St Michael's House, 1392 Hazelton Boulevard, Burlington, Ontario L7P 4V3
    *Tel: 905 332 9240          Email: sistersofthechurch@sympatico.ca*
51 Gates Lane, St Elizabeth Village, Hamilton, Ontario L9B 1T8
    *Tel & Fax: 905 387 5659*

# AUSTRALIA

*Arrived in Australia 1892.   Established as a separate Province 1965.*

LINDA MARY SHUTTLE CSC
*(Provincial, assumed office November 1999)*
*Email: lindacsc@ausnet.net.au*

| | | |
|---|---|---|
| Audrey Floate | Fiona Cooper | Helen Jamieson |
| Elisa Helen Waterhouse | Frances Murphy | Rosamund Duncan |

### Addresses in Australia

Sisters of the Church, 29 Lika Drive, Kempsey, NSW 2440
> *Tel: 2 6562 2313     Fax: 2 6562 2314     Email: infoaus@sistersofthechurch.org*

Apt.9/66-70 Parramatta Road, Camperdown, NSW 2050
PO Box M191, Missenden Road, NSW 2050
> *Tel & Fax: 2 9516 2407        Email: francescsc@ozemail.com.au*

Unit 15/75 St John's Road, Glebe, NSW 2037          *Tel & Fax: 2 9660 8020*

Apt 310/99 River Street, South Yarra, Victoria 3141        *Tel & Fax: 3 9827 1658*

32 Gillard Street, Burwood, Newcomb, Victoria 3125
> *Tel: 3 9808 4565            Email: elisahelencsc@westnet.com.au*

# SOLOMON ISLANDS

*Arrived in Solomon Islands 1970.   Established as a separate Province 2001.*

KATHLEEN KAPEI CSC
*(Provincial, assumed office 26 September 2004)*
*Email: kkapei@yahoo.com.au*
PHYLLIS SAU CSC *(Assistant Provincial)*
*Email: phyllissauu@yahoo.co.uk*

| | | |
|---|---|---|
| Agnes Maeusia | Joan Yupe | Rose Houte'e |
| Anna Caroline Vave | Joanna Suunorua | Roselyn Tego |
| Beglyn Tiri | Kate Furi | Ruth Faith Ruu |
| Belinda Seai | Lilian Mary Manedika | Ruth Hope Sosoke |
| Caroline Hariden | Linesu Raru | Selina Selimaoma |
| Daisy Gaoka | Lucia Sadias | Veronica Vasethe |
| Dorah Palmer | Margaret Mary Engo | Vivian Marie |
| Doreen Awaisi | Margosa Funu | Von Amevuvlian |
| Emily Mary Ikai | Mary Judith Tongisetonu | Winifred Kinilokea |
| Esther Teku | Mary Leingala | Winifred Sofia |
| Evelyn Yaiyo | Muriel Tisafa'a | Kamagiogamana |
| Florence Mola | Patricia Kalali | |
| Florence Sakua | Rachel Teku | *Novices:* 19 |
| Janet Karane | Rebecca Margaret Sulupi | *Postulants:* 5 |
| Jennifer Clare | Rose Glenda Kimanitoro | |

### Addresses in the Solomon Islands

Tetete ni Kolivuti, Box 510, Honiara

PO Box A7, Auki, Malaita              *Tel: 40423*

Patteson House, Box 510, Honiara
*Tel: 22413   Fax: 27582  Email: csc@welkam.solomon.com.sb*

St Gabriel's, c/o Hanuato'o Diocese, Kira Kira, Makira/Ulawa Province   *Fax: 50128*

St Mary's, Luesalo, Diocese of Temotu, Santa Cruz

St Scholastica's House, PO Box 510, Honiara

### Associates
Associates are men and women who seek to live the Gospel values of Simplicity, Chastity and Obedience within their own circumstances. Each creates his/her own Rule of Life and has a Link Sister or Link House. They are united in spirit with CSC in its life of worship and service, fostering a mutually enriching bond.

### Community History
*A Valiant Victorian: The Life and Times of Mother Emily Ayckbowm 1836-1900 of the Community of the Sisters of the Church*, Mowbray, London, 1964.

Ann M Baldwin CSC, *Now is the Time: a brief survey of the life and times of the Community of the Sisters of the Church*, CSC, 2005.

### Community Publication
*Newsletter*, twice a year, the editor of which is Sister Judith (West Harrow, UK, address, *Email: judithcsc@mac.com*). Information can be obtained from any house in the community and by email.

### Community Wares
Books by Sister Sheila Julian Merryweather: *Colourful Prayer*; *Colourful Advent*; *Colourful Lent*. All published by Kevin Mayhew, Buxhall, Stowmarket.
Some houses sell crafts and cards. Vestments are made in the Solomon Islands.

### Guest and Retreat Facilities
Hospitality is offered in most houses. Ham Common and Tetete ni Kolivuti have more accommodation for residential guests as well as day facilities. Programmes are offered at Ham Common: please apply for details. Please contact individual houses for other information.

### Office Book used by the Community
The Office varies in the different Provinces. Various combinations of the Community's own Office book, the New Zealand psalter, the UK *Common Worship* and the most recent prayer books of Australia, Canada and Melanesia are used.

### Bishops Visitor
| | |
|---|---|
| UK | Rt Revd Peter Price, Bishop of Bath and Wells |
| Australia | Rt Revd Graeme Rutherford, Assistant Bishop of Newcastle |
| Canada | Rt Revd Ralph Spence, Bishop of Niagara |
| Solomon Islands | Rt Revd Dr Terry Brown, Bishop of Malaita |

### Address of Affiliated Community
Community of the Love of God  (*Orthodox Syrian*)
Nazareth, Kadampanad South 691553, Pathanamthitta District, Kerala, INDIA

# Community of the Sisters of the Love of God

## SLG

Founded 1906

Convent
of the Incarnation
Fairacres
Oxford OX4 1TB
UK
Tel: 01865 721301
Fax: 01865 250798
Email:
sisters@slg.org.uk
Guest Sister:
guests@slg.org.uk

**Matins**
6.00 am (6.15 am Sun)

**Terce & Mass** 9.05 am

**Sext** 12.15 pm

**None**
2.05 pm (3.05 pm Sun)

**Vespers** 5.30 pm

**Compline**
8.35 pm (8.05 pm Sun)

**Office Book:** SLG Office

**Registered Charity:**
No. 261722;
SLG Charitable Trust Ltd:
registered in England
990049

A contemplative community with a strong monastic tradition founded in 1906, which seeks to witness to the priority of God and to respond to the love of God - God's love for us and our love for God. We believe that we are called to live a substantial degree of withdrawal, in order to give ourselves to a spiritual work of prayer which, beginning and ending in the praise and worship of God, is essential for the peace and well-being of the world. Through offering our lives to God within the Community, and through prayer and daily life together, we seek to deepen our relationship with Jesus Christ and one another. The Community has always drawn upon the spirituality of Carmel; life and prayer in silence and solitude is a very important dimension in our vocation. The Community also draws from other traditions, and our Rule is not specifically Carmelite. Another important ingredient is an emphasis on the centrality of Divine Office and Eucharist together in choir, inspired partly by the Benedictine way of life.

SISTER MARGARET THERESA SLG
*(Revd Mother, installed 24 June 2007)*

| | |
|---|---|
| Sister Josephine | Sister Helen Columba |
| Sister Mary Magdalene | Sister Catherine |
| Sister Mary Margaret | Sister Julie |
| Sister Benedicta | Sister Shirley Clare |
| Sister Isabel | Sister Avis Mary |
| Sister Adrian | Sister Alison |
| Sister Anne | Sister Tessa |
| Sister Jane Frances | Sister Raphael |
| Sister Mary Kathleen | Sister Raine |
| Sister Edwina | Sister Barbara |
| Sister Esther Mary | Sister Stephanie Thérèse |
| Sister Barbara June | Sister Clare |
| Sister Susan | Sister Freda |
| Sister Edmée | Sister Judith |
| Sister Christine | Sister Eve |
| Sister Cynthia | Sister Elizabeth |
| Sister Rosemary | Sister Helen |

**Obituaries**

| | |
|---|---|
| 7 Oct 2005 | Sr Mary Joseph, aged 86, professed 42 years |
| 8 Nov 2006 | Sister Margaret Clare, aged 94, professed 64 years |
| 4 May 2007 | Sister Patricia Thomas, aged 60, professed 26 years |
| 21 May 2007 | Sister Ellinor, aged 83, professed 36 years |

### Oblates and associates

The Community includes Oblate Sisters, who are called to the contemplative life in the world rather than within the monastic enclosure. There are three other groups of associates: Priest Associates, Companions, and the Fellowship of the Love of God. Information about all these may be obtained from the Reverend Mother at Fairacres.

### Community Publication: *Fairacres Chronicle.*

Published twice a year by SLG Press (see under Community Wares).

### Community Wares

SLG Press publishes the *Fairacres Chronicle* and a range of books and pamphlets on prayer and spirituality. Contact details:

The Editor, SLG Press, Convent of the Incarnation, Fairacres, Oxford OX4 1TB, UK
*Tel: 01865 241874  Fax: 01865 790860*

Best to telephone: Mon-Fri 10.30 am- 12 noon, & Mon-Thu in afternoons. A call answering service is in place for voicemail if there is no-one currently in the office.

*Email:*     General matters: *editor@slgpress.co.uk*

            Orders only: *orders@slgpress.co.uk*              Website: *www.slgpress.co.uk*

### Guest and Retreat Facilities

There is limited accommodation for private retreats, for both men and women, at Fairacres. Please write to or email the Guest Sister to make a booking.

*Email: guests@slg.org.uk*

### Most convenient time to telephone:

10.30 am - 12 noon; 3.30 pm - 4.30 pm; 6.00 pm - 7.00 pm

Sunday and Friday afternoons are ordinarily covered by an answer phone, but messages are cleared after Vespers.

### Bishop Visitor: Rt Revd Michael Lewis, Bishop of Middleton

*A Sister at work in SLG Press*

# Community of the Sisters of Melanesia

## CSM

*Founded 1980*

*KNT/Headquarter*
*Verana'aso*
*PO Box 19*
*Honiara*
SOLOMON ISLANDS

*First Office, Mattins &*
*Mass*
*5.45 am*

*Morning Office*
*7.45 am*

*Mid-day Office &*
*Intercession*
*11.55 am*

*Afternoon Office*
*1.30 pm*

*Evensong & Meditation*
*5.30 pm*

*Compline*
*8.45 pm*

*Office Book*
*CSM Office Book*
*(adapted from*
*MBH Office book)*

The community of the Sisters of Melanesia is a sisterhood of women in Melanesia. It was founded by Nester Tiboe and three young women of Melanesia on 17 November 1980. Nester believed that a Religious community of women in Melanesia was needed for the work of evangelism and mission, similar to the work of the Melanesian Brotherhood, founded by Brother Ini Kopuria.

On 17 November 1980, the four young women made their promises of Poverty, Celibacy, and Obedience to serve in the community. The ceremony took place at St Hilda's Day at Bunana Island and officiated by the Most Reverend Norman Kitchener Palmer, the second Archbishop of the Province of Melanesia.

The community aims to offer young women in Melanesia an opportunity of training for ministry and mission, so that they may serve Christ in the church and society where they live. To provide pastoral care for women and teenage children and uphold the Christian principles of family life. To be in partnership with the Melanesian Brotherhood and other Religious communities by proclaiming the Gospel of Jesus Christ in urban and rural areas in the islands. To give God the honour and glory, and to extend His Kingdom in the world.

### Addresses of other houses in the Solomon Islands

Joe Wate Household, Longa Bay, Waihi Parish, Southern Region, Malaita

Marau Missionary Household, Guadalcanal

NAT Household, Mbokoniseu, Vutu, Ghaobata Parish, East Honiara, Guadalcanal

Sir Ellison L. Pogo Household, Honiara

### Community Wares

Vestments, altar linen, weaving and crafts.

### Associates

The supporters of the Community of the Sisters of Melanesia are called Associates, a group established in 1990. It is an organization for men and women, young and old, and has over one thousand members, including many young boys and girls. All promise to uphold the Sisters in prayer, and they are a great support in many ways. The Associates of the Community of the Sisters of Melanesia are in the Solomon Islands, Australia and Canada.

SISTER CATHERINE ROSSER CSM
*(Head Sister, assumed office 26 September 2006)*
SISTER SUSSY LISAGITA CSM *(Assistant Head Sister)*

Sister Lydia Dora
Sister Phylistus Autedi
Sister Phylistus Pwai
Sister Kate Collin
Sister Ella Itopa
Sister Naomi
Sister Mildred
Sister Elizabeth Olehe
Sister Florence
Sister Hilda
Sister Dora Toke
Sister Patricia
Sister Olivia
Sister Jennifer
Sister Margaret
Sister Ellina
Sister Janet Olonia

Sister Mary Blessed
Sister Dorothy
Sister Ireen
Sister Julian
Sister Noelyn
Sister Rachael
Sister Serah Para
Sister Sandra Mary
Sister Mary Lulo
Sister Unice
Sister Elizabeth
Sister Sussy Great
Sister Nestar Tetei
Sister Nestar Legala
Sister Phylistus Sau
Sister Hellen Kolikisi
Sister Lorettalyn

Sister Miriam Matena
Sister Jennifer Forau
Sister Herodias
Sister Rogilyn Gaelona
Sister June Anu
Sister Alice Iwa
Sister MaryFord Rugu
Sister Edira Fay
Sister Joyce Buta
Sister Ellen Hiniva
Sister Kate Awakeni

*Novices:* 27
*Aspirants:* 10

**Bishop Visitor:** Most Revd Sir Ellison Pogo, Archbishop of Melanesia

*Sisters outside the Honiara house*

# Community of the Transfiguration

## CT

*Founded 1898*

495 *Albion Avenue*
*Cincinnati, Ohio* 45246
*USA*
Tel: 513 771 5291
Fax: 513 771 0839
Email: ctsisters@aol.com
Website:
www.ctsisters.org

**Lauds, Morning Prayer**
*6.30 am*

**Holy Eucharist**
*7.00 am*

**Noon Office**
*12.30 pm*

**Evensong**
*5.00 pm*

**Compline**
*8.30 pm*

**Office Book**
*CT Office Book*
*& the Book of Common Prayer*

**Bishop Visitor**
*Rt Revd Christopher Epting*

The Community of the Transfiguration, founded in 1898 by Eva Lee Matthews, is a Religious community of women dedicated to the mystery of the Transfiguration. Our life is one of prayer and service, reflecting the spirit of Mary and Martha, shown forth in spiritual, educational and social ministries. The Mother House of the community is located in Cincinnati, Ohio, where our ministries include hospitality, retreats, a school, a retirement/nursing home and a recreation center.

The community also offers a retreat ministry on the West Coast; and in the Dominican Republic, the Sisters minister to malnourished children and their families through medical clinics and a school.

The Sisters live their life under the vows of poverty, chastity and obedience. The motto of the community is Benignitas, Simplicitas and Hilaritas - Kindness, Simplicity and Joy.

**Other addresses**
St Mary's Memorial Home,
    469 Albion Avenue, Cincinnati, Ohio 45246, USA

Bethany School,
    555 Albion Avenue, Cincinnati, Ohio 45246, USA
    www.bethanyschool.org

Sisters of the Transfiguration, 1633 "D" Street,
    Eureka, California 95501, USA

St Monica's Center,
    10022 Chester Road, Cincinnati, Ohio 45215, USA

Dominican Republic Ministry:
    Sister Jean Gabriel CT, DMG # 13174 *or*
    Sister Johanna Laura CT, DMG # 13173 *or*
    Sister Priscilla Jean CT, DMG # 19105
Agape Flights, 100 Airport Avenue, Venice, Florida
34285, USA        Email: ct_sisters@yahoo.com

**Community Publication:** *The Quarterly*

**Community History**
Mrs Harlan Cleveland, *Mother Eva Mary CT: The
    story of a foundation*, Morehouse, Milwaukee, 1929.
Sibyl Harton, *Windfall of Light: a study of the Vocation
    of Mother Eva Mary CT*, Roessler, Cincinnati, 1968.

**Guest and Retreat Facilities:** These are available.

**Associates**
The Community has Associates and Oblates.

# Fikambanan'ny Mpanompovavin 1 Jesoa Kristy

## (Society of the Servants of Jesus Christ)

## FMJK

*Founded 1985*

*Convent Hasina, BP 28*
*Ambohidratrimo 105*
*Antananarivo 101*
*MADAGASCAR*

The FMJK sisters were founded by Canon Hall Speers in 1985. They live in the village of Tsinjohasina, on the high plateau above the rice fields, situated some fifteen kilometres from Antananarivo, the capital of Madagascar. The sisters work in the village dispensary and are active in visiting, Christian teaching and pastoral work in the villages around. They are an independent community but have been nurtured by a connection with the Community of St Mary the Virgin, Wantage, in the UK.

SISTER JACQUELINE FMJK
*(Masera Tonia, assumed office 5 June 2002)*
SISTER CHAPINE FMJK *(Prioress)*

Sister Ernestine
Sister Georgette
Sister Isabelle
Sister Odette
Sister Voahangy
Sister Vololona
Sister Fanja

**Other house**
Antaralava, Soamanandray, BP 28,
Ambohidratrimo 105, Antananarivo 101,
Madagascar

**Community Wares**
We make crafts and embroidery.

**Office Book:** FMJK Office and Prayer Book

**Bishop Visitor:** Most Revd Remi Rabenirina,
Archbishop of the Indian Ocean

**6.00 am**
Morning meditation

**6.30 am**
Morning Prayer

**9.00 am**
Silent Prayer for the Nation

**12.10 pm**
Midday Prayer &
midday meditation

**3.00 pm**
Silent Prayer for the Nation

**4.30 pm**
Silent prayer

**5.00 pm**
Evening Prayer

**8.00 pm**
Compline

# Korean Franciscan Brotherhood

## KFB

*Founded 1994*

156 *Balsan-Ri,*
*Nam-Myeon,*
*Chuncheon* 200-922,
*REPUBLIC OF KOREA*

Tel: 33 263 4662
Fax: 33 263 4048

Email:
kfb1993@kornet.net

Web site:
www.francis.or.kr

*Morning Prayer,*
*Eucharist & Meditation*
*6.00 am*

*Midday Prayer*
*12 noon*

*Evening Prayer*
*6.00 pm*

*Night Prayer &*
*Meditation*
*9.30 pm*

The Korean Franciscan Brotherhood is a community in formation in the Anglican Church of Korea. It is supported by the Society of St Francis through various ways, such as visits and the loan of an SSF brother (currently Christopher John SSF) as a mentor to KFB. The community aims to contribute to the building up of God's kingdom by a life of witness through prayer, hospitality and service.

Our friary is in rural Gangwondo, 90 km northeast of Seoul. We offer hospitality at the friary, manage the nearby diocesan retreat house, take part in some children's and young people's ministry, as well as preaching and leading spirituality and other programmes.

BROTHER STEPHEN KFB
(*Guardian, assumed office 2006*)
Brother Lawrence

### Third Order & Associates
We have a Friends' Association with about 130 members, about half of whom are young people. Members make a simple promise to help us by whatever way they can.

### Community Publication
The quarterly community newsletter is available in printed form (donation appreciated) or at the Web site.

### Community Wares
Block mounted icon prints, candles.

### Guest and Retreat Facilities
We have two guest rooms for single or small group use. Guests can share in worship and meals with the community. There are many walks around the friary and through its completely natural surroundings. As well as regular retreatants, visitors from overseas are welcome, or those making stopovers in Korea. We are about three hours by bus from Incheon International Airport. Accommodation is by donation.

### Office Book
The Daily Office SSF (in Korean translation)

### Bishop Protector
Most Revd Francis Park, Bishop of Seoul,
Presiding Bishop of Korea

# Little Brothers of Francis

## LBF

*Founded 1987*

*Franciscan Hermitage*
*Eremophilia*
*PO Box 162*
*Tabulam, NSW 2469*
*AUSTRALIA*

Email:
mailbag@
franciscanhermitage.
org

**Website:**
www.
franciscanhermitage.
org

*Bishop Visitor*
*Rt Revd Graeme*
*Rutherford,*
*Assistant Bishop of*
*Newcastle, NSW*

We are a community of Brothers who desire to deepen our relationship with God through prayer, manual work, community, and times of being alone in our hermitages. We follow the Rule written by Saint Francis for Hermitages in which three or four brothers live in each fraternity. As others join us we envisage a federation of fraternities with three or four brothers in each.

The sources of inspiration for the LBF are:

**1. Gospels:** Central to our spirituality, and the main source material for our meditation and prayer life.

**2. St Francis:** Francis would recall Christ's words and life through persistent meditation on the Gospels, for his deep desire was to love Christ and live a Christ-centred life. He was a man of prayer and mystic who sought places of solitude, and hermitages played a central role in his life. Significant events, like the initiation of the Christmas Crib tradition, happened at the hermitage at Greccio, and he received the stigmata while he was at the hermitage at Mount La Verna. Though the early brothers embraced a mixed life of prayer and ministry, Francis wanted places of seclusion - hermitages, for the primacy of prayer, in which three or four brothers lived.

**3. St Francis's Rule for Hermitages:** In his brief rule for life within the hermitage, Francis set out the principles that are important.

a. Liturgy of the Hours is the focus, and sets the rhythm of the daily prayer.

b. Each hermitage was to have at the most four Brothers, which meant they would be both 'little' and 'fraternal'.

c. Brothers could withdraw for periods of solitude.

d. Hermitages were not to be places/centres of ministry.

**4. Desert Fathers:** The stories and sayings of the Desert Fathers contain a profound wisdom for any who are serious about the inner spiritual journey. This is why they have held such prominence in monastic circles in both East and West down through the centuries, and why they are a priority source for us.

Each Brother has responsibility for certain areas of the community's life. Decision-making is by consensus.

Brother Wayne LBF
Brother Howard LBF
Brother Geoffrey Adam LBF

*Novices:* 1

*With the suppoet of the fraternity, each brother is to develop his own rhythm of prayer, soltiude, and manual labour.*

*Vigil Office*
*followed by Lectio Divina*
*2.00 am or 4.00 am*

*Meditation*
*6.00 am - 7.00 am*

*Angelus followed by Morning Prayer*
*7.00 am*

*Terce    9.00 am*

*Angelus followed by Midday Prayer*
*12 noon*

*None    3.00 pm*

*Angelus, Evening Prayer & Prayer Time*
*6.00 pm - 7.00 pm*

*Compline*
*8.00 pm*

## Friends

The friends of the Little Brothers of Francis are those who feel a spiritual affinity with the Brothers and desire to deepen their prayer life and to support the Brothers in their life and witness. They have an independent organisation, with its own office-bearers and requirements for membership. Contact : Canon Bruce Maughan, 122 Shrapnel Road, Canon Hill, Queensland 4170, AUSTRALIA.

## Community Publication

*Bush Telegraph.*
Contact the Brothers for a subscription which is by donation.

## Community Wares

Honey, jam, marmalade, cards and hand-carved holding crosses.

## Guest and Retreat Facilities

There is a guest cabin for one person or possibly two.

*Brother Wayne with a local sheep farmer and his Wiltshire horn ram on loan for the LBF flock's breeding season.*

# The Melanesian Brotherhood

# MBH

*Founded 1925*

**SOLOMON ISLANDS REGION**
*The Motherhouse of the*
*Melanesian Brotherhood*
*Tabalia*
*PO Box 1479*
*Honiara*
SOLOMON ISLANDS

**PAPUA NEW GUINEA REGION**
*Dobuduru Regional*
*Headquarters*
*Haruro*
*PO Box 29*
*Popondetta*
*Oro Province*
PAPUA NEW GUINEA

**SOUTHERN REGION**
*Tumsisiro Regional*
*Headquarters*
*PO Box 05*
*Lolowai*
*Ambae*
VANUATU

**Email:**
mbhches@solomon.
com.sb

**Website:**
www.orders.
anglican.org/mbh

The Melanesian Brotherhood was founded by Ini Kopuria, a native Solomon Islander from Guadalcanal, in 1925. Its main purpose was evangelistic, to take and live the Gospel in the most remote islands and villages throughout the Solomon Islands, among people who had not heard the message of Christ. The Brotherhood's method is to live as brothers to the people, respecting their traditions and customs: planting, harvesting, fishing, house building, eating and sharing with the people in all these things. Kopuria believed that Solomon Islanders should be converted in a Melanesian way.

Today, the work of the Brotherhood has broadened to include work and mission among both Christians and non-Christians. The Melanesian Brotherhood now has three regions: Solomon Islands, Papua New Guinea, and Southern (Vanuatu & Polynesia diocese). They have also opened two households and a community centre in the large island of Palawan, the Philippines. There is a Region for Companions and Brothers in Europe.

Following an ethnic conflict in the Solomon Islands 2000-2003, the Melanesian Brotherhood have been increasingly called upon as peace makers and reconcilers, work for which they were awarded the United Nations Pacific Peace Prize in 2004.

The Brotherhood has also led missions in New Zealand, Australia, Philippines and UK (2000 and 2005); their missionary approach includes music, dance and a powerful use of drama.

The Brotherhood aims to live the Gospel in a direct and simple way following Christ's example of prayer, mission and service. The Brothers take the vows of poverty, chastity and obedience, but these are not life vows but for a period of three years, which can be renewed. They train for three years as novices and normally make their vows as Brothers at the Feast of St Simon and St Jude.

## Community Publications
*Spearhead Toktok* [Solomon Islands] and *Partnership Toktok* [Philippines] (both occasional)
*Companions' Newsletter* for the Europe Region (once a year) - contact Brian Macdonald-Milne, address under 'Companions' below.

## Community History and other books
Brian Macdonald-Milne, *The True Way of Service: The Pacific Story of the Melanesian Brotherhood, 1925-2000*, Christians Aware, Leicester, 2003.

*Timetable of the Main House*

**First Office and Mattins**
5.50 am
(6.20 am
Sun & holidays)

**Holy Communion**
6.15 am
(7.15 am on
Sun & holidays)

**Morning Office**
8.00 am

**Midday Office**
12 noon
(Angelus on
Sun & holidays)

**Afternoon Office**
1.30 pm
(not Sun & holidays)

**Evensong** 5.30 pm
(6.00 pm
Sun & holidays)

**Last Office** 9.00 pm

**Office Book**
*Offices and Prayers
of the
Melanesian Brotherhood
1996
(not for public sale)*

**Bishop Visitor**
The Most Revd Sir Ellison
Pogo,
Archbishop of Melanesia,
Father
of the Brotherhood

BROTHER CAULTON WERIS MBH
*(Head Brother, assumed office November 2004)*
BROTHER ALPHONSE GARIMAE *(Assistant Head Brother)*
[LEADERSHIP ELECTIONS NEXT DUE AT THE OCT 2007 CHAPTER]

*Professed Brothers:* 399
(Solomon Islands: 236; Southern Region: 72; PNG: 91)
*Novices:* 260
(Solomon Islands: 150; Southern Region: 50; PNG: 60)

# SOLOMON ISLANDS REGION

## CENTRAL MELANESIA SECTION
BROTHER BRESIN RUADI *(Section Elder Brother)*

Central Headquarters, Tabalia, Guadalcanal
Norman Kitchener Palmer Household
St Barnabas Cathedral Working Household
Bishopsdale Working Household
David Sale Household, Komukama
Palawan Mission, Philippines
Bishop Patteson Theological College, Kohimarama

## CENTRAL SOLOMONS SECTION
BROTHER CULLWICK HAPI *(Section Elder Brother)*

Thomas Peo Section Headquarters, Koloti
Ini Kopuria Household, Kolina
Olimauri Household, Mbambanakira
Calvary Household, Surapau
Selwyn Rapu Working Household
Derick Vagi Working Household

## MALAITA SECTION
BROTHER GEORGE PASA *(Section Elder Brother)*

Airahu Section Headquarters
Apalolo Household, South Malaita
Funakwa'a Household, East Kwaio
Wairura Household
New Dawn Range Working Household, West Kwaio
Urutao Working Household, North Malaita
Kokom Working Household, Auki
Tasman Working Household, Nukumanu Atoll (PNG)

## YSABEL SECTION
BROTHER ABRAHAM SIRO *(Section Elder Brother)*

Welchman Section Headquarters, Sosoilo
Poropeta Household, Kia
Alfred Hill Working Household

Hulon Working Household, Yandina, Russell Islands
John Pihavaka Household, Gizo
Noro Working Household
Pupuku Working Household

**HANUATO'O SECTION**
>  BROTHER ALICK PALUSI *(Section Elder Brother)*

Fox Section Headquarters
Simon Sigai Household
Star Harbour Working Household

Ulawa Working Household
Johnnie Kuper Working Household, Pamua

**TEMOTU SECTION**
>  BROTHER MATHIAS LEEMAN *(Section Elder Brother)*

Makio Section Headquarters
Lata Working Household

Utupua Working Household

# SOUTHERN REGION
BROTHER THOMAS LOLOVAG *(Regional Head Brother)*
BROTHER FISHER YOUNG *(Regional Secretary)*
BROTHER JAMES TOVILE *(Regional Companions Secretary)*

**VANUATU SECTION**
>  BROTHER BADDELEY HANGO *(Section Elder Brother)*

Tumsisiro Regional Headquarters
Canal Household, Santo Town
Hinge Household (Lorevuilko, East Santo)
Suriau Household (Big Bay, Santo Bush)
Surunleo Household, Bwatnapni (Central Pentecost)

Saratabulu Household (West Ambae)
Noel Seu Working Household,
(South Ambae)
Patteson Household (Port Vila)

**BANKS & TORRES SECTION**
>  BROTHER FRESHER DIN *(Section Elder Brother)*

Sarawia Section Headquarters

# PAPUA NEW GUINEA REGION
BROTHER ALPHAEUS DUK *(Regional Head Brother)*
BROTHER DAVIS CYPRIAN *(Regional Secretary)*
BROTHER JOHN BODGER YAWOTA *(Regional Companions Secretary)*

**POPONDOTA SECTION**
>  BROTHER CHILLION MONGAGI *(Section Elder Brother)*

Dobuduru Regional Headquarters, Popondetta
St Christopher's Workshop
Wanigela Household

Berubona Working Household
Damara Household, Safia
Nindewari Household

## PORT MORESBY SECTION
BROTHER SAMSON GIS *(Section Elder Brother)*

Port Moresby Section Headquarters, Oro Village
Cape Rodney Household
Morata Working Household
Pivo Household

## DOGURA SECTION
BROTHER TONY AREWA *(Section Elder Brother)*

Mawedama Section Headquarters, Sirisiri, Dogura

| | |
|---|---|
| Iapoa Household | Pumani Household |
| Samarai Island Working Household | Podagha Project Household |

## AIPO RONGO SECTION
BROTHER STANFORD GULKUM *(Section Elder Brother)*

Aiome Section Headquarters, Aganmakuk

| | |
|---|---|
| Kinibong Household | Marvol Household, Ilu Mamusi |
| Aum Household, Tsendiap | Nambayufa Household, Siane Valley |

## NEW GUINEA ISLANDS SECTION
BROTHER ALFRED MOGEL *(Section Elder Brother)*

Akolong Section Headquarters
Aseke Household, Au (Gasmata)
Hosea Sakira Working Household, Ura (Cape Gloucester)

*Companions*
The Melanesian Brotherhood is supported both in prayer, in their work and materially by the Companions of the Melanesian Brotherhood (C.O.M.B.).

For more information about becoming a Companion, please contact:

| | | |
|---|---|---|
| Revd Brian Macdonald-Milne | or | Companions Chief Secretary |
| 39 Way Lane, Waterbeach | | PO Box 1479 |
| Cambridge CB25 9NQ, UK | | Honiara |
| *Email: bj.macdonaldmilne@homecall.co.uk* | | SOLOMON ISLANDS |

Alongside Companions, the Brotherhood also has associates whose ministry is more closely associated with the community, except that they do not take the threefold vow. They work voluntarily without wages just like the brothers.

*Guest and Retreat Facilities*
CHESTER RESTHOUSE, PO Box 1479, Honiara, SOLOMON ISLANDS, offers a Christian welcome. Eight twin-bedded rooms, self-catering, £13 per room per night.
   All the Brotherhood's headquarters and section headquarters can provide simple accommodation for visitors. Retreats can be made by prior arrangement with the relevant Chaplain at Central, Regional or Section headquarters.

# Order of the Holy Cross OHC

*Founded 1884*

*Holy Cross Monastery
& Novitiate
PO Box 99 (1615 Rt.
9W)
West Park
NY 12493-0099
USA*
Tel: 845 384 6660
Fax: 845 384 6031
Email: davidbohc@
hcmnet.org

**Website:**
www.holycross-
monastery.com

*Mattins* 7.00 am

*Holy Eucharist
8.30 am
(9.00 am Sun & major
feast days)*

*Midday Prayer* 12 noon

*Vespers* 5.00 pm

*Compline* 7.40 pm
*Monday is the Monks'
sabbath - no scheduled
liturgies.*

*Office Book:*
*OHC Monastic Breviary*

The Order of the Holy Cross is a contemporary Benedictine monastic community open to both clergymen and laymen. The principles which govern the Order's life are in two documents: The Rule, written by James Otis Sargent Huntington, the founder of the Order, and the Rule of St Benedict.

The liturgical life of each house centers around the corporate praying of the Daily Office and the celebration of the Holy Eucharist. Members also spend time in private prayer and meditation.

The work of the Order is varied, as members are encouraged to find ways to use their own unique talents in ministry. Houses of the Order vary from traditional monastic retreat/conference centers of hospitality to active inner-city urban houses. Members of the Order are engaged in preaching, counseling and spiritual direction, in teaching, in parish work, in evangelism, in retreat work, and in ministry to alcoholics, addicts and those with AIDS. The Order has a special ministry of building the monastic life in the Anglican Church in Africa.

**Other Addresses**

Mount Calvary Retreat House, PO Box 1296, Santa Barbara, CA 93102,
USA
*Tel: 805 962 9855   Fax: 805 962 4957*

Holy Cross Priory, 204 High Park Avenue, Toronto, Ontario M6P 2S6,
CANADA
*Tel: 416 767 9081   Fax: 416 767 4692*

Incarnation Priory, 1601 Oxford Street, Berkeley, CA 94709,
USA
*Tel: 510 548 3406   Fax: 510 649 0881*

Mariya uMama weThemba Monastery, PO Box 6013, Grahamstown 6141,
SOUTH AFRICA
*Tel: 46 622 8111     Fax: 46 622 6424*

**Community History**
Adam Dunbar McCoy OHC, *Holy Cross: A Century of Anglican Monasticism*, Morehouse-Barlow, Wilton, CT, 1987.

### FATHER DAVID BRYAN HOOPES OHC
*(Superior, assumed office 1999)*
BROTHER ROBERT LEO SEVENSKY OHC *(Assistant Superior)*

Father Anthony-Gerald Stevens
Brother Michael Stonebraker
Father Thomas Schultz
Father Christian George Swayne
Brother Laurence Harms
Brother Samuel De Merell
Father Rafael Campbell Dixon
Brother William Sibley
Father Bede Thomas Mudge
Brother Ronald Haynes
Father Brian Youngward
Father Nicholas Radelmiller
Father Roy Parker
Brother Adrian Gill
Father Adam D. McCoy
Father Carl R Sword
Brother William Brown

Father Bernard Van Waes
Brother Timothy Jolley
Father James Robert Hagler
Father Leonard Abbah
Brother Reginald-Martin Crenshaw
Father Richard Paul Vaggione
Brother Cecil R Couch
Brother Lary Pearce
Father Andrew Colquhoun
Brother John Forbis
Brother Scott Wesley Borden
Brother Kevin Patrick Cagle
Brother Bernard Jean Delcourt
Brother James Randall Greve

*Novices:* 5

#### Obituaries
5 May 2006        Father Douglas Brown, aged 62, professed 23 years
13 Sep 2006       Father Allan E Smith, aged 83, professed 45 years

#### Associates
Associated with the Order are groups of clergy and lay people who participate in varying degrees in the prayer and work of Holy Cross. Information about these groups can be had by writing to any of the houses.

#### Community Publication
*Holy Cross*, published twice a year. (Cost - donation.)

#### Community Wares
Incense (West Park); Coffee and tea (Santa Barbara).

#### Guest and Retreat Facilities
WEST PARK: 39 rooms at US$70 per day (accommodation for couples and individuals). Guest House is closed Mondays, Christmas and August.
SANTA BARBARA: 19 rooms at US$70 per day. Guest House closed on Mondays, for two weeks in January and for the month of August.
TORONTO: 2 double rooms; 1 single. Canadian $60 per day (couple), $40 (single).
BERKELEY: 2 rooms (for couples or single) at US$40 per person (no meals served).
GRAHAMSTOWN: 19 rooms (doubles or singles) - closed Mondays, Christmas and January.

*Bishop Visitor:* Rt Revd Mark S Sisk
*Deputy Bishop Visitor:* Rt Revd Ann E Tottenham

# Order of the Holy Paraclete

## OHP

*Founded 1915*

St Hilda's Priory
Sneaton Castle, Whitby
North Yorkshire
YO21 3QN
UK
Tel: 01947 602079
Fax: 01947 820854
Email:
ohppriorywhitby
@btinternet.com
**Website:**
www.ohpwhitby.org

*Morning Prayer* 7.15 am
*(7.30 am Sat & Sun)*

*Eucharist*
*7.45 am  (Wed & Fri)*
*8.00 am (Sat)*
*9.30 am (Sun)*
*12.30 pm*
*(Mon, Tue & Thu)*

*Midday Office* 12.40 pm
*12.15 pm (Tue & Thu)*
*12 noon (Sat)*

*Vespers* 6.00 pm
*(4.30 pm Sun)*

*Compline* 9.00 pm
*(8.30 pm Fri)*

*Office Book: OHP Office*

Founded as an educational order, the sisters have diversified their work in UK to include hospitality, retreats and spiritual direction, hospital chaplaincy, inner city involvement, preaching and mission, and development work overseas.

The Mother House is at St. Hilda's Priory, Whitby. Some sisters work in the adjacent Sneaton Castle Centre, which caters for a wide variety of day and residential groups. Other houses are in York, Hull and Sleights (near Whitby).

Overseas, the Order's long-standing commitment to Africa has been extended in exciting new developments: raising awareness of AIDS and providing a home for abused girls in Swaziland, and fostering vocations to Religious life in Ghana.  In response to perceived local interest and support, two new convents have been built: one in Jachie, Ashanti, where there is also an Eye Clinic run by a Ghanaian sister; the other in Johannesburg alongside St. Benedict's House, the retreat and conference Centre run by the sisters.

Central to the Order's life in all its houses are the Divine Office and Eucharist, and a strong emphasis on corporate activity.

## Houses in the UK

**Beachcliff,** 14 North Promenade, Whitby, North Yorkshire YO21 3JX
*Tel: 01947 601968      Email: ohpbeaccliff@hotmail.co.uk*

**Caedmon,** 30 Castle Road, Whitby, YO21 3QW
*Tel: 604645           Email: srheather@connectfree.co.uk*

**St Oswald's Pastoral Centre,** Woodlands Drive, Sleights, Whitby, North Yorkshire YO21 1RY
*Tel: 01947 810496      Email: ohpstos@globalnet.co*

**1A Minster Court,** York YO7 2JJ
*Tel: 01904 620601     Email: ohpyork@onetel.com*

**OHP Hull,** 9 Cranbourne Street, Spring Bank, Hull HU3 1PP          *Tel: 01482 586861    Fax: 01482 213114*
*Email: ohphull@cranhull.fsnet.co.uk*

## Houses in Africa

**Jachie,** Convent of the Holy Spirit, PO Box AH 9375, Ahinsan, Kumasi Ashanti, GHANA, West Africa
*Tel: 203432   Email: ohpjac@yahoo.com*

**The Sisters OHP,** Poste Restante, Piggs Peak, SWAZILAND
*Tel: 437 1514      Email: jdean@africaonline.co.sz*

The Sisters OHP, **Ikhaya Lokuthula**
*Tel: 0027 11 435 4725      Email: sisters@stben.co.za*
**St Benedict's Retreat House, (including** Ikhaya Lokuthula), PO Box 27,
Rosettenville 2130, REPUBLIC OF SOUTH AFRICA
*Tel: 11 435 3662   Fax: 11 435 2970    Email: sisters@stben.co.za*

SISTER DOROTHY STELLA OHP
*(Prioress, assumed office 15 July 2005)*
SISTER HEATHER FRANCIS OHP *(Sub-Prioress)*

| | | |
|---|---|---|
| Sister Kathleen | Sister Heather | Sister Marion Eva |
| Sister Ursula | Sister Muriel | Sister Judith |
| Sister Barbara Maude | Sister Mary Margaret | Sister Erika |
| Sister Sophia | Sister Anita | Sister Maureen Ruth |
| Sister Margaret Irene | Sister Margaret Shirley | Sister Margaret Anne |
| Sister Olive | Sister Nancye | Sister Jocelyn |
| Sister Marjorie | Sister Patricia | Sister Barbara Ann |
| Sister Rosa | Sister Gillian | Sister Carole |
| Sister Constance | Sister Hilary Joy | Sister Mavis |
| Sister Catherine | Sister Maureen | Sister Rachel |
| Sister Janet | Sister Grace | Sister Linda |
| Sister Philippa | Sister Janette | Sister Aba |
| Sister Alison | Sister Janet Elizabeth | Sister Pam |
| Sister Michelle | Sister Betty | Sister Helen |
| Sister Mary Nina | Sister Benedicta | Sister Karan |
| Sister Stella Mary | Sister Caroline | |
| Sister Lucy | Sister Margaret Elizabeth | *Novices:* 4 |

*Obituaries*
16 Sep 2005  Sister Bridget Mary, aged 91, professed 65 years
27 Sep 2006  Sister Marion, aged 85, professed 39 years

*Tertiaries and Associates*
THE OHP TERTIARY ORDER is a fellowship of women and men, united under a common discipline, based on the OHP Rule, and supporting one another in their discipleship.  Tertiaries are ordinary Christians seeking to offer their lives in the service of Christ, helping the Church and showing love in action.  They value their links with each other and with the Sisters of the Order, at Whitby and elsewhere, and when possible they meet together for mutual support in prayer, discussion and ministry.  The Tertiary Order is open to communicant members of any Trinitarian Church.

THE OHP ASSOCIATES are friends of the Order who desire to keep in touch with its life and work while serving God in their various spheres.  Many have made initial contact with the Sisters through a visit or parish mission, or via another Associate. All are welcome, married or single, clergy or lay, regardless of religious affiliation.

*Community Publication: OHP Newsletter*, twice a year.  Write to The Publications Secretary at St Hilda's Priory.  Annual subscription: £4.50 for the UK, £5.50 for the rest of Europe and £7.00 for the rest of the world.

*Community History*
A Foundation Member, *Fulfilled in Joy,* Hodder & Stoughton, London, 1964 *(out-of-print).*
Rosalin Barker, *The Whitby Sisters,* OHP, Whitby, 2001.

*Community Wares*
Cards and craft items. St Hilda's Priory has a shop selling books, cards, church supplies and religious artefacts.          *Email: sneatonshop@btinternet.com*

*Guest and Retreat Facilities*
ST HILDA'S PRIORY: six rooms (four single; one double; one twin) available in the Priory or nearby houses. Individuals or small groups are welcome for personal quiet or retreat, day or residential. If requested in advance, some guidance can be provided. There is no programme of retreats at the Priory. Contact the Guest Sister with enquiries and bookings.

SNEATON CASTLE CENTRE: seventy-one rooms (one hundred and twenty beds). The Centre has conference, lecture and seminar rooms with full audio-visual equipment, and recreational facilities. There is a spacious dining room and an excellent range of menus. Guests are welcome to join the community for worship or to arrange their own services in the Chapel.
Contact the Bookings Secretary, Sneaton Castle Centre, Whitby YO21 3QN.
*Tel: 01947 600051*
See also the website: *www.sneatoncastle.co.uk*

ST OSWALD'S PASTORAL CENTRE: 13 rooms (16 beds). 3 self-catering units.

*Most convenient time to telephone:*
9.00 am - 5.00 pm, Mon-Fri; 10.00 am - 12 noon Sat

*Bishop Visitor:* Most Revd John Sentamu, Archbishop of York

*Registered Charity:* No. 271117

*Archbishop Sentamu of York with novice sisters from Ghana.*

# Order of Julian of Norwich

## OJN

*Founded 1985*

2812 *Summit Avenue,*
*Waukesha*
*WI* 53188-2781
*USA*

Tel: 262 549 0452
Fax: 262 549 0670

Email:
ojn
@orderofjulian.org

**Website:**
www.
orderofjulian.org

*Morning Prayer*
*6.00 am*

*Mass*
*7.00 am*

*Noonday Office*
*12 noon*

*Evensong*
*5.00 pm*

*Compline*
*8.30 pm*

The Order of Julian of Norwich is a contemplative semi-enclosed Religious order of nuns and monks in the Episcopal Church, living together in two houses. We profess traditional vows of poverty, chastity, and obedience, with the added vow of prayer 'in the spirit of our Blessed Mother Saint Julian', the fourteenth-century English anchoress and our patron.

The ministry of the Order to the Church is to be a community of prayer and contemplative presence, expressed in communal liturgical worship in chapel and in the silence and solitude of the cell. Gregorian Chant is used for most of the four-fold Divine Office of the Book of Common Prayer. The Eucharist is the centre of our life, the genesis of our work of contemplative and intercessory prayer. This primary apostolate supports a limited exterior apostolate of the teaching of classical contemplative spirituality by retreats, spiritual direction, study and writing.

Founded in 1985 by the Revd John Swanson, the Order was canonically recognized by the Episcopal Church in 1997, and is affiliated with the Conference of Anglican Religious Orders in the Americas. For further information on the Order or its affiliates, please address the Guardian.

THE REVD FATHER GREGORY FRUEHWIRTH OJN
*(Guardian, assumed office 14 April 2003)*

Revd Father John-Julian Swanson
Sister Cornelia Barry
Sister Monica Clark
Revd Mother Hilary Crupi
Sister Therese Poli
Brother Barnabas Leben
Sister Miriam Motley

*Novices: 1 Postulants: 1*

### Associates and Oblates

ASSOCIATES
Friends of the Order, desiring a spiritual bond with the Julian Community who keep a simple Rule (one daily Office, Sunday Mass, annual reports to the Warden of Associates) and pledge financial support for the Order.

OBLATES
Persons committed to live the Order's spiritual and contemplative charism in the
world under an adaptation of regular vows. They have a Rule of: two BCP Offices
daily; three per cent of their tithe to the Order; three hours contemplative prayer a
week; a four-day silent retreat annually; Sunday Mass and seven Holy days of
Obligation, etc. They make a semi-annual report to the Warden of Oblates.

*Other address*
Llewelyn House, 59104 County Road D, Eastman, WI 54626-8139, USA   *Tel: 608 874
4495      Fax: 608 874 4885*
*Email: llewelynhouse@orderofjulian.org*

*Office Book*
The Book of Common Prayer of the Episcopal Church of the USA for Morning
Prayer; OJN Chantbook for other Offices

**Community Publication**
*JuliaNews* (newsletter) & *Julian Jottings* (essays), both quarterly. Subscription free.
Contact Sister Monica OJN.

**Community History**
Teunisje Velthuizen, ObJN,
*One-ed into God: The first decade of the
Order of St Julian of Norwich,*
The Julian Press, 1996.

**Community Wares**
The Julian Shop has books, religious
articles, many pamphlets written by
members.
*Email: julianshop@centurytel.net*

**Guest and Retreat Facilities**
Two guest rooms at each house.
There is no charge.

**Bishop Visitor**
Rt Revd Edwin Leidel,
retired Bishop of
Eastern Michigan

*Father Gregory sowing seeds*

# Order of St Anne at Bethany

# OSA

*Founded 1910*

*25 Hillside Avenue*
*Arlington*
MA 02476-5818
*USA*
Tel: 781 643 0921
Fax: 781 648 4547
Email:
bethanyconvent
@aol.com

*Morning Prayer*
*6.30 am*

*Eucharist*
*7.30 am or 8.00 am*

*Midday prayers*
*12 noon*

*Evensong*
*5.00 pm*

*Compline*
*as announced*

*Office Book*
*SSJE Office Book*

We are a small multi-cultural community of women committed to witnessing to the truth that, as Christians, we belong to this age, this society; and that it is here and now that we demonstrate to the Church and the world that the Religious Life lived in community is relevant, interesting, fulfilling and needed in our world and our times.

We are three Filipinas, one American and one Bahamian, and we strive to recognize and value the diversity of persons and gifts. We believe that God has a vision for each one of us and that opportunities to serve the Church and the world are abundant. For this to become real, we know that our spirits and hearts must be enlarged to fit the dimensions of our Church in today's world and the great vision that God has prepared for our Order. We are especially grateful for our continuing ministry within the Diocese of Massachusetts and with the Bethany House of Prayer. In this, we are assisted and encouraged by our four Alongsiders, our Associates, our Bishops and the clergy who minister to us.

The Rule of the Order of St Anne says our houses may be small, but our hearts are larger than houses. Our community has always been 'people-oriented' and we derive a sense of joy and satisfaction in offering hospitality at our Convent, at the Bethany House of Prayer and in our beautiful chapel.

Always constant in our lives are our personal prayer and our corporate worship, our vows of Poverty, Celibacy and Obedience, our commitment to spiritual growth and development of mind and talents, and our fellowship with one another and other Religious communities, as friends and sisters.

SISTER ANA CLARA OSA
*(Superior, assumed office 1992)*

Sister Olga                    Sister Maria Agnes
Sister Felicitas              Sister Maria Teresa

*Associates*
We have an associate program and continue to receive men and women into this part of our life.

**Community Wares**
Communion altar bread

**Bishop Visitor**
Rt Revd M. Thomas Shaw SSJE, Bishop of Massachusetts

**Community History and Books**
Sister Johanna OSA (editor), *A Theme for Four Voices*, privately printed, Arlington, Mass., 1985

**Guest and Retreat Facilities**
The Bethany House of Prayer is situated at 181 Appleton Street on the grounds of the Convent and Chapel. It sponsors, coordinates and offers a variety of programs and events including Quiet Days, Special Liturgies, contemplative prayer, spiritual direction, parish day-retreats, hospitality and workshops. For more information call 781 648 2433.

---

## Order of St Benedict

10 ‑ 11.45

### Burford

### OSB

*Founded 1941*

*Priory of Our Lady*
30 *Priory Lane, Burford*
*Oxfordshire*
OX18 4SQ
*UK*

Tel: 01993 823605

Email: information
@burfordosb.org.uk

Website: www.
burfordosb.org.uk

*Registered Charity:*
No. 221617

Burford Priory is home to a community of Benedictine nuns and monks. By a common life of prayer, manual work and study, they try to create an atmosphere of stillness and silence in which the Community and its guests are enabled to be open and receptive to the presence of God.

While the recitation of the Office and celebration of the Eucharist constitute the principal work of the Community, the ministry of hospitality, the care of the grounds (which comprises a large organic kitchen garden, formal gardens and woodland), the maintenance of the historic Priory buildings, and the income generating crafts provide manual work for the members of the Community and those guests who wish to share it.

The Priory seeks to be a place of encounter and reconciliation. The early concern of the Community was to pray for Christian unity; and the Community enjoys links with Baptist, Lutheran, Orthodox and Roman Catholic communities. This ecumenism has broadened to include dialogue with people of other faiths, particularly those with a monastic tradition, and those who are seeking a spiritual way, either within or outside an established religious tradition.

RT REVD BROTHER STUART BURNS OSB
*(Abbot, elected 14 October 1996)*
Sister Scholastica Newman
Sister Mary Bernard Taylor
Sister Gabriel Allatt
Brother Thomas Quin
Brother Anthony Hare
Brother Philip Dulson
Sister Mary Kenchington

*Novices: 1      Postulants: 1*

**Lauds** *6.45 am*
*(7.00 am Sun &*
*Solemnities)*

**Terce** *9.00 am*

**Eucharist**
*12.00 noon (10.30 am Sun &*
*Solemnities)*

**None** *2.00 pm*

**Vespers** *5.30 pm*

**Compline** *9.00 pm*

**Vigil**
*8.30 pm Sat & Eve of*
*Solemnities*

**Office Book:** *Burford Office*

*Friends*: There is a Friends' Association.
                Contact: *friends@burfordosb.org.uk*

**Guest and Retreat Facilities**
Eight-bedroomed retreat house, with six single rooms and
two twin-bedded rooms.
                Contact: *bookings@burfordosb.org.uk*

*Most convenient time to telephone:* 10.00 am - 11.45 am

**Community History**
*Burford Priory - a brief history of the house and its owners,*
Headstart History, 1999              ISBN: 1 85943 1402

**Community Wares**
Incense, printing (hand press) cards and letter heads, hand-
written icons using traditional materials, block mounted
icon prints, Chinese brush painted cards and mounted
photograph cards.    Contact: *craftsales@burfordosb.org.uk*

*Bishop Visitor:* Rt Revd Stephen Oliver, Bishop of Stepney

---

# Order of St Benedict

# Camperdown

# OSB

*Founded 1975*

*Benedictine Monastery*
PO Box 111
*Camperdown*
*Victoria* 3260
AUSTRALIA

Tel: 3 5593 2348
Fax: 3 5593 2887

Email: benabbey@
dodo.com.au

The community was founded in the parish of St Mark, Fitzroy, in the archdiocese of Melbourne on 8 November 1975, when the first two monks were clothed. In 1980, after working in this inner city parish for five years, and after adopting the Rule of Saint Benedict, they moved to the country town of Camperdown in the Western District of Victoria.   Here the community lives a contemplative monastic life with the emphasis on the balanced life of prayer and work that forms the Benedictine ethos.

In 1993, the Chapter decided to admit women and to endeavour to establish a mixed community of monks and nuns.  To this end, two nuns came from Malling Abbey (UK) and one has transferred her stability to Camperdown.

The community supports itself through the operation of a printery, icon reproduction, manufacture of incense, crafts and a small guest house.  A permanent monastery has now been built and the monastery church was consecrated by the diocesan bishop in February 1995.  On 8 November 2000, in the presence of a congregation of over 300 friends, the community celebrated its silver jubilee of foundation at a concelebrated Mass in St Mark's, Fitzroy, at which the Archbishop of Melbourne presided.   On July 11th 2002, the community elected the founder, Dom Michael King, as the first Abbot and he was blessed by the

*Website*
www.
benedictineabbey
.com.au

*Vigils*
*4.30 am*

*Lauds*
*6.30 am*

*Terce &*
*Conventual Mass*
*8.15 am*

*Sext*
*11.45 am*

*None*
*2.10 pm*

*Vespers*
*5.00 pm*

*Compline*
*7.30 pm*

*Office Book*
*Camperdown breviary*
*with a two-week cycle*
*of the Psalter*
*and seasonal and*
*sanctoral variations.*

Bishop Visitor in the Abbey Church on the Feast of the Transfiguration, August 6th 2002.

In 2005, the Chapter decided to ask for aggregation to the Subiaco Congregation of the Benedictine Confederation. This application was received favourably and we are now in a period of probation that will end with aggregation being granted on July 11, 2007. This is an historic step for an Anglican community to be given the opportunity to live its life aggregated to the Congregation, thereby receiving the benefits of such a world-wide body but retaining its Anglican ethos - a great step in ecumenism.

THE RT REVD DOM MICHAEL KING OSB
*(Abbot, elected 11 July 2002)*
Dom Placid Lawson
Sister Mary Philip Bloore
Sister Raphael Stone
Brother Ephraem Curry

*Novices: 1*

*Oblates*
There is a small group of clerics and lay people who form the Oblates of St Benedict attached to the community. The group numbers seventy persons from Australia, New Zealand and Canada following the Benedictine life according to their individual situations. Oblates usually visit the monastery once a year and keep in regular contact with the parent community.

*Community Publication*
The Community produces a newsletter yearly in December.

*Community Wares*
Printing, icons, cards, incense, devotional items.

*Guest and Retreat Facilities*
There is a small guest house (St Joseph's), which can accommodate six people, open to men and women, for private retreats and spiritual direction. Guests eat with the community and are welcome to attend the services in the church. A donation of $50.00 per day is suggested.

*Abbot Visitor:* Rt Revd Dom Bruno Marin OSB
*Confessor:* Rt Revd David Farrer, Bishop of Wangaratta
*Diocesan Bishop:*
            Rt Revd Michael Hough, Bishop of Ballarat

# Order of St Benedict

# Community of St Mary at the Cross, Edgware

# OSB

*Founded 1866*

*St Mary at the Cross*
*Priory Field Drive*
*Hale Lane*
*Edgware*
*Middlesex* HA8 9PZ
*UK*

Tel: 020 8958 7868
Fax: 020 8958 1920

Email:
nuns.osb.edgware
@btclick.com

**Website:** www.
edgwareabbey.org.uk

**Bishop Visitor**
*Rt Revd Peter Wheatley,*
*Bishop of Edmonton*

**Registered Charity:**
*No. 209261*

With its dedication to St Mary at the Cross, this community has a special vocation to stand with Christ's Mother beside those who suffer. From its earliest days in Shoreditch, where Mother Monnica Skinner and Revd Henry Nihill worked together as co-founders, the sisters were drawn to the desperately poor and sick people around them. Awareness of the needs of many 'incurable children', led to the building of a hospital, marking the beginning of the community's life work.

Time passes and needs change; over the years the community's work has evolved to meet the present needs of elderly frail people for nursing or residential care. This care provision continues in Henry Nihill House at Edgware Abbey, where Residents enjoy close links with the community, its worship and its life.

From its foundation, the heart of the community's vocation lay in prayer; the Divine Office and the Eucharist were and are central to its life, love finding its expression in a care for those in need. Today many people are welcomed at the abbey, finding there a place of peace; all are offered Benedictine hospitality and given space for rest and renewal, with the opportunity to share in the community's worship.

RT REVD DAME MARY THÉRÈSE ZELENT OSB
*(Abbess, elected 30 March 1993)*
VERY REVD DAME MARY EANFLEDA BARBARA JOHNSON OSB
*(Prioress)*
Dame Ruth Mary Catherine Campbell

*Intern Oblate:* Raili Lappalainen

*Ethiopian Orthodox:*
Sister Atsede Bekele
Sister Tirsit Eguale

**Obituaries**
14 Mar 2006    Dame Teresa Mary Hastie
aged 93, professed 57 years

**Oblates:** Our Oblates are part of our extended Community family: living outside the cloister; following the spirit of the Holy Rule of St Benedict; bonded with the Community in prayer and commitment to service.

*Readings
and Lauds*

*7.00 am   (7.30 am Sun)*

*Midday Office*

*11.55 am  (except Sun)*

*Vespers*
*5.30 pm*
*(4.40 pm Fri)*

*Compline*
*7.30 pm*

*Mass*
*7.45 am weekdays*
*11.00 am once a week 11.00*
*am  Sun & feast days*

*Holy Hour:*
*4.40 pm on Fri*
*(Vespers and Benediction)*

*First Fri of month:*
*11.55 am*
*Exposition and prayer,*
*ending in Holy Hour.*

*Office Book*
*The Divine Office.*
*The Community has its*
*own form of Compline.*

*Community Publication*
*Abbey Newsletter*, published yearly.  There is no charge but donations are welcome.  Obtainable from the Convent.

*Community Wares*
CLOISTER CRAFTS     Small Convent Craft Shop.  Goods available include printed and hand-crafted cards for many occasions, devotional items, attractive hand-crafted goods, a good range of books, including new publications.

*Guest and Retreat Facilities*
Only minutes from the M1, the Convent offers an excellent:

DAY CONFERENCE CENTRE
Open 9 am - 6 pm, the Centre has space for about fifty people: ideal for church groups, training days, family parties etc.  It is fully wheel-chair accessible.  Closed Holy Week and the Christmas holiday.

GUEST ACCOMMODATION
*Loreto* - a small comfortable guest house with seven bedrooms.  Hospitality for up to seven days for rest and retreat.

*St Raphael's*
Six spacious ground floor bedrooms, in pleasant surroundings.

*Quiet Days* - a welcome is given to anyone needing space in their lives for prayer, study or reflection.  Please note that there is a recommended tariff which covers basic costs for guest facilities etc. but special arrangements can be made with Mother Abbess for anyone who cannot afford these costs.  Requests for booking forms may be made by telephone, Monday-Friday, 9.00 am - 4.30 pm, or by post to the Guest Mistress.

*Prayer Link:*     Many people, often whole parishes, are linked with the Community in a simple commitment to prayer and intercession.

*Monastic experience:*  Applications are considered from women who wish to spend up to three months living alongside the Community and sharing in its life and worship. (There is no long-term accommodation for men.)

# Order of St Benedict

# Elmore Abbey

# OSB

*Founded 1914*

*Elmore Abbey*
*Church Lane*
*Speen, Newbury*
*Berkshire* RG14 1SA
*UK*

Tel: 01635 33080
Email: elmore.abbey
@virgin.net
Website: www.
elmoreabbey.org

**Vigils** *5.30 am*

**Lauds** *8.00 am*

**Terce** *10.00 am*

**Sext** *12.00 noon*

**None** *4.00 pm*

**Vespers** *6.00 pm*

**Compline** *8.30 pm*

**Mass**
*8.00 am Mon – Sat*
*(with Lauds)*
*10.00 am Sun*

The monastery aims to provide an environment within which the traditional monastic balance between worship, study and work may be maintained with a characteristic Benedictine stress upon corporate worship and community life. To this end, outside commitments are kept to a minimum.

VERY REVD DOM SIMON JARRATT OSB
*(Conventual Prior, elected 13 December 2005)*
(RT REVD) DOM KENNETH NEWING OSB *(Sub-Prior)*
Dom Francis Hutchison
Dom Bruce De Walt
Brother Hugh Kelly

*Oblates*
An extended confraternity of oblates, numbering over 300 men and women, married and single, seek to live according to a rule of life inspired by Benedictine principles. From the start, the community has believed in the importance of prayer for Christian unity and the fostering of ecumenism. Details can be obtained from the Oblate Master.

*Community Publication*
*Elmore Abbey Record*, yearly, write to the Cellarer.

Books:
Augustine Morris, *Oblates: Life with Saint Benedict* £4.25.
Simon Bailey, *A Tactful God: Gregory Dix*, £12.99.

*Guest and Retreat Facilities*
There is a small guest house with accommodation for up to four wishing to stay for a personal retreat or period of quiet. Guests are admitted to the Oratory, the Guests' Common Room, the Refectory and the front garden.

*Most convenient time to telephone*
9.30 am - 9.50 am; 10.30 am - 11.45 am; 2.30 pm - 3.45 pm; 5.00 pm - 5.30 pm
*Tel & answerphone: 01635 33080*

*Bishop Visitor:*
Rt Revd Dominic Walker OGS, Bishop of Monmouth

*Office Book:* Elmore Abbey Office books

*Registered Charity:*
Pershore Nashdom & Elmore Trust - No. 220012

# Order of St Benedict

## Malling Abbey

## OSB

*Founded 1891*

*St Mary's Abbey*
*52 Swan Street*
*West Malling, Kent*
ME19 6JX
*UK*
Tel: 01732 843309

**Vigils**
*4.30 am   (5.00 am Sun)*

**Lauds**
*6.50 am   (8.10 am Sun)*

**Eucharist**
*7.30 am   (9.00 am Sun)*

**Terce** *8.45 am*

**Sext** *12.00 noon*

**None** *3.00 pm*

**Vespers** *4.45 pm*

**Compline** *7.25 pm*

**Office Book**
*Malling Abbey Office*

**Bishop Visitor**
*Rt Revd John Waine*

Saint Benedict sees the monastery as a school of the Lord's service where a united community endeavours to grow in stability, conversion of life and obedience within the enclosure. The call of God is the essential requirement for admission to the novitiate to share in the life of prayer, study and manual work in the house and grounds. The period of training before final profession is normally six years. The guest house offers hospitality to those wishing to share the worship and peace of the Abbey for a few days.

MOTHER ABBESS MARY JOHN MARSHALL OSB
*(elected 27 September 1990)*
SISTER MARY STEPHEN PACKWOOD OSB *(Prioress)*
SISTER MARY MARK BROOKSBANK OSB *(Sub-Prioress)*

| | |
|---|---|
| Sister Macrina Banner | Sister Felicity Spencer |
| Sister Mary Ignatius Conklin | Sister Bartimaeus Ives |
| Sister Mary Simon Corbett | Sister Seonaid Crabtree |
| Sister Ruth Blackmore | Sister Mary Michael Wilson |
| Sister Mary Cuthbert Archer | Sister Miriam Noke |
| Sister Mary Francis Tillard | Sister Mary Owen DeSimone |
| Sister Mary Gundulf Wood | Sister Margaret Joy Harris |
| Sister Mary David Best | *Novices:* 1 |

Sister Jean CHF

**Obituaries**

| | |
|---|---|
| 23 Mar 2006 | Sister Mary Augustine Dalgarno, aged 89, professed 56 years |
| 14 May 2006 | Sister Phyllis Ella CHF, aged 93, professed 45 years |
| 3 Sep 2006 | Sister Anastasia Feast, aged 89, professed 50 years |

**Oblates**

Oblates are men and women who feel called by God to follow the Benedictine way, but outside the cloister. They affirm their baptismal commitment by a promise of conversion of life worked out in a personal rule based on Saint Benedict's Rule. As members of the oblate family, they are united to the community and to their fellow oblates in mutual love and  fellowship. Oblates share in the community's worship by praying the Office, though not necessarily at the same time as at the abbey.  The minimum is two Offices daily and if possible these are Lauds and Vespers. Eucharist: attendance at least once a week. Retreat at least two days annually, at the abbey or elsewhere. Regular Prayer and *lectio*. Rule: to be read through at least annually.

*Community Wares*
There are cards and booklets printed and painted at the abbey on sale at the Guest House.

*Guest and Retreat Facilities*
We offer no organised retreats apart from those for our oblates.  Those wishing to make a private retreat are welcome to do so at the Guest House.

*Most convenient time to telephone*:   10 am - 11.30 am, 3.15 pm - 3.45 pm.

---

# Order of St Benedict

# Servants of Christ Priory

# OSB

*Founded 1968*

*28 West Pasadena Avenue*
*Phoenix*
*AZ 85013 2002*
*USA*
Tel: 602 248 9321
Email:
cderijk@cox.net

*Morning Prayer*
*6.00 am*

*Mass*  *6.30 am*

*Midday Prayer*
*12 noon*

*Evening Prayer*
*4.30 pm*

*Compline*
*8.00 pm*

A community united in love for God and one another following the Benedictine balance of prayer, study and work reflects the life of the monks.  Outside engagements are accepted as long as they do not interfere with the monastic routine.

THE VERY REVD CORNELIS J. DE RIJK OSB
*(Prior, assumed office November 1985)*
The Revd Lewis H. Long

*Oblates*
Oblates follow a rule of life consistent with the Rule of St Benedict adapted to their lifestyle.  Those in the metropolitan Phoenix area meet once a month at the monastery.

*Community Wares*
We have a gift shop which stocks Prayer Books, Bibles, hymnals, (including BCP-hymnal combo & BCP-Bible combo), religious books and jewelry.  We also supply altar bread and candles to numerous parishes.

*Guest and Retreat Facilities*
We have two single rooms and two double rooms for individuals who wish to come and participate in our life. Day guests are also welcome.  Guests have use of the grounds, the library, and share meals with the community.  We are closed in August.

*Bishop Visitor*
Rt Revd Kirk Stevan Smith, Bishop of Arizona

*Office Book:*  The Book of Common Prayer of the Episcopal Church of the USA

# Order of St Benedict Busan OSB

Founded 1993

810-1 Baekrok-ri
Habuk-myon
Yangsan-shi
Kyungnam 626-860
SOUTH KOREA

Tel: 55 384 1560

Mobile: 010 9335 1560

Email: bundo1993@
hanmail.net

**Morning Prayer**
6.20 am

**Eucharist**
7.00 am (Wed only)

**Day Office (Intercessions)**
12 noon

**Evening Prayer**
5.30 pm

**Compline**
8.00 pm

**Office Book**
Korean Common Prayer Book

**Bishop Visitor**
Rt Revd Solomon Yoon,
Bishop of Busan

There has been an Anglican community in Seoul for many years, but it was the wish of Bishop Bundo Kim to establish a community in Busan - in the south of Korea. Thus it was that in 1993, the Order of St Benedict was founded in Busan City. In four years, sufficient money was raised by the Diocese to buy a more spacious, rural accommodation in Yangsan (to the north of Busan), offering more room for retreats, and for community and parish work.

SISTER MARTHA HAN OSB
*(Senior Sister, assumed office 1998)*
Sister Michaela

### Community Publication
Summer and Christmas Newsletters. Contact Sister Martha re donations.

### Associates
There is an informal group of Associates.

*Our Lady in the garden*

### Guest and Retreat Facilities
There are three guest rooms for private retreats, with good kitchen and bathroom facilities. For larger groups, Korean-style accommodation is used. There are no restrictions on length of stay, and both men and women are welcome. There is no set charge but by donation only.

***Most convenient time to telephone:*** 9.30 am - 7.00 pm

# St Gregory's Abbey Three Rivers OSB

*Founded 1939*

St Gregory's Abbey
56500 Abbey Road
Three Rivers
Michigan 49093-9595
USA
Tel: 269 244 5893
Fax: 269 244 8712
Email: abbotand
@net-link.com

**Website:** saintgregorys-
abbeythreerivers.org

**Matins**
*4.00 am*
*(5.30 am Sun &
solemnities, with Lauds)*

**Lauds**
*6.00 am*

**Terce & Mass**
*8.15 am  (8.30 am Sun
& solemnities)*

**Sext**
*11.30 am (12 noon Sun &
solemnities, with None)*

**None**
*2.00 pm*

**Vespers**
*5.00 pm*

**Compline**
*7.45 pm*

St Gregory's Abbey is the home of a community of men living under the Rule of St Benedict within the Episcopal Church. The center of the monastery's life is the Abbey Church, where God is worshipped in the daily round of Eucharist, Divine Office, and private prayer. Also offered to God are the monks' daily manual work, study and correspondence, ministry to guests, and occasional outside engagements.

RIGHT REVD ANDREW MARR OSB
*(Abbot, elected 2 March 1989)*
VERY REVD AELRED GLIDDEN OSB *(Prior)*

Father Benedict Reid*          Brother Martin Dally
Father Jude Bell              Brother Abraham Newsom
Father William Forest         Brother Cuthbert

*resident elsewhere*

***Community Publications and History***
*Abbey Newsletter*, published four times a year. A subscription is free.  To be added to the mailing list, write to the Abbey Business office.

The book *Singing God's Praises* was published in the Fall of 1998.  It includes articles from community newsletters over the past sixty years and also includes a history of St Gregory's.  Copies can be bought from the Abbey, price $20 a copy, postpaid.

***Community Wares:*** The Abbey sells a calendar each year featuring photographs taken by one of the monks.

***Guest and Retreat Facilities***
Both men and women are welcome as guests.  There is no charge, but $30 per day is 'fair value for services rendered' that is not tax-deductible.  For further information and arrangements, contact the guest master by mail, telephone or e-mail at *guestsga@net-link.net.*

***Associates***
We have a Confraternity which offers an official connection to the Abbey and is open to anyone who wishes to join for the purpose of incorporating Benedictine principles into their lives.  For further information and an application form, please write the Father Abbot.

***Office Book:*** The community uses home-made books based on the Roman Thesaurus for the Benedictine Office.

***Bishop Visitor:*** Rt Revd Arthur Williams,
                    suffragan Bishop of Ohio (retired)

# Order of St Helena

## OSH

*Founded 1945*

*Convent of St Helena*
*PO Box 426*
*701 Blooming Grove*
*Turnpike*
*Vails Gate*
*NY 12584-0426*
*USA*
Tel: 845 562 0592
Fax: 845 569 7051

Email: cintra
@comcast.net

*Website:* www.osh.org

**Matins**
*7.00 am*
*(7.30 am Sat & Sun)*

**Eucharist**
*7.30 am*
*(8.00 am Sat & Sun)*

**Diurnum**
**and intercessions**
*noon*

**Vespers**
*5.00 pm*

**Compline**
*7.30 pm*

The Order of St Helena witnesses to a contemporary version of traditional monasticism, taking a threefold vow of Poverty, Celibate Chastity and Obedience. Our life in community is shaped by the daily Eucharist and fourfold Office, plus hours of personal prayer and study, and from this radiates a wide range of ministries.

As an Order, we are not restricted to any single area of work but witness and respond to the Gospel, with individual sisters engaging in different ministries as they feel called by God and affirmed by the community. Our work is thus wonderfully varied: sisters work in parishes as priests or as pastoral assistants; they lead retreats, quiet days and conferences;work with the national Church and various organizations; offer spiritual direction; are psychotherapists; teach; serve in hospital chaplaincies and community service programs. Seven sisters are ordained priests.

The convents in Vails Gate, NY, and Augusta, Georgia, have guest houses and offer retreats and conferences.

In 1997, the Order adopted a new style of governance and no longer has a superior or single sister as head. Instead, the Order was led by a four-member Leadership Council, with responsibility and ultimate authority vested equally in all four members. Beginning in 2007, the Order will be led by a three-member Council.

*Leadership Council:*

SISTER CINTRA PEMBERTON OSH
REVD SISTER ELLEN FRANCIS POISSON OSH
*(Minister of Vocations)*
SISTER CORNELIA RANSOM OSH

| | |
|---|---|
| Revd Sister Mary Michael | Sister Ann Prentice |
| Sister Ruth Juchter | Sister Mary Lois Miller |
| Sister Ellen Stephen | Sister Veronica Aryeequaye |
| Sister Jean Campbell | Sister Deborah Magdalene |
| Revd Sister Carol Andrew | Sister Linda Elston |
| Sister Barbara Lee | Sister Mary Therese |
| Sister Benedicta | Revd Sister Sophia Woods |
| Sister Elsie Reid | Revd Dr Sister Claire Tenny |
| Revd Sister Rosina Ampah | |
| Sister Linda Julian | *Novices:* 3 |
| Sister June Thomas | |

*Associates*
ASSOCIATES - open to all women and men. Write to the Secretary for Associates at the Vails Gate Convent.

**Community Publication**
*saint helena*, published quarterly, free of charge. Write to the Convent of St Helena at Vails Gate for a subscription.

**Other Addresses**
Convent of St Helena, 3042 Eagle Drive, Augusta, GA 30916-5645, USA
       *Tel: 706 798 5201   Fax: 706 796 0079*
       *Email: conventofsthelena@comcast.net*

Convent of St Helena, 134 East 28th Street, New York, NY 10016-8156, USA
       *Tel: 212 889 1124   Fax: 815 846 4771       Email: ljulian@ix.netcom.com*

**Community Wares and Books**
Hand-made rosaries - *write to* Sister Mary Lois at the New York convent.
Hand-done copper enamels with religious themes - *write to* Sister Ellen Stephen at the Vails Gate convent.
Sister Cintra Pemberton OSH, *Soulfaring: Celtic Pilgrimage then and now*, SPCK, London, & Morehouse, Harrisburg, PA, 1999.
Doug Shadel and Sister Ellen Stephen OSH, *Vessel of Peace: The voyage toward spiritual freedom*, Three Tree Press, 1999.

**Community History**
A history is in process, being written by The Revd Sister Mary Michael.

**Guest and Retreat Facilities**
CONVENT OF ST HELENA, VAILS GATE, NEW YORK - Seventeen rooms, no restrictions, cost by donation.
CONVENT OF ST HELENA, AUGUSTA, GEORGIA - Fifteen rooms, no restrictions, cost by donation.

**Office Book**
The Saint Helena Breviary, Monastic Edition, which includes all the music in plainchant notation, is now published. It follows closely the BCP of the Episcopal Church of the USA. The focus is on inclusive language and expanded imagery for God, following principles set forth by the Standing Commission for Liturgy and Music of the Episcopal Church, USA. The Saint Helena Psalter, extracted from the Breviary, was published by Church Publishing, Inc., in November 2004.

**Bishop Visitor**: Rt Revd Steven Charleston,
       Dean of the Episcopal Divinity School, Cambridge, Massachusetts

**Registered Charity No**: US Government 501 (c)(3)

# Sisterhood of the Holy Nativity

## SHN

*Founded 1882*

*Bethlehem-by-the-Lake*
*W1484 Spring Grove*
*Road*
*Ripon*
*WI 54971-8655*
*USA*
Tel: 920 748 5332

Email: srboniface
@hotmail.com

*Website*
*www.*
*episcopalian.org/shn*

**Matins**  *6.30 am*

**Eucharist**  *7.00 am*

**Diurnum**
**(Noonday Prayer)**
*12 noon*

**Vespers**  *5.30 pm*

**Compline**  *8.00 pm*

**Office Book**
*The Monastic Breviary,*
*published by the*
*Order of the Holy Cross*

Ours is a mixed life, which means that we combine an apostolic ministry with a contemplative lifestyle. The Rule of the Sisterhood of the Holy Nativity follows the model of the Rule of St Augustine of Hippo. As such, we strive to make the love of God the motive of all our actions. The four 'charisms', which undergird our life, are Charity, Humility, Prayer, and Missionary Zeal. Each of these spiritual gifts we desire to develop in our lives both for the fraternal unity they foster among us, and for the power they provide for the work of evangelistic ministry.

Our ministries are varied. We have an extensive ministry with children, working at summer camps, teaching Sunday School and conducting Vacation Church Schools. Sisters travel to conduct retreats, teaching and preaching missions. Many of the Sisters offer Spiritual Direction. We built a smaller Convent and moved here in December 1999 in order to provide additional staff at St. Mary's Retreat House and to free Sisters for outside ministry.

SISTER BONIFACE SHN
*(Revd Mother, assumed office March 2007)*
SISTER MARGARETTA SHN *(Assistant Superior)*

| | |
|---|---|
| Sister Elsbeth | Sister Abigail |
| Sister Mary Frances | |
| Sister Columba | *Novices:* 1 |
| Sister Kathleen Marie | *Postulants:* 1 |
| Sister Charis | |

**Obituaries**

| | |
|---|---|
| 23 Sep 2006 | Sister Ruth Angela, aged 101, professed 67 years |
| 8 Feb 2007 | Sister Maria, aged 60, professed 15 years, Revd Mother 1996-2007 |

**Associates and Oblates**

ASSOCIATES are men and women who connect themselves to the prayer life and ministry of the community, and keep a Rule of Life. Membership is open to adult (lay and clerical) members of the Episcopal Church.

OBLATES can be men or women who desire a closer connection with the Community and are able to commit to spending at least three weeks each year living and working with the Sisters at one of our Houses. We have seven Oblates and have seven Novice Oblates.

*Other Addresses*
St. Mary's Retreat House, 505 East Los Olivos Street, Santa Barbara, CA 93105 USA
*Tel: 805 682 4117          Email: st_marysretreat@yahoo.com*
*Website: stmarysretreathouse.com*

*Community Publication*
We put out an occasional newsletter, *Sisters of the Holy Nativity*. If interested contact:
St Mary's Retreat House, 505 E. Los Olivos St, Santa Barbara, CA 91305, USA *(Email: st_marysretreat@yahoo.com)*.
There is no charge, though we occasionally make an appeal for donations.

*Guest and Retreat Facilities*
St Mary's Retreat House provides retreats for groups or individuals, with accommodation for twenty-four. It is located on seven beautiful acres within the Santa Barbara city limits with a view of the mountains. The House is closed on Thursdays. The suggested donation is $150.00 for a weekend or a Monday to Wednesday retreat. We do not accept same day reservations. The House is closed during the week after Christmas and during the Triduum and Easter Week.
   The Mother House can accommodate one or two guests. An offering is accepted.

*Bishop Visitor:* Rt Revd Russell E Jacobus, Bishop of Fond du Lac

---

# Sisterhood of St John the Divine

# SSJD

Founded 1884

St John's Convent
233 Cummer Avenue
Toronto
Ontario M2M 2E8
Canada
Tel: 416 226 2201
ext. 301
Fax: 416 222 4442
Emails:
convent@ssjd.ca
guesthouse@ssjd.ca

**Website:** www.ssjd.ca

Morning Prayer
8.30 am

Holy Eucharist
12 noon (8.00 am Sun)

Noon Office
12 noon (when Eucharist
not at 12 noon)

Evening Prayer
5.00 pm

Compline
8.10 pm

Office Book
Book of Alternative
Services 1985

The Sisterhood of St John the Divine is a contemporary expression of the Religious life for women within the Anglican Church of Canada. Founded in Toronto in 1884, we are a prayer- and gospel-centred monastic community, bound together by the call to live out our baptismal covenant through the vows of poverty, chastity and obedience. Living as we do in a time of change, these vows anchor us in the life of Jesus and in the transforming experience of the Gospel. Nurtured by our founding vision of prayer, community and ministry, we are open and responsive to the needs of the Church and the contemporary world, continually seeking the guidance of the Holy Spirit in our life and ministry.

St John's Convent is a centre of prayer, community, and mission, which nurtures and supports the life of the whole Sisterhood. The Convent's mission includes: a guest house where individuals and groups are welcomed, and share in the community's prayer and liturgy; regularly scheduled retreats; availability of Sisters to preach, teach, speak, lead retreats and quiet days; programs which help people to build bridges between our secular culture, the Church, and the monastic tradition; discernment programs for those seeking guidance in their life and work; the offering of spiritual direction; embroidered white church linens; music and liturgical leadership for the Church; ecumenical outreach; and partnership with St John's Rehab Hospital.

The Sisterhood supports St John's Rehab Hospital through membership of the Hospital Corporation and Board of Directors, and through its presence on the Hospital staff. The Sisters advocate for a vision of health care which expresses SSJD's mission and values in a multi-faith, multi-cultural setting, and provides spiritual and pastoral support for patients, staff and volunteers.

*Community History and Books*
Sister Eleonora SSJD, *A Memoir of the Life and Work of Hannah Grier Coome, Mother-Foundress of SSJD*, Toronto, Canada, OUP, London, 1933 (out of print).

*The Sisterhood of St John the Divine 1884-1984*, published 1931 as *A Brief History*; 4th revision 1984, available at the Convent for $4.00.

Sister Constance Joanna SSJD, *From Creation to Resurrection: A Spiritual Journey*, Anglican Book Centre, Toronto, 1990.

Sister Constance SSJD, *"Other Little Ships": The memoirs of Sister Constance SSJD*, Patmos Press, Toronto, 1997.

SISTER ELIZABETH ANN ECKERT SSJD
*(Reverend Mother, assumed office 13 April 2005)*
SISTER MARGARET MARY WATSON SSJD *(Assistant to the Reverend Mother)*

Sister Constance Murphy
Sister Joyce Bodley
Sister Helena Ward
Sister Philippa Watson
Sister Margaret Ann Macfarlane
Sister Wilma Grazier
Sister Thelma-Anne McLeod
Sister Jean Marston
Sister Beryl Stone
Sister Merle Milligan
Sister Doreen McGuff
Sister Patricia Forler
Sister Madeleine Mary Salter
Sister Jocelyn Mortimore
Sister Margaret Ruth Steele

Sister Sarah Jean Thompson
Sister Anitra Hansen
Sister Jessica Kennedy
Sister Constance Joanna Gefvert
Sister Valerie Clarke
Sister Brenda Jenner
Sister Anne Norman
Sister Peta-Ann Jackson
Sister Elizabeth Rolfe-Thomas
Sister Helen Claire Gunter
Sister Susan Elwyn
Sister Louise Manson
Sister Dorothy Handrigan
Sister Amy Hamilton

*Novices:* 1

## Obituaries

| | |
|---|---|
| 9 Nov 2005 | Sister Marilyn Fowler, aged 77, professed 52 years |
| 1 Jan 2006 | Sister Teresa Keen, aged 80, professed 42 years |
| 23 Apr 2007 | Sister Nora Lynch, aged 90, professed 62 years |

### Associates and Oblates

Our approximately nine hundred associates are women and men who follow a Rule of Life and share in the ministry of the Sisterhood. The Sisterhood of St John the Divine owes its founding to the vision and dedication of the clergy and lay people who became the first Associates of SSJD. A year of discernment is required before being admitted as an Associate to see if the Associate Rule helps the person in what she/he is seeking; and to provide the opportunity to develop a relationship with the Sisters and to deepen the understanding and practice of prayer. The Associate Rule provides a framework for the journey of faith. There are three basic commitments: belonging in a parish; the practice of prayer, retreat, study of scripture, and spiritual reading; and the relationship with SSJD. Write to the Sister in the SSJD house nearest to you for further information.

We have a small but growing number of Oblates. Oblate are women who wish to make a promise of prayer and service in partnership with the Sisterhood. Each Oblate develops her own Rule of Life in partnership with the Oblate Director, her spiritual director, and a support group. A year of discernment is also required, as well as an annual residency program. Write to Sister Doreen in Victoria, BC, for more information.

### Community Publication

*The Eagle* (newsletter). Contact the Convent Secretary. Published quarterly. $10.00 suggested annual donation.

***Bishop Visitor:*** Rt Revd Colin Johnson

*Addresses of other Houses*
St John's House/Maison St Jean,
   840 Notre Dame Avenue, St Lambert, Quebec J4R 1R8
   *Tel: 450 671 5898 Fax: 450 671 5996 Email: maison@ssjd.ca*
   A community of Sisters committed to being a praying presence in the Diocese of Montreal. We offer hospitality and spiritual nourishment to those who come for shorter or longer periods, and an outreach ministry to the Diocese and beyond.

St John's House, BC,
3937 St Peter's Road, Victoria, British Columbia V8P 2JP
   *Tel: 250 920 7787 Fax: 250 920 7709 E-mail: bchouse@ssjd.ca*
   A community of Sisters committed to being a praying presence in the Diocese of British Columbia. Prayer, intentional community, hospitality, and mission are at the heart of our life in the Diocese and beyond.

*Community Wares: Wings* - a book of poems by Sisters; *Songs for Celebration* - music and words by Sisters Thelma-Anne & Rosemary Anne; printed cards calligraphed by Sisters; cards with photo taken by Sisters. Good selection of books on spiritual growth - not SSJD. All for sale at the Convent (but not by mail).

*Guest and Retreat Facilities*
Guest House has thirty-seven rooms (forty-two people) used for rest, quiet time and retreats. Contact the Guest Sister at the Convent for details about private accommodation, scheduled retreats, quiet days and other programs.
   The Sisters in Montréal, QC, and in Victoria, BC, also take guests and conduct retreats - contact these houses for detailed information.

---

# Sisterhood of St Mary

*Founded 1929*

St Andrew's Mission
PO Haluaghat
Mymensingh
BANGLADESH

*Bishop Visitor*
Rt Revd Michael Baroi,
Bishop of Dhaka

The community is located on the northern border of Bangladesh at the foot of the Garo hills in India. The community was formed in Barisal at the Sisterhood of the Epiphany, and was sent here to work among the indigenous tribal people, side by side with St Andrew's Brotherhood already working in the area. The membership of the Sisterhood has always been entirely indigenous. The first sisters were Bengalis. The present sisters are the fruit of their work - all are Garo. They take the vows of Poverty, Purity and Obedience and live a very simple life. They lead a life of prayer and formation of girls. They also look after the Church and do pastoral work among women and children in the Parish.

Sister Mira Mankhin
*(Sister Superior, assumed office 2002)*
Sister Anita Raksam *(Assistant Superior)*
Sister Bregita Doffo      Sister Mala Chicham
*Novices: 2*

**Obituaries**
2006     Sister Charu Sangma

# Sisters of Charity (UK) SC

Founded 1869

237 Ridgeway
Plympton
Plymouth
PL7 2HP
UK

Tel: 01752 336112

Email: plympton
sisters@tiscali.co.uk

**Morning Prayer**
*8.00 am*

**Vespers**
*5.00 pm*

**Compline**
*7.00 pm*

**Office Book**
*Daily Prayer*

**Registered Charity:**
No. X33170

A Community following the Rule of St Vincent de Paul and so committed to the service of those in need. The Sisters are involved in parish work and the Community also has a nursing home in Plympton.

MOTHER ELIZABETH MARY SC
*(Revd Mother, assumed office 21 April 2003)*
SISTER GABRIEL MARGARET SC *(Assistant)*

Sister Faith Mary
Sister Theresa
Sister Angela Mary
Sister Rosamund
Sister Hilda Mary
Sister Faith Nicolette
Sister Margaret Veronica
Sister Mary Joseph
Sister Clare *(priest)*
Sister Mary Patrick

### Obituaries
8 Nov 2006   Sister Mary Theresa, aged 85,
professed 55 years, Revd Mother 1987-2003

### Oblates and Associate Members
The Community has a group of Oblates and Associate Members, formed as a mutual supportive link. We do not provide a rule of life; instead we ask our Oblates and Associate Members to add to their existing rule the daily use of the Vincentian Prayer.

Oblates are also asked to use the Holy Paraclete hymn and one of the Daily Offices, thereby joining in spirit in the Divine Office of the Community. Oblates are encouraged to make an annual retreat.

Associate Members support us by their prayers and annual subscription.

### Other addresses
Saint Vincent's Nursing Home, Fore Street, Plympton, Plymouth PL7 1NE                    *Tel: 01752 336205*

### Guest and Retreat Facilities
We welcome individuals for Quiet Days.

*Most convenient time to telephone*: 4.00 pm - 6.30 pm

*Bishop Visitor:* Rt Revd Robert Evens, Bishop of Crediton

# Sisters of Charity (USA) SC

*Founded 1869*

*The Episcopal Sisters of Charity*
PO Box 755
*Martinsburg*
*West Virginia* 25402
USA
or
1657 *Swan Pond Road*
*Martinsburg*
*West Virginia* 25404
USA

Tel: 304 250 7346
Email: sisofchr
@hotmail.com

*Morning Prayer* 8.00 am

*Noonday Prayer*
12 *noon*

*Evening Prayer* 5.00 pm

*Compline is said privately*

*Office Book*
*Order of Saint Helena's Breviary*

*Bishop Visitor*
*Rt Revd W Michie Klusmeyer*

"Charity is the name you bear", Saint Vincent de Paul wrote to his daughters, "Charity is the robe in which you are clothed with its three parts: Love of God, Love among yourselves and Love of the Poor." As a Vincentian community, we combine a life of prayer with service to those in need whom our founder, Saint Vincent de Paul, saw as Christ in the world. Some of our activities include: retreat work, pro bono spiritual direction to those with limited incomes, assisting low income families, and work in mission churches. We provide hospitality to the lesbian and gay community of West Virginia's Eastern Panhandle by offering an open and affirming Eucharist with fellowship, as well as a weekly Eucharist celebration for the elderly in our rural neighbourhood. We serve in our parish churches and in our diocese on the Committee to End Racism. Our outreach also includes travelling to Haiti to work with the sick, and providing supplies and donations to that country.

REVD SISTER JULIAN HOPE SC
*(Sister-in charge)*
Sister Mary Martha          Sister Miriam
*Novices: 1*

**Oblates and Associate members**
The Community has a group of Oblates and Associate Members, formed as a mutual supportive link. We do not provide a rule of life; instead we ask our Oblates and Associate Members to add to their existing rule the daily use of the Vincentian prayer. Oblates are also asked to use the Holy Paraclete hymn and one of the Daily Offices, thereby joining in spirit in the Divine Office of the Community. Oblates are encouraged to make an annual retreat, if possible at one of the Community houses. Oblates and Associate Members support us by their prayers and annual subscription.

**Community Publication**
*The Mustard Seed* - a newsletter sent free.

**Community Wares:** Rosaries and chaplets

**Guest and Retreat Facilities**
Retreat house with sitting room, coffee room, two meeting rooms and a religious library. Ten acres of land. Day retreats for groups of up to twenty. Two guest rooms for individual retreatants (men or women). Meals $5 per person per meal plus a donation.

**Most convenient time to telephone**: 9.00 am - 8.00 pm ET

# Sisters of the Incarnation SI

*Founded 1981*

*The House of the Incarnation*
6 *Sherbourne Terrace*
*Dover Gardens*
*SA* 5048
AUSTRALIA

Tel: 08 8296 2166

Email: sisincar
@chariot.net.au

**Office Book**
*A Prayer Book for Australia (1995 edition) for Morning and Evening Prayer, and Compline; Midday Office is from another source.*

The sisters live under vows of poverty, chastity and obedience in a simple life style, and seek to maintain a balance between prayer, community life and work for each member and to worship and serve within the church. They combine the monastic and apostolic aspects of the Religious Life. The monastic aspects include prayer, domestic work at home, community life and hospitality. The sisters are engaged in parish ministry and with priestly responsibility for two parishes.

The community was founded in the diocese of Adelaide in 1981 as a contemporary expression of the Religious Life for women in the Anglican Church. In 1988, the two original sisters made their Profession of Life Intention within the Sisters of the Incarnation, before the Archbishop of Adelaide, the Visitor of the community. One member was ordained to the diaconate in 1990 and the priesthood in 1993. The governing body of the community is its chapter of professed sisters, which elects the Guardian, and appoints an Episcopal Visitor and a Community Advisor. The community is not endowed; the sisters work to earn sufficient for their needs.

SISTER PATRICIA SI
(*Guardian, assumed office 1981*)
Sister Juliana (*priest*)

**Friends**
The community has a group of Friends who share special celebrations and significant events, many of whom have supported the community from the beginning, while others become Friends as we touch their lives. There is no formal structure.

***Bishop Visitor:*** Rt Revd Dr K Rayner

*The sisters with their Bishop Visitor.*

# Society of the Holy Cross

## SHC

*Founded 1925*

3 Jeong-dong
Jung-ku
Seoul 100-120
KOREA

Tel: 2 735 7832
or 2 735 3478
Fax: 2 736 5028
Email: holycross25
@yahoo.com

**Website:**
www.sister.or.kr

*Morning Prayer*
*6.15 am*

*Holy Eucharist  6.45 am*

*Midday Prayer*
*12.30 pm*
*(12 noon Sun & great feast days)*

*Evening Prayer*
*5.00 pm*

*Compline  8.00 pm*

*Office Book*
*Revised Common Prayer for Morning & Evening Prayer and Compline; & SHC material for Midday Office*

The community was founded on the feast day of the Exaltation of the Holy Cross in 1925 by the Rt Revd Mark Trollope, the third bishop of the Anglican Church in Korea, admitting Postulant Phoebe Lee and blessing a small traditional Korean-style house in the present site of Seoul. The Community of St Peter, Woking, Surrey in England, sent seventeen Sisters as missionaries to Korea between 1892 and 1950, who nourished this young community for a few decades. Sister Mary Clare CSP, who was the first Mother Superior of this community, was persecuted by the North Korean communists and died during the 'death march' in the Korean War in 1950. This martyrdom especially has been a strong influence and encouragement for the growth of the community.

Our spirituality is based on a modified form of the Augustinian Rule harmonized with the Benedictine one. Bishop Mark Trollope, the first Visitor, and Sister Mary Clare CSP compiled the Divine Office Book and the Constitution and Rule of the Community. The activities that are being continuously practised even now include pastoral care in parishes, running homes for the elderly and those with learning difficulties, teaching at the Anglican University, and counselling people.

We explore a program for vocation one weekend each month and a spiritual prayer meeting and workshop monthly with people who want to improve their spiritual life. We also conduct Quiet Hours and Retreats individually or in groups. We lead contemplation based on Ignatian Spirituality. It was a great occasion for us to celebrate the 80th anniversary of the community's foundation on 14 September 2005. Sister Catherine was made deacon on 25 May 2006 and ordained priest 29 April 2007 in St Mary & St Nicholas Cathedral, Seoul.

SISTER ANGELA SHC
*(Reverend Mother, assumed office 1 Jan 2007)*
SISTER HELEN ELIZABETH SHC *(Assistant Superior)*

| | |
|---|---|
| Sister Monica | Sister Monica Alma |
| Sister Phoebe Anne | Sister Martha Joanna |
| Sister Edith | Sister Theresa |
| Sister Cecilia | Sister Grace |
| Sister Maria Helen | Sister Helen Juliana |
| Sister Etheldreda | Sister Lucy Edward |
| Sister Catherine | Sister Martha |
| Sister Maria Clare | Sister Prisca |
| Sister Pauline | |

*Novices: 1    Postulants: 1*

*Obituaries*

| | |
|---|---|
| 4 Jan 2006 | Sister Esther, aged 85, professed 58 years |
| 3 Feb 2006 | Sister Tabitha, aged 98, professed 71 years, Revd Mother 1971-79 |
| 27 Oct 2006 | Sister Maria Agnes, aged 83, professed 59 years |

*Friends and Associates*

FRIENDS are men and women from all walks of life who desire to have a close link with the community. They follow a simple Rule of Life, which includes praying for the Sisters and their work. Friends also form a network of prayer, fellowship and mutual support within Christ's ministry of wholeness and reconciliation. About one hundred members come together for the annual meeting in October at the Motherhouse. The committee members meet bi-monthly at the convent.

ASSOCIATES: about thirty friends have been trained in the last two years, and nine of them promised to be the Associate Members on 3 May 2007.

*Other Addresses*

St Anne's Convalescent Home for Elderly People,
619-28 Onsuri, Kilsang, Kangwha, Inch'on, 417-840 South Korea
*Tel: 32 937 1935    Fax: 32 937 0696*
*Email: anna1981@kornet.net        Website: www.oldanna.or.kr*

St Bona House for Mentally Retarded People,
2-4 Neamni, Kadok, Chongwon, Chungbuk 363-853, South Korea
*Tel: 82 43 297 8348        Fax: 82 43 298 3156*
*Email: sralma@chollian.net        Website: www.bona.or.kr*

*Community Publication*

*Holy Cross Newsletter,* published occasionally, in Korean.
Sister Catherine SHC, *Holy Vocation* (booklet for the SHC 75th anniversary, 2000)
Contact Sister Catherine at the Mother House.

*Community History*

Jae Joung Lee, *Society of the Holy Cross 1925-1995,* Seoul, 1995 (in Korean).
Sisters Maria Helen & Catherine, *The SHC: the First 80 Years,* 2005

*Community Wares*

Wafers and wine for Holy Eucharist, vestments and church linen, and the following items: prayer books, Bibles, hymnals, cards, crosses, candles, candle-stands, bells, cruets etc.

*Guest and Retreat Facilities*

The Community occasionally organizes retreats and quiet days for Christians. At present, just seven rooms are available for guests.

*Bishop Visitor*

Most Revd Francis K Park, Bishop of Seoul, Presiding Bishop of Korea

# Society of the Precious Blood (UK)

## SPB

*Founded 1905*

*Burnham Abbey
Lake End Road
Taplow, Maidenhead
Berkshire* SL6 OPW
UK
Tel & Fax:
01628 604080
Email:
burnhamabbey@
btinternet.com

**Website:**
www.burnhamabbey
.org

*Lauds* 7.30 am

*Eucharist*
9.30 am

*Angelus & Sext*
12.00 noon

*Vespers* 5.30 pm

*Compline*
8.30 pm

*Office Book*
SPB Office Book

*Registered Charity:*
No. 900512

We are a contemplative community whose particular work within the whole body of Christ is worship, thanksgiving and intercession. Within these ancient Abbey walls, which date back to 1266, we continue to live the Augustinian monastic tradition of prayer, silence, fellowship and solitude. The Eucharist is the centre of our life, where we find ourselves most deeply united with Christ, one another and all for whom we pray. The work of prayer is continued in the Divine Office, in the Watch before the Blessed Sacrament and in our whole life of work, reading, creating, and learning to live together. This life of prayer finds an outward expression in welcoming guests, who come seeking an opportunity for quiet and reflection in which to deepen their own spiritual lives.

SISTER MARY BERNARD SPB
*(Reverend Mother, assumed office 30 January 2003)*

| | |
|---|---|
| Sister Margaret Mary | Sister Mary Benedict |
| Sister Dorothy Mary | Sister Victoria Mary |
| Sister Jane Mary | Sister Miriam Mary |
| Sister Mary Laurence | Sister Elizabeth Mary |
| Sister Mary Philip | Sister Grace Mary |

### Obituaries
4 Oct 2005          Sister Mary Luke, aged 94

### Companions and Oblates
Oblates (16 in number at present) are men and women who feel drawn by God to express the spirit of the Society, united with the Sisters in their life of worship, thanksgiving and intercession. They live out their dedication in their own situation and make a yearly Promise.

Men and women who desire to share in the prayer and work of the Society but cannot make as full a commitment to saying the Office may be admitted as Companions.

### Community History
Sister Felicity Mary SPB, *Mother Millicent Mary of the Will of God,* Macmillan, London, 1968.

Booklets and leaflets on the history and life of the Abbey and the Community.

### Community Wares
The Sisters find a creative outlet in producing cards, rosaries, holding crosses and other crafts (for sale in the Guest House).

**Community Publications:** *Newsletter,* yearly at Christmas. *Companions/Oblates Letter,* quarterly.

*Guest and Retreat Facilities:* We have a small guest house with four single rooms for individual (unconducted) retreats.

*Most convenient time to telephone*: 10.30 am - 12 noon, 3 pm - 4.30 pm, 7 pm - 8 pm

*Bishop Visitor:* Rt Revd Stephen Cottrell, Bishop of Reading

---

# Society of the Precious Blood

## (Lesotho)

## SPB

*Founded 1905*

*Priory of Our Lady Mother of Mercy*
PO Box 7192
*Maseru* 100
LESOTHO
Tel: 00266 58859585

*Morning Prayer 6.15 am*

*Eucharist 7.00 am*

*Terce 9.45 am*

*Midday Office 12 noon*

*Evening Prayer 5.30 pm*

*Compline 8.00 pm*

*Office Book*
*Daily Prayer &*
*An Anglican Prayer Book 1989,*
*CPSA*

*Bishop Visitor*
*awaiting ecletion*

Five Sisters of the Society of the Precious Blood at Burnham Abbey came to Masite in Lesotho in 1957 to join with a community of African women, with the intention of forming a multi-cultural contemplative community dedicated to intercession. In 1966, this community at Masite became autonomous, although still maintaining strong ties of friendship with Burnham Abbey. In 1980, a House of Prayer was established in Kimberley in South Africa, which has developed a more active branch of the Society.

SISTER ELAINE MARY SPB
(*Prioress, assumed office 24 September 1997*)

| | |
|---|---|
| Sister Josephine Mary | Sister Diana Mary |
| Sister Theresia Mary | Sister Cicily Mary |
| Sister Magdalen Mary | Sister Camilla Mary |
| Sister Lucia Mary | *Intern Oblates:* 2 |
| Sister Mary Dominic | *Novices:* 1  *Postulants:* 1 |

**Oblates and Companions**
The Community has thirteen oblates (in South Africa, Zambia, New Zealand and the UK), and eighty-six Companions and Associates (in Lesotho, South Africa and the UK). All renew their promises annually. Oblates are sent prayer material regularly. Companions and Associates receive quarterly letters and attend occasional quiet days.

**Other House**
St Monica's House of Prayer, 46 Green Street, West End, Kimberley, 8301 SOUTH AFRICA *Tel: 053 832 7331*

**Community Publication**
Annual *Newsletter;* apply to the Prioress. No charge.

**Community Wares:** Cards, crafts, religious booklets.

**Guest and Retreat Facilities**
Small guest house with three bedrooms. There is no fixed charge. It is closed in winter (mid-June to mid-August). Both men and women are welcome for retreats, which may be private or accompanied by a Sister. We also welcome anyone who wishes to share our life for a few months, to live with us in the Priory.

# Society of the Sacred Advent

## SSA

*Founded 1892*

*Community House*
*34 Lapraik Street*
*Albion*
*QLD* 4010
*AUSTRALIA*
Tel: 07 3262 5511
Fax: 07 3862 3296
Email:
sistersofssa_bne
@bigpond.com

*Quiet time*
*6.00 am*

*Morning Prayer*
*6.30 am*
*(7.00 am Sun & Mon)*

*Eucharist*
*7.00 am*
*(7.30 am Sun)*

*Midday Prayer*
*12 noon*

*Evensong 5.30 pm*

*Compline*
*7.30 pm*
*(8.00 pm Wed & Sat)*

The Society of the Sacred Advent exists for the glory of God and for the service of His Church in preparation for the second coming of our Lord and Saviour Jesus Christ.

Members devote themselves to God in community under vows of poverty, chastity and obedience. Our life is a round of worship, prayer, silence and work. Our Patron Saint is John the Baptist who, by his life and death, pointed the way to Jesus. We would hope also to point the way to Jesus in our own time, to a world which has largely lost touch with spiritual realities and is caught up in despair, loneliness and fear.

As part of our ministry, Sisters may be called to give addresses, conduct Retreats or Quiet Days, or to make themselves available for spiritual direction, hospital chaplaincy and parish work. The aim of the Community is to grow in the mind of Christ so as to manifest Him to others. The Society has two Schools, St Margaret's and St Aidan's and two Sisters are on each of the School Councils.

SISTER EUNICE SSA
*(Revd Mother, assumed office 21 March 2007)*

| | |
|---|---|
| Sister Dorothy | Sister Beverley |
| Sister June Ruth | Sister Gillian |
| Sister Sandra | *Novices: 1* |

**Community Publication**
There is a Newsletter, twice yearly. For a subscription, write to Sister Sandra SSA. The cost is A$5 per year.

**Community History**
Elizabeth Moores, *One Hundred Years of Ministry*, published for SSA, 1992.

**Community Wares:** Cards and crafts.

**Bishop Visitor**
Rt Revd Godfrey Fryar, Bishop of Rockhampton

**Guest and Retreat Facilities**
There are twenty single rooms. Both men and women are welcome. The facilities are closed over Christmas and in January.

**Office Book**
A Prayer Book for Australia; *The Daily Office SSF* is used for Midday Prayer.

*Fellowship and Company*

THE FELLOWSHIP OF THE SACRED ADVENT

Since 1925, the work of the Community has been helped by the prayers and work of a group of friends known as the Fellowship of the Sacred Advent. They have a simple Rule of Life.

THE COMPANY OF THE SACRED ADVENT began in 1987.

This is a group of men and women, clergy and lay, bound together in love for Jesus Christ and His Church in the spirit of St John the Baptist. It seeks to proclaim the Advent challenge: 'Prepare the Way of the Lord.' Members have a Rule of Life and renew their promises annually.

Members of the Fellowship and Company are part of our extended Community family. The Sisters arrange Retreats and Quiet Days and support them with their prayers, help, or spiritual guidance, as required.

---

# Society of the Sacred Cross

## SSC

Founded 1914
(Chichester);
moved to Wales in 1923

Tymawr Convent
Lydart, Monmouth
Gwent
NP25 4RN
UK
Tel: 01600 860244
or 860808

Email:
tymawrconvent
@btinternet.com

**Website:**
www.
churchinwales.org.
uk/tymawr/index.
html

The community, part of the Anglican Church in Wales, lives a monastic, contemplative life of prayer based on silence, solitude and learning to live together, under vows of poverty, chastity and obedience, with a modern rule, Cistercian in spirit. At the heart of our corporate life is the Eucharist with the daily Office and other times of shared prayer spanning the day. All services are open to the public and we are often joined by members of the neighbourhood in addition to our visitors. Our common life includes study, recreation and work in the house and extensive grounds. It is possible for women and men, married or single, to experience our life of prayer by living alongside the community for periods longer than the usual guest stay. Hospitality is an important part of our life at Tymawr and guests are most welcome. We also organise and sponsor occasional lectures and programmes of study for those who wish to find or develop the life of the spirit in their own circumstances. The community is dedicated to the crucified and risen Lord as the focus of its life and the source of the power to live it.

*Community Wares*

The Border series of books, co-published by Tymawr Convent & Canterbury Press. Authors: John Polkinghorne, Una Kroll, Esther de Waal & Jane Williams. Obtainable from Tymawr at £3 each.

Colour photographs cards of Tymawr available at 60p each (including envelope).

*Morning Prayer*
*7.00 am*

*Terce*
*8.45 am*

*Eucharist*
*12.00 noon*

*Evening Prayer*
*5.30 pm*

*Silent Corporate Prayer*
*8pm*

*Compline*
*8.30 pm*

*Office Book*
*Celebrating Common Prayer, with additional SSC material.*

*Bishop Visitor*
*Rt Revd Dominic Walker OGS, Bishop of Monmouth*

*Registered Charity:*
*No. 1047614*

*Most convenient time to telephone:*
6.45 pm – 8.00 pm only,
except Mondays,
Fridays and Sundays.

SISTER MARY JEAN SSC
*(Revd Mother, assumed office 2 July 1998)*
SISTER GILLIAN MARY SSC *(Assistant)*

| Sister Anne | Sister Cara Mary |
|---|---|
| Sister Veronica Ann | Sister Emma Joy |
| Sister Lorna Francis* | Sister Vivien Michael |
| Sister Heylin Columba* | Sister Laurie |

* *Living the contemplative life away from Tymawr.*

**Obituaries**
19 Sep 2005 Sister Mary Janet, aged 65, professed 39 years
1 Apr 2006    Sister Rosemary, aged 90, professed 55 years
19 Aug 2006 Sister Clare, aged 90, professed 61 years

**Oblates and Associates**
There are forty-six Oblates, living in their own homes, each having a personal Rule sustaining their life of prayer. One hundred and eighteen Associates, women and men, have a simple commitment. Three Companion Brothers, who are priests, live a life of prayer as a 'cell' under a Rule inspired by SSC's Rule. One Companion Sister lives a solitary life of prayer under vow. Three months are spent annually with SSC. There are also two residents who live alongside the community.

**Community History**
Sister Jeanne SSC, *A Continuous Miracle*,
(privately printed).

**Community Publication**
*Tymawr Newsletter*, yearly at Advent. Write to the above address.

**Guest and Retreat Facilities**
The community offers facilities for individual guests and small groups. There are five rooms (one double) in the guest wing of the Main House for full board. Michaelgarth, the self-catering guest house offers facilities for individuals or groups (five singles and two doubles), and also for day groups. The Old Print House offers full facilities for day groups of up to eight. Individuals may have private retreats with guidance from a member of the community. The community occasionally organises retreats and study days. Pilgrimages round the grounds, on a variety of themes, can be arranged. Please write with a stamped addressed envelope for details.

# Society of the Sacred Mission

## SSM

*Founded 1893*

*Office Book*
*Celebrating Common Prayer*

*Bishops Visitor*
*Rt Revd Tom Butler,*
*Bishop of Southwark*
*(PROVINCE OF EUROPE)*

*Most Revd Philip Freier,*
*Archbishop of Melbourne*
*(SOUTHERN PROVINCE)*

*Rt Revd Thabo*
*Makgoba,*
*Bishop of Grahamstown*
*(SOUTHERN AFRICAN*
*PROVINCE)*

Founded in 1893 by Father Herbert Kelly, the Society is a means of uniting the devotion of ordinary people, using it in the service of the Church. Members of the Society share a common life of prayer and fellowship in a variety of educational, pastoral and community activities in England, Australia, Japan, Lesotho, and South Africa.

### PROVINCE OF EUROPE
JONATHAN EWER SSM
*(Provincial, assumed office April 2001)*

| | |
|---|---|
| Clement Mullenger | *Associates:* |
| Frank Green | Linda Bosworth |
| Andrew Longley | David Bosworth |
| Ralph Martin | Margaret Moakes |
| Andrew Muramatsu | Paul Golightly |
| Edmund Wheat | John Davis |
| Colin Griffith | Garry Finch |
| Tanki Mofana | Elizabeth Baker |
| Mary Hartwell | Robin Baker |
| Elizabeth Macey | Marcus Armstrong |
| Michael Maasdorp | Joan Golightly |

**Obituaries**
1 Nov 2005  Alban Perkins, aged 97, professed 72 years

**Addresses**
30 Bourne Street, London SW1W 8JJ
*Tel: 020 7259 0499          Email: j_ewer@yahoo.com*

*Provincial Administrator:*
The Well, Newport Road, Willen MK15 9AA, UK
*Tel: 01908 242190          Email: ssmlondon@yahoo.co.uk*

St Antony's Priory, Claypath, Durham DH1 1QT, UK
*Tel: 0191 384 3737          Email: durham.ssm@which.net*

1 Linford Lane, Milton Keynes, Bucks MK15 9DL, UK
*Tel: 01908 663749*

**Community History**
Herbert H Kelly SSM, *An Idea in the Working*, SSM Press, Kelham, 1908.
Alistair Mason, *SSM: History of the Society of the Sacred Mission*, Canterbury Press, Norwich, 1993.

**Community Publication**
*SSM News* (newsletter of the Province of Europe)
The Secretary, SSM Newsletter, The Well, Newport Road, Willen MK15 9AA, UK

## SOUTHERN PROVINCE
### MATTHEW DOWSEY SSM
*(Provincial, assumed office November 2004)*

| | | |
|---|---|---|
| Laurence Eyers | Dunstan McKee | *lay members:* |
| John Lewis | Christopher Myers | Geoff Pridham |
| Henry Arkell | Margaret Dewey | Stuart Smith |
| David Wells | Steven de Kleer | Lynne Rokkas |
| Francis Horner | Gregory Stephens | Joy Freier |

### Addresses

St John's Priory, 14 St John's Street, Adelaide, SOUTH AUSTRALIA 5000
*Tel: 8 8223 1014   Fax: 8 8223 2764*          *Email: ssm.adelaide@bigpond.com*

St Michael's Priory, 75 Watson's Road, Diggers Rest, Victoria 3427, AUSTRALIA
*Tel: 03 9740 1618   Fax: 03 9740 0007*          *Email: ssm.melbourne@bigpond.com*

**Community Publication:** *Sacred Mission*   (newsletter of the Southern Province):
Editor, St Michael's Priory, 75 Watson's Road, Diggers Rest, VIC 3427, AUSTRALIA

## SOUTHERN AFRICAN PROVINCE
*(re-founded September 2004)*
### MICHAEL LAPSLEY SSM
*(Provincial, assumed office September 2004)*

| | | |
|---|---|---|
| William Nkomo | Moiloa Mokheseng | Thato Tjakata |
| Robert Stretton | Keketso Sebotsa | Mosuoe Rahuoane |
| Mosia Sello | Joseph Motaung | |
| Moeketsi Motojane | Thetsane Lebina | *Novices: 2* |
| Moeketsi Khomongoe | Samuel Monyamane | |

### Addresses

33 Elgin Road, Sybrand Park, Cape Town, SOUTH AFRICA, 7708
*Tel: 21 696 4866   Email: michael.lapsley@attglobal.net*

SSM Priory, PO Box 1579, Maseru 100, LESOTHO
*Tel: 22315979      Fax: 22310161*                 *Email: priorssm@ilesotho.com*

### Companions and Associates (applicable to all provinces)
COMPANIONS: are men and women who support the aims of the Society without being closely related to any of its work.  They consecrate their lives in loving response to a vocation to deepen their understanding of God's will, and to persevere more devotedly in commitments already made: baptism, marriage or ordination.
ASSOCIATES: are those who support the aims of the Society, and actively share in its work.

# Society of St Francis

## SSF

Founded *1919 (USA)*
*1921 (UK)*

The Society of St Francis has diverse origins in a number of Franciscan groups which drew together during the 1930s to found one Franciscan Society. SSF in its widest definition includes First Order Brothers, First Order Sisters (CSF), Second Order Sisters (OSC) and a Third Order. The First Order shares a common life of prayer, fraternity and a commitment to issues of justice, peace and the integrity of creation. In its larger houses, this includes accommodation for short-term guests; in the city houses, the Brothers are engaged in a variety of ministries, chaplaincies and care for poor people. The Brothers are also available for retreat work, for counselling and for sharing in the task of mission in parishes and schools. They also undertake work in Europe and there are houses in America, Australasia and the Pacific, and are supportive to incipient communities in Zimbabwe and Korea.

*(Minister General, election Summer 2007)*

**Minister General**
Email: brdaniel@
ozemail.com.au

## EUROPEAN PROVINCE
SAMUEL SSF

*(Minister Provincial, assumed office 1 July 2002)*
BENEDICT SSF *(Assistant Minister)*

**Minister Provincial**
*(European Province)*
Email:
ministerssf
@franciscans.org.uk

**European Province Website:**
www.franciscans.org.uk

*Office Book*
The Daily Office SSF

*Bishop Protector*
Rt Revd Michael Perham,
Bishop of Gloucester

*European Province SSF*
*Registered Charity:*
No. 236464

| | |
|---|---|
| Alan Michael | Julian |
| Amos | Kentigern John |
| Andrew | Kevin |
| Angelo | Malcolm |
| Anselm | Mark Edmund |
| Arnold | Martin |
| Augustine Thomas | Martin Philip |
| Austin | Maximilian |
| Bart | Nathanael |
| Benjamin | Nicholas Alan |
| Christian | Oswin Paul |
| Colin Wilfred | Paschal |
| Damian | Paul Anthony |
| David Jardine | Philip Bartholomew |
| Desmond Alban | Raphael |
| Donald | Raymond Christian |
| Edmund | Reginald |
| Edward | Robert Coombes |
| Giles | Ronald |
| Hugh | Thomas Anthony |
| James Anthony | Vincent |
| James William | Wilfrid |
| Jason Robert | |
| John | |

*Novices:* 1
*Postulants:* 1

*Obituaries*

| | |
|---|---|
| 11 Apr 2007 | Geoffrey, aged 85, professed 56 years |
| 17 May 2007 | Bernard, aged 78, professed 45 years |
| 22 May 2007 | Roger Alexander, aged 74, professed 29 years |

*Third Order* - see page 173 for the Third Order SSF.

*Companions*

Companions are individual Christians who wish to associate themselves with the Society through prayer, friendship and in seeking to live the spirit of the Gospel in the way of St Francis. For more information about becoming a Companion contact: The Secretary for Companions, Hilfield Friary, Dorchester, Dorset DT2 7BE, UK.

*Addresses*

The Friary, **Alnmouth**, Alnwick, Northumberland  NE66 3NJ
　　　*Tel: 01665 830213    Fax: 01665 830580    Email: alnmouthssf@franciscans.org.uk*
Bentley Vicarage, 3a High Street, **Bentley**, Doncaster DN5 0AA
　　　*Tel: 01302 872240*
St Clare's House, 2 Fourlands Road, **Birmingham** B31 1EX
　　　*Tel: 0121 475 4482                      Email: birminghamssf@franciscans.org.uk*
St Matthias's Vicarage, 45 Mafeking Road, **Canning Town**, London E16 4NS
　　　*Tel: 020 7511 7848*
The Friary, 6A Stour Street, **Canterbury**, Kent CT1 2BD
　　　*Tel: 01227 479364                      Email: canterburyssf@franciscans.org.uk*
St Mary-at-the-Cross, **Glasshampton**, Shrawley, Worcestershire WR6 6TQ
　　　*Tel: 01299 896345    Fax: 01299 896083    Email: glasshamptonssf@franciscans.org.uk*
The Friary of St Francis, **Hilfield**, Dorchester, Dorset DT2 7BE
　　　*Tel: 01300 341345    Fax: 01300 341293    Email: hilfieldssf@franciscans.org.uk*
The Vicarage, **Holy Island**, Berwick-upon-Tweed, Northumberland TD15 2RX
　　　*Tel: 01289 389216                      Email: holyislandssf@franciscans.org.uk*
House of the Divine Compassion, 42 Balaam Street, **Plaistow**, London E13 8AQ
　　　*Tel: 020 7476 5189                      Email: plaistowssf@franciscans.org.uk*
10 Halcrow Street, **Stepney**, London E1 2EP
　　　*Tel: 020 7247 6233 or 020 7377 0230    Email: stepneycsf@franciscans.org.uk*

*Community History:* Petà Dunstan, *This Poor Sort: A History of the European Province of the Society of Saint Francis*, DLT, London, 1997, £19.95 + £2 p&p.

*Community Publications: franciscan*, three times a year, for which an annual subscription is £6.00 (£7.00 from January 2008). Write to the Subscriptions Secretary at Hilfield Friary. Books available from Hilfield Friary book shop include: *The Daily Office SSF*, £10.00 + £2 p&p.

*Community Wares:* Hilfield Friary shop has 'Freeland' cards & traidcraft goods.

*Guest and Retreat Facilities*

HILFIELD    The friary has eight bedrooms (one twin-bedded) for men and women guests. Individually-guided retreats are available on request. There are facilities for day guests and for groups of up to forty. The Hilfield project *(www.HilfieldProject. co.uk)*, established in 2006, is an initiative at the Friary to work for peace among people of different faiths and to care for the environment. It offers facilities in three

*Addresses for ANZ*
*Province*

*The Hermitage*
PO Box 46
*Stroud*
NSW 2425
AUSTRALIA
Tel: 2 4994 5372
Fax: 2 4994 5527
Email:
ssfstrd@bigpond.
com

*The Friary*
115 *Cornwall St*
*Annerley*
*Brisbane*
QLD 4103
AUSTRALIA
Tel: 7 3391 3915
Fax: 7 3391 3916
Email: BrDonald@
franciscan.org.au
**Website:**
www.franciscan.
org.au

*Friary of the Divine*
*Compassion*
PO Box 13-117
*Hillcrest*
*Hamilton*
AOTEOROA NEW ZEALAND
Tel: 7 856 6701
Fax: 7 856 6901
Email: friary
@franciscan.org.nz
**Website:**
www.franciscan.
org.nz

**Office Book**
*The Daily Office SSF*

self-catering houses for families and groups to meet, pray and focus on issues of justice, peace and the integrity of creation. The friary is normally closed from Sunday afternoon until Tuesday morning.

ALNMOUTH    The Friary has twelve rooms (including one twin-bedded) for men or women guests. Some conducted retreats are held each year and individually-guided retreats are available on request. The friary is closed for twenty-four hours from Sunday afternoon.

GLASSHAMPTON    The guest accommodation, available to both men and women, comprises five rooms. Groups can visit for the day, but may not exceed fifteen people. The friary is closed from noon on Mondays for twenty-four hours.

## AUSTRALIA/NEW ZEALAND PROVINCE

SSF friars went from England to Papua New Guinea in the late 1950s and the first Australian house was established in 1964. The first New Zealand house followed in 1970. In 1981, the Pacific Province was divided into two: Australia/ New Zealand and the Pacific Islands.

ALFRED BOONKONG SSF
*(Minister Provincial, assumed office 1 May 2003)*
CHRISTOPHER JOHN SSF *(Assistant Minister)*

| | | |
|---|---|---|
| Brian | Donald Campbell | Nathan-James |
| Bruce-Paul | Gabriel Maelasi | Noel-Thomas |
| Damian Kenneth | Graham | William |
| Daniel | Lionel | *Novices: 3* |

**Community Publication**
*Franciscan Angles*, New Zealand, & *Franciscan Angles*, Australia, published three times a year. To be put on the mailing list, write to the Hamilton or Brisbane address. Subscription is by donation.

**Community Wares:** Holding Crosses (Stroud and Brisbane)

**Guest and Retreat Facilities**
There is limited accommodation for short stay guests available in the Brisbane and Hamilton friaries, and the Hermitage at Stroud. Payment is by donation. The old monastery of the Clares at Stroud is also available for accommodation. For bookings tel: 2 4969 7100.

**Bishops Protector**
Rt Revd George Connor, Bishop of Dunedin
*(Protector General)*
Most Revd Roger Herft, Archbishop of Perth
*(Deputy Protector for Australia)*

*Little Portion Friary*
PO Box 399
*Mount Sinai*
NY 11766/0399
USA
Tel: 631 473 0533
Fax: 631 473 9434
Email:
mtsinaifriary@s-s-f.org

*San Damiano*
573 *Dolores Street*
*San Francisco, CA* 94110
USA
Tel: 415 861 1372
Fax: 415 861 7952
Email:
judehillssf@aol.com

*Divine Providence Friary*
*Rua Acurua* 180
*- Vila Ipojuca*
05053-000 *Sao Paulo-SP*
BRAZIL
Tel: (11) 3672 5454
Email: freicezar@
hotmail.com

Minister Provincial
Tel: 415 861 7951
Fax: 415 861 7952
Email: judehillssf
@aol.com

**Province of the
Americas Website**
www.s-s-f.org

*Office Books:*
BCP, SSF *Office Book*
& CSF *Office Book.*

*Bishop Protector:*
Rt Revd Johncy Itty,
Bishop of Oregon

## PROVINCE OF THE AMERICAS

The Province of the Americas of SSF was founded as the Order of St Francis in 1919 by Father Claude Crookston, who took the name Father Joseph. Under his leadership the community developed, based first in Wisconsin and then on Long Island, New York. The Order originally combined a monastic spirituality with a commitment to missions and evangelizing. In 1967, the OSF friars amalgamated with the Society in the UK and became the American Province of SSF.

Our lives are structured around our times together of formal prayer and the Eucharist, which give our lives a focus. Brothers engage in a wide variety of ministries: community organizing, missions, work in parishes and institutions, counselling and spiritual direction, study, the arts, serving the sick and infirm and people with AIDS, the homeless, workers in the sex industry, political work for the rights of people who are rejected by society. We come from a wide variety of backgrounds and cultural traditions. Living with each other can be difficult, but we work hard to find common ground and to communicate honestly with each other. God takes our imperfections and, in the mystery of Christ's body, makes us whole.

JUDE SSF
*(Minister Provincial , assumed office May 2005)*
CLARK BERGE SSF *(Assistant Minister)*

| | | |
|---|---|---|
| Antonio Sato | Guire | Richard Jonathan |
| Cezar | Ivanildo | Robert Hugh |
| Derek | Jon Bankert | Thomas |
| Donald Luke | Jonathan | |
| Dunstan | Leo-Anthony | *Novices:* 5 |
| | | *Postulants:* 4 |

**Obituaries**
13 Dec 06  Justus, aged 58 years, professed 30 years,
Minister Provincial 1993-2002

**Community Publication:** *The Little Chronicle,* four times a year, by donation. Write to: The Editor TLC, 573 Dolores Street, San Francisco, CA 94110, USA.

**Guest and Retreat Facilities**
There is a guest house at Little Portion Friary (Mount Sinai address), with twelve rooms, accommodating a maximum of sixteen guests. It is closed on Mondays. If there is no answer when telephoning, please leave a message on the answering machine.

*Chapter gathering of the SSF Province of the Americas*

## PACIFIC ISLANDS PROVINCE
### *Papua New Guinea Region*
LAURENCE HAUJE SSF
*(Regional Minister, Papua New Guinea Region)*

Anthony Kambuwa
Charles Iada
Clifton Henry
Dominic Ombeda
Gilson Kira
Ham Kavaja
Lester Meso

Lester Raurela
Lucas
Oswald Dumbari
Owen Paul
Philip Etobae
Robert Eric
Rodney Benunu

Selwyn Suma
Smith Tovebae
Wallace Yovero
Worrick

*Novices:* 7

### *Obituaries*
17 Dec 2006          Timothy Joseph, aged 48, professed 27 years

### *Addresses*

All Saints' Friary
Dipoturu, PO Box 78
Popondetta 241
Oro Province, PNG

Saint Margaret's Friary
Katerada, PO Box 78
Popondetta 241
Oro Province, PNG

Martyrs' House
PO Box 78
Popondetta,
Oro Province, PNG
*Tel & fax: 3297 491*

Saint Mary of the
          Angels Friary
Haruro, PO Box 78
Popondetta 241
Oro Province, PNG
*Tel: 329 7060*

Saint Francis Friary
Koke, PO Box 1103
Port Moresby, NCD
PNG
*Tel & fax: 320 1499*
*Email:*
     *ssfpng@online.net.pg*

Philip Friary
Ukaka, PO Box 22
Alotau
Milne Bay Province
PNG

## Pacific Islands Province
*Solomons Islands Region*

Athanasius Faifu SSF
*(Regional Minister, Solomon Islands Region)*

| | |
|---|---|
| Allan Lafumana | Lent Fugai |
| Andrew Manu | Luke Manitara |
| Anthony Huta Awao | Manasseh Birahu |
| Benjamin Tabugau | Martin Tawea |
| Colin | Matthew Melake |
| Comins Romano | Nathanael Gari |
| Ezekiel Kelly | Nathanael Volohi |
| Francis Christopher Saemala | Noel Niki |
| George | Patteson Kwa'ai |
| Hartman Dena | Samson Amoni |
| Hill Cliff Tahaangi | Samson Siho |
| Hilton Togara | Steven Watson Hovu |
| Hudson Filiga | Thomas Hereward Peleba |
| Isom Waisi | Wellington Hugo Maake |
| James Sou | Winston Paoni |
| John Kogudi | |
| Jonas Balugna | *Novices:* 17 |

### Addresses

Patteson House
PO Box 519
Honiara
Guadalcanal
Solomon Islands
*Tel: 22386*
*Regional Office*
   tel & fax: *25810*

St Bonaventure Friary
Kohimarama
   Theological College
PO Box 519
Honiara, Guadalcanal
Solomon Islands
*Tel: 50128*

Saint Francis Friary
PO Box 7
Auki, Malaita Province
Solomon Islands
*Tel: 40054*

San Damiano Friary
Diocese of Hanuato'o
Kira Kira
Makira Ulawa Province
Solomon Islands
*Tel: 50031*

Michael Davis Friary
PO Box 519
Honiara
Guadalcanal
Solomon Islands

La Verna Friary/
                   Little Portion
Hautambu
PO Box 519
Honiara
Guadalcanal
Solomon Islands

Holy Martyrs Friary
Luisalo
PO Box 50
Lata
Temotu Province
Solomon Islands

**Bishop Protector:** Rt Revd Richard Naramana, Bishop of Ysabel

# Society of St John the Divine

## SSJD

Founded *1887*

Cottage 252
Umdoni Retirement Village
PO Box 300
Pennington 4184, Natal
SOUTH AFRICA

Tel: 039 975 3194
Email: maryevelyn
@polka.co.za

**Prayer Time** *7.30 am*
*(7.15 am Tue)*

**Angelus & Morning Prayer**
*8.30 am*

**Midday Office & Angelus**
*12.15 pm*

**Angleus & Evening Office**
*5.00 pm*

**Compline** *8.00 pm*

**Prayer Time**
*8.30 - 9.00 pm*

**Office Book**
*An Anglican Prayer Book
1989 (South African) for
Morning & Evening Prayer.
Our own SSJD book for
Midday Office & Compline.*

**Bishop Visitor**
*Bishop Rubin Phillip,
Bishop of Natal*

The Society has never been a large community, with just sixty professions over a century, and has always worked in Natal. Originally the community ran schools and orphanages, but handed the last of its institutions to the diocese in 1968, and moved to Durban from Pietermaritzburg. In 1994, after the death of the older Sisters, the four of us who remained moved to a house that was more central in Durban.

We moved to Umdoni Retirement Village in 2003. Our involvement outside the village is limited as we now have no transport of our own. Sister Hilary is now living in Durban, working full time in the office of St Mary's church, Greyville, and she is also a lay minister and very active in the prayer ministry in the parish of St Thomas's, Durban. Because of her age, she cannot live in the retirement village with us, but does come to visit us here when possible. Her address is: c/o The Bowdens, 105, 11th Avenue, Morningside, Durban, 4001.

SISTER MARGARET ANNE SSJD
(*Sister-in-charge, assumed office May 1994*)

Sister Mary Evelyn        Sister Hilary
Sister Sophia

### Community Publication

Two newsletters are sent out each year to Oblates, Associates and Friends in about May and Advent. The Advent newsletter also goes to a much wider circle of friends.

### Community History

Sister Margaret Anne SSJD, *What the World Counts Weakness*, privately published 1987. Copies are still available from us at Umdoni Retirement Village, price R10.00.

### Community Wares

Crocheted girdles for clergy and lay ministers.

### Oblates and Associates

These are people who are linked with us and support us in prayer.
*Oblates:* There are two, non-resident, who support us in prayer. They renew their oblation annually.
*Associates:* There are over a hundred, some overseas. They have a Rule of Life and renew their promises annually.
*Friends:* There are about ninety of them, who have a simple Rule of Life, and like the Oblates and Associates meet with the Sisters quarterly, if they live in South Africa.

# Society of St John the Evangelist

## (UK)

## SSJE

*Founded 1866*

*St Edward's House*
*22 Great College Street*
*Westminster*
*London* SW1P 3QA
*UK*
Tel: 020 7222 9234
Fax: 020 7799 2641

Email *(for superior):*
frpeter@ssje.org.uk

**Website:**
www.ssje.org.uk

**Mattins**
*7.00 am (7.30 am Sun)*

**Eucharist**
*7.30 am (8.00 am Sun)*

**Terce**
*9.00 am*

**Sext**
*12 noon*

**Evensong**
*6.30 pm*

**Compline**
*9.30 pm*

*A Registered Charity*

The Society of Saint John the Evangelist is the oldest of the Anglican orders for men, out of which the North American Congregation (and others worldwide) grew. We have been at the forefront of the Religious life since then, and have pioneered a new and more flexible way into the Community for the twenty-first century. New members first of all become 'Seekers' and then take simple annual vows as 'Internal Oblates' and live alongside us for a period of years before coming into First Vows. In this way, we escape the rigidity of the old system as people these days come from a much wider background than was formerly the case.

We seek to make use of their individual God-given talents as they seek to become what our Founder, Father Benson, envisaged: mission priests and lay brothers, based on their Community and its prayer life, but proclaiming Christ to the world. So we are engaged in running quiet days and retreats, both within and outside the House, counselling and spiritual direction. We look to befriend people whose English is limited and teach then as well as helping with students from overseas. We work in liturgics and preach and run parish missions. St Edward's House is a centre for private retreats and hospitality and is used by many religious and charitable groups for meetings, prayer etc.

FATHER PETER HUCKLE SSJE
*(Superior, assumed office 7 March 2002)*
BROTHER JAMES SIMON SSJE
*(Assistant Superior and Novice Guardian)*

| | |
|---|---|
| Father Alan Bean | Father David Campbell |
| Father James Naters | Father Peter Palmer |

*Obituaries*
27 Feb 06          Brother Gerald Perkins, aged 74,
                                    professed 30 years

*The Fellowship of St John*
The Fellowship was completely revamped in 1998 and this is an on-going process. It seeks to become a group of members, lay and ordained, who, through the connection with SSJE, seek to deepen their own spiritual life through a number of simple obligations. It has its own committee and the Father Superior is the Warden.

There are members throughout the country: those in

London and the South East meet regularly in St Edward's House. The Newsletter is sent out to some five hundred subscribers and organisations every month, including people in Australia, Canada, Europe, South Africa and New Zealand, where we have a link parish.

People wanting to be associated with SSJE in this way serve a year's probation and are then admitted. Further details may be obtained from the Contacts' Officer, Brother James Simon.

### Community Publication

*Newsletter*, published monthly, editor c/o St Edward's House.
All enquiries to Brother James Simon (*Contacts Officer*). £6 per annum.

### Guest and Retreat Facilities

Three conducted retreats are held each year; and there are Quarterly Quiet Days. Individual retreatants are welcomed and there are also facilities for Quiet Days. There are nineteen single rooms.
*Email for guest master:* guestmaster@ssje.org.uk

*Most convenient time to telephone:* 9.30 am - 8.30 pm

*Bishop Visitor:* Rt Revd Dominic Walker OGS, Bishop of Monmouth

---

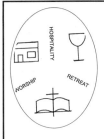

# THE COMMUNITY OF THE WORD OF GOD

In a small guest house adjoining their home, members of the Community offer hospitality to those seeking a short period of prayer, rest or study, amidst the busyness of inner-city life. They also welcome any who, loving the Word of God, would like to explore the possibility of community life.

*For further information contact:*
Secretary C. W. G., 90 Kenworthy Road, London E9 5RA

The Community of the Word of God was founded in 1972 in Hackney, E. London, where it still has its home. Members are evangelical, lay Christians who feel called by God to a shared life of prayer, hospitality and witness. They take as their pattern of life the example of the early church in the book of Acts, seeking to share the love of Jesus and to encourage each other in their work and witness. Some members follow secular occupations, others are involved in voluntary work in church or the local area while others are available to welcome those who come to the community house. They are also involved in the organisation of retreats.

# Society of St John the Evangelist

## (North American Congregation)

## SSJE

*Founded 1866*

*The Monastery*
980 *Memorial Drive*
*Cambridge, MA* 02138
*USA*

Tel: 617 876 3037
Fax: 617 876 5210
Email:
monastery@ssje.org
**Website:** www.ssje.org

*Morning Prayer* 6.00 *am*

*Eucharist* 7.45 *am*

*Midday Prayer* 12.30 *pm*

*Evening Prayer* 6.00 *pm*

*Compline* 8.30 *pm*

*Office Book*
*BCP of ECUSA,*
*and the Book of Alternate*
*Services of the Anglican*
*Church of Canada*

*Bishop Visitor*
*Rt Revd Arthur Walmsley*

The Society of St John the Evangelist was founded in the parish of Cowley in Oxford, England, by Richard Meux Benson in 1866. SSJE is the oldest Religious order for men. The presence of the Society in North America dates from 1870, when SSJE came to Boston. The brothers of the North American Congregation live at the monastery in Cambridge, Massachusetts, near Harvard Square, and at Emery House, a rural retreat sanctuary in West Newbury, Massachusetts. They gather throughout the day to pray the Divine Office, and live under a modern Rule of Life, adopted in 1997. At profession, they take vows of poverty, celibacy and obedience.

SSJE's guesthouses offer hospitality to many. Guests may come individually or attend a group retreat focused on some area of prayer and spirituality. SSJE brothers lead these retreats and programs in their own houses and throughout North America in parishes, dioceses and conference centers. SSJE brothers also serve as preachers and teachers, spiritual directors and confessors. One of the brothers, Thomas Shaw, is Bishop of Massachusetts. SSJE's publishing ministry, COWLEY PUBLICATIONS, provides books for ongoing theological exploration and spiritual formation. Several times a year, SSJE brothers serve as chaplains for pilgrimages in Israel/Palestine sponsored by St George's College, Jerusalem. In recent years, they have been leading retreats and teaching in Anglican churches and seminaries in East Africa. Nearer to home, brothers are engaged part-time in ministries to students and young adults, persons living with HIV/AIDS, the homeless, the deaf and Asian-Americans.

CURTIS ALMQUIST SSJE
*(Superior, assumed office 13 May 2001)*
GEOFFREY TRISTRAM SSJE *(Deputy Superior)*
DAVID VRYHOF SSJE *(Assistant Superior)*

Paul Wessinger
David Allen
John Oyama *(in Japan)*
Bernard Russell
Thomas Shaw
John Goldring
Jonathan Maury
Eldridge Pendleton
James Koester
John Mathis

Mark Brown
Kevin Hackett
Robert L'Esperance
Timothy Solverson
Roy Cockrum
Bruce Neal
Jude Smith

*Novices: 2*

*Associates*
The Fellowship of Saint John is composed of men and women throughout the world who desire to live their Christian life in special association with the Society of Saint John the Evangelist. They have a vital interest in the life and work of the community and support its life and ministries with their prayers, encouragement and gifts. The brothers of the Society welcome members of the Fellowship as partners in the gospel life, and pray for them by name during the Daily Office, following a regular cycle. Together they form an extended family, a company of friends    abiding in Christ and seeking to bear a united witness to him as "the Way, the Truth and the Life", following the example of the beloved Disciple. For further information, contact the Director of the Fellowship of Saint John, 980 Memorial Drive, Cambridge, MA 02138, USA.

*Other house*
Emery House, 21 Emery Lane, West Newbury,
MA 01985, USA    *Tel: 978 462 7940   Fax: 978 462 0285*

*Community History:* This is now being written.

*Community Publication*
*Cowley:* for a subscription, write to SSJE at the Cambridge, Massachusetts, address. The suggested donation is US$20 annually. This publication is also available on the community's website (www.ssje.org).

*Guest and Retreat Facilities*
**Monastery Guesthouse** in Cambridge, MA - sixteen rooms - US$75 per night/ US$40 for full-time students.
**Emery House** in West Newbury, MA - seven hermitages and four rooms - US$75 per night/ US$40 for full-time students.

COWLEY PUBLICATIONS
Books published by Cowley Publications are obtainable from:
*in the USA*
        Website: www.cowley.org

*in Canada*
Anglican Book Centre, 80 Hayden Street, Toronto, Ontario M4Y 3G2, CANADA
        *Tel: 416 924 1332   Fax: 416 924 2760*
        Website: www.anglicanbookcentre.com
*in the UK & Europe*
Columba, 55a Spruce Avenue, Blackrock, Co. Dublin, IRELAND
        *Tel: 1 294 2560     Fax: 1 294 2564*
        Website: www.columba.ie

*in Australia*
John Garratt Bookroom, 32 Glenvale Crescent, Private Bag 400, Mulgrave, Victoria 3170, AUSTRALIA    *Tel: 300 650 878    Fax: 395 453 222*
        Website: www.johngarratt.com.au

# Society of St Margaret

## (Boston)

## SSM

Founded *1855*
*(Boston Convent founded 1873)*

*St Margaret's Convent*
*17 Highland Park Street*
*Boston*
*MA 02119-1436*
*USA*

Tel: 617 445 8961
Fax: 617 445 7120
Email: ssmconvent
@ssmbos.com

**Website:**
www.ssmbos.com

*Morning Prayer*
*6.00 am*

*Eucharist  7.30 am*

*Noon Office  12 noon*

*Evening Prayer*
*5.30 pm*

*Compline  8.30 pm*

*Office Book*
*Book of Common Prayer*
*of the Episcopal Church of*
*the USA*

St Margaret's Convent, Boston, is one of four autonomous convents that comprise the Society of St Margaret founded by John Mason Neale. The American Convent was founded in 1873 to administer the Children's Hospital in Boston. Today, our mission as an Episcopal Religious community of women is to find Jesus present in worship, in the common life, and in ministries that concentrate on responding to the needs of the times. The Sisters' lives are centered on the Eucharist; from the Lord's Table we share our lives with one another at the table of the common life and go out in ministry to serve those in whom Jesus continues his incarnate life. Our houses are houses of hospitality, and all are welcome to join us for the Daily Office and the Eucharist. We also welcome individuals and groups who seek a place for retreats or private prayer time in an atmosphere of quiet, nurturing silence. Our sisters find the opportunity for mission in many places: schools, prisons, parishes, nursing homes, and homeless shelters. We value one another and our diverse ages, backgrounds, ministries and gifts.

SISTER CAROLYN SSM
*(Mother Superior, assumed office March 2002)*
SISTER ADELE MARIE SSM *(priest)  (Assistant Superior)*

| | |
|---|---|
| Sister Esther | Sister Claire Marie |
| Sister Bernardine | Sister Mary Gabriel |
| Sister Lucy Mary | Sister Adele |
| Sister Catherine | Sister Julian |
| Louise *(priest)* | Sister Christine |
| Sister Jane Margaret | Sister Marie Therese |
| Sister Rosemary | Sister Brigid |
| Sister Marjorie Raphael | Sister Elizabeth |
| Sister Marion | Sister Promise |
| Sister Mary Michael | Sister Beatrice |
| Sister Emily Louise | Sister Grace |
| Sister Mary Eleanor *(priest)* | Sister Sarah Margaret |
| Sister Gloria | Sister Kristina Frances |
| Sister Marie Margaret | |
| Sister Ann | *Novices: 2* |

**Obituaries**
16 Dec 2005        Sister Joan Margaret, aged 99,
professed 68 years

**Associates**
Associates of one Convent of the Society of St Margaret are Associates of all. They have a common Rule, which is

flexible to circumstances. They include men and women, lay and ordained. No Associate of the Society may be an Associate of any other community.

*Addresses of other houses*
St Margaret's Convent, Port-au-Prince, HAITI          *Tel: 509 222 2011*
  *Mailing address:*
St Margaret's Convent, Port-au-Prince, c/o Agape Flights, Inc., 100 Airport Avenue, Venice, FL 34285-3901, USA          *Email: mariemargaretssm@yahoo.com*

Neale House, 50 Fulton Street, New York, NY 10038-1800, USA
*Tel: 212 619 2672   Email: sisters@trinitywallstreet.org*

St Margaret's House, 47 Jordan Road, New Hartford, NY 13413-2385, USA
*Tel: 315 724 2324   Email: ssmsistersCNY@aol.com*

*A profession in the Boston Convent chapel*

**Community Publication**
*St Margaret's Quarterly.*  For information, contact the Editor at the Boston Convent. The subscription rate is $5.

**Community History**
Sister Catherine Louise SSM, *The House of my Pilgrimage: a History of the American House of the Society of Saint Margaret*, privately published, 1973.
Sister Catherine Louise SSM, *The Planting of the Lord: The History of the Society of Saint Margaret in England, Scotland & the USA;* privately published, 1995.

**Community Wares**
Haitian Gift Shop, with cards, crafts and altar linens for sale for the benefit of the Scholarship Fund for Holy Trinity School in Port-au-Prince.  Available both at the Convent in Boston and in Port-au-Prince.

*Guest and Retreat Facilities*
All our houses have facilities for guests and retreatants.  For costs and details of facilities, contact the house you are interested in.

*Bishop Visitor:* Rt Rev David Joslin, Assisting Bishop of Rhode Island

# Society of St Margaret

## (Hackney)

## SSM

Founded 1855
(St Saviour's Priory 1866)

St Saviour's Priory
18 Queensbridge Road
London E2 8NS
UK

Tel: 020 7739 9976

Email:
ssmpriory@aol.com

**Leader of the community**
020 7613 1464

**Guest Bookings**
020 7739 6775
Fax: 020 7739 1248

*(Sisters are not available on Mondays)*

**Website:** www.
stsaviourspriory.m
org.uk

St Saviour's Priory is one of the autonomous Houses which constitute the Society of St Margaret founded by John Mason Neale. Exploring contemporary ways of living the Religious life, the community seeks, through a balance of prayer and ministry, to respond to some of the needs that arise amongst the marginalised in East London. The Office is four-fold and the Eucharist is offered daily. The Sisters' outreach to the local community includes: working as staff members (lay or ordained) in various parishes; supporting issues of justice and racial equality; supporting the gay community; Sunday Stall and Drop in Centre; Dunloe Centre for the homeless and alcoholics; complementary therapy; tutoring, individual spiritual direction and retreats; dance workshops; art work and design. The Sisters also share their community building and resources of worship and space with individuals and groups.

THE REVD SISTER HELEN LODER SSM *(priest)*
*(Leader of the Community, assumed office 17 February 2001)*
THE REVD SISTER JUDITH BLACKBURN SSM *(priest)*
& SISTER MOIRA JONES SSM *(Assistant Leaders)*
Sister June Atkinson
Sister Frances (Claire) Carter
Sister Elizabeth Crawford
Sister Pauline (Mary) Hardcastle
Sister Anna Huston
Sister Enid Margaret Jealous
Sister Sue Makin
Sister Pamela Radford
Sister Mary Michael (Lilian) Stokes

*Novices: 1*

**Obituaries**

| | | |
|---|---|---|
| 8 Nov 2005 | Sister Joyce Anderson, aged 100, | professed 50 years |
| 6 Feb 2006 | Sister Marjorie Kelly, aged 77, | professed 47 years |
| 7 Feb 2007 | Sister Beatrice Follows, aged 91, | professed 54 years |

*Associates and Friends*

*Associates* make a long term commitment to the Society of St Margaret, following a Rule of Life and helping the Community where possible. An Associate of one SSM house is an Associate of all the houses. There are regular quiet days for Associates who are kept in touch with community developments.

**Morning Prayer** *7.15 am*
*(7.30 am Sun)*
*followed by*
**Eucharist**
*(12.15 pm on major feasts)*

**Midday Office**
*12.45 pm*

**Evening Prayer** *5.00 pm*

**Night Prayer** *8.30 pm*

**Office Book**
*Celebrating Common Prayer*

**Bishop Visitor**
*Rt Revd Dominic Walker*
*OGS, Bishop of Monmouth*

**Registered Charity:**
No 230927

*Friends of St Saviour's Priory* commit themselves to a year of mutual support and friendship and are invited to regular events throughout the year.

**Community Publication:** *The Orient,* yearly.   Write to The Orient Secretary at St Saviour's Priory.   Brochures about the Community are available at any time on request.

**Community Wares:**   Traidcraft, South American Toybox, cards, books and religious items for sale.

**Community History**
*Memories of a Sister of S. Saviour's Priory,* Mowbray, 1904.
*A Hundred Years in Haggerston,* published by St Saviour's Priory, 1966.
*(Both now out of print, but available for loan from St Saviour's Priory.)*
Sister Catherine Louise SSM, *The Planting of the Lord: The History of the Society of Saint Margaret in England, Scotland & the USA;* privately published, 1995.

**Guest and Retreat Facilities**
Six single rooms for individual guests.   Excellent facilities for non-residential group meetings.

**Most convenient time to telephone:** 10.30 am - 1.00 pm (Not Mondays).

---

# Society of St Margaret
## (Uckfield)
## SSM

*Founded 1855*

*St Margaret's Convent*
*Hooke Hall*
*250 High Street*
*Uckfield*
*East Sussex*
TN22 1EN
UK
Tel: 01825 766808

The Convent at Hooke Hall is one of the autonomous Houses which constitute the Society of St Margaret, founded by John Mason Neale.  The Sisters' work is the worship of God, expressed in their life of prayer and service.  They welcome visitors as guests and retreatants, and are involved in spiritual direction and parish work.  At Chiswick they care for elderly women in a nursing home and have guests.   There is a semi-autonomous house and a branch house in Sri Lanka.

MOTHER CYNTHIA CLARE SSM
*(Mother Superior, assumed office 2 March 2000)*
SISTER MARY PAUL SSM *(Assistant Superior)*

Sister Raphael Mary
Sister Mary Michael
Sister Rita Margaret
Sister Eleanor
Sister Jennifer Anne

Sister Lucy
Sister Barbara
Sister Elizabeth
Sister Sarah

**Obituaries**
17 Feb 2006  Sr Rosamond, aged 90, professed 63 years

Email: egmotherssm
@hotmail.com

*Matins* 7.15 *am*
(7.30 *am Sun & Wed*)

*Eucharist* 8.00 *am*
(9.30 *am Sun &* 11 *am*
*Wed in the parish church*)

*Midday Office &*
*Litany of the Holy Name*
12.30 *pm*

*Vespers*
5.00 *pm* (4.45 *pm Sun*)

*Compline* 8.00 *pm*

*Office Book*
'A Community Office'
printed for St Margaret's
Convent, East Grinstead

*Bishop Visitor*
Rt Revd John Hind,
Bishop of Chichester

*Registered Charity:*
No. 231926

St Margaret's Convent
157 St Michael's Road
Polwatte
Colombo 3
SRI LANKA

*Bishop Visitor*
Rt Revd Duleep de
Chickera,
Bishop of Colombo

## Associates

Associates observe a simple Rule, share in the life of prayer and dedication of the community, and are welcomed at all SSM convents.

*Other address:* St Mary's Convent & Nursing Home Burlington Lane, Chiswick, London W4 2QF, UK
*Tel: 020 8 994 4641          Fax: 020 8995 9796*

### Community Publication

*St Margaret's Chronicle,* Newsletter three times a year. Write to the Editor at St Margaret's Convent. £2.00 per annum, including postage and packing.

### Community History

Sister Catherine Louise SSM, *The Planting of the Lord: The History of the Society of Saint Margaret in England, Scotland & the USA;* privately published, 1995.

Pamela Myers, *Building for the future: A Nursing History 1896 to 1996 to commemorate the centenary of St Mary's Convent and Nursing Home, Chiswick,* St Mary's Convent, Chiswick, 1996.

*Doing the Impossible: a short sketch of St Margaret's Convent, East Grinstead 1855-1980,* privately published, 1984. Postscript 2000.

### Guest and Retreat Facilities

There are six beds, primarily for individual retreats. Day retreatants are welcome both as individuals and in groups of up to twelve people. Some Sisters are available for support in these retreats. Donations appreciated.

*Most convenient time to telephone:*
10.00 am - 12 noon, 7.00 pm - 8.00 pm.

### SEMI-AUTONOMOUS HOUSES OVERSEAS

The Sisters run a Retreat House, a Hostel for young women, a Home for elderly people, and are involved in parish work and church embroidery.

SISTER CHANDRANI SSM
*(Sister Superior, assumed office 2006)*
Sister Lucy Agnes
Sister Jane Margaret
Sister Mary Christine

*Novices:* 1

### Other address

A children's home:
St John's Home, 133 Galle Road, Moratuwa, SRI LANKA

# Society of St Margaret

## (Walsingham)

## SSM

*Founded 1855*
*(Walsingham Priory founded 1955)*

*The Priory of Our Lady*
*Bridewell Street*
*Walsingham*
*Norfolk NR22 6ED*
*UK*
Tel: 01328 820340
*(Revd Mother)*
Tel: 01328 820901
*(Sisters & guests)*

**Readings**
**& Morning Prayer**
*7.00 am (6.30 am Thu)*

**Mass**
*9.30 am (7.10 am Thu)*
*(No Mass on Sun in Sisters' Chapel)*

**Midday Prayer**
*12.45 pm*

**Evening Prayer** *5.00 pm*

**Night Prayer** *8.45 pm*

**Office Book**
*The Divine Office*

**Registered Charity**
*No . 25515*

In January 1994, the Priory of Our Lady at Walsingham reverted to being an autonomous house of the Society of St Margaret. The Sisters are a Traditional Community whose daily life is centred on the Eucharist and the daily Office, from which flows their growing involvement in the ministry of healing, and reconciliation in the Shrine, the local parishes and the wider Church. They welcome guests for short periods of rest, relaxation and retreat, and are available to pilgrims and visitors. They also work in the Sacristy, the Shrine Shop and the Education Department of the Shrine.

MOTHER MARY CLARE SSM
*(Revd Mother, assumed office 18 April 2006)*

| | |
|---|---|
| Sister Mary Teresa | Sister Wendy Renate |
| Sister Joan Michael | Sister Phyllis |
| Sister Christina Mary | Sister Mary Joan |
| Sister Alma Mary | Sister Jane Louise |
| Sister Columba | Sister Carolyne Joseph |
| Sister Francis Anne | |

*Emails:*
Revd Mother: mothermaryclare@ssmargaret.com
Bursar: alma@walsingham.f9.co.uk

*Obituaries*
8 Apr 2007      Sister Mary Kathleen, aged 80,
professed 50 years

*Associates*
There are Associates, and Affiliated Parishes and Groups.

*Community Publication*
Community booklet, *Wellspring*, published annually in the autumn. Write to the Priory for information. £3.50, including postage.

*Community History*
Sister Catherine Louise SSM, *The Planting of the Lord: The History of the Society of Saint Margaret in England, Scotland & the USA*; privately published, 1995.

*Community Wares*      Cards (re-cycled) and embroidered; books; Breviary and Missal markers; Religious objects (statues, pictures, rosary purses etc).

*Guest and Retreat Facilities*
St Margaret's Cottage, (self-catering) for women and men,

families and small groups. One single room (bed sit, ensuite) on the ground floor, suitable for a retreatant, and three twin rooms upstairs.

*Most convenient time to telephone:*
10.30 am - 12.30 pm; 2.30 pm - 4.30 pm; 6.30 pm - 8.30 pm.

*Bishop Visitor:* Rt Revd Peter Wheatley, Bishop of Edmonton

# Society of St Paul SSP

*Founded 1958*

2728 *Sixth Avenue*
*San Diego*
*CA* 92103-6397
*USA*

Tel: 619 542 8660
Email:
anbssp@earthlink.net

*Office Book*
*Book of Common Prayer*
*of the*
*Episcopal Church of the*
*USA*

*Bishop Visitor*
*Rt Revd*
*James R Mathes,*
*Bishop of San Diego*

The Society of St Paul began in Gresham, Oregon in 1958. Early ministry included nursing homes, a school, and commissary work in the Mid-East and Africa. In 1959, SSP was the first community for men to be recognized by the canons of the Episcopal Church in the United States. The brothers live a life of prayer and are dedicated to works of mercy, charity and evangelism.

In 1976, the order moved its mother house and the novitiate of the monastery to Palm Desert, California, providing facilities for a retreat and conference center until 1996.

In 2001, the brothers moved to St Paul's Cathedral in San Diego. In particular, we are involved at St Paul's Senior Homes and Services, the Uptown Faith Community Services, Inc., Dorcas House, a foster home for children whose parents are in prison in Tijuana, Mexico, and St Paul's Cathedral ministries.

THE REVD CANON BARNABAS HUNT SSP
(*Rector, assumed office 1989*)
THE REVD CANON ANDREW RANK SSP (*Associate Rector*)

*Fellowship of St Paul*
The Fellowship of St Paul, our extended family, is an association of Friends, Associates and Companions of the Society of St Paul, who live a Rule of Life centered on the Glory of God. Fellowship members support the Society and one another with their love, prayers and commitment. Fellowship members reflect the spirit of the Society of St Paul wherever they may be.

*Community Publication*
*St Paul's Printer.* Subscription is by donation. Contact The Revd Canon Barnabas Hunt at the San Diego address.

# Society of the Sisters of Bethany

## SSB

*Founded 1866*

7 Nelson Road
Southsea
Hampshire  PO5 2AR
UK
Tel: 02392 833498

Email: ssb@
sistersofbethany.
org.uk

**Website:** www.
sistersofbethany.
org.uk

**Mattins** *7.00 am*

**Mass** *7.45 am*
*(8.00 am Sun; 9.30 am
Wed & alternate Sats)*

**Terce** *9.15 am*

**Midday Office** *12.00 noon*

**Vespers** *5.00 pm*

**Compline** *8.00 pm*

**Office Book**
*Anglican Office book with
adaptations*

By prayer and activity, the Sisters seek to share in the work of reconciling the divided Churches of Christendom and the whole world. At the heart of each Sister's vocation is a call to prayer. Praying in the Spirit which unites us all to Christ and in Christ, for the wholeness of broken humanity, for the integrity of creation, for the peace of the world and for the Kingdom of God.

The Community prays daily for the unity of Christians. The intention of the Eucharist every Thursday is for Unity and is followed by their Office for Unity. On Fridays a three-hour Prayer Watch is kept in Chapel, and in addition each Sister has her own special intentions.

Each Sister makes the offering of herself in the hidden life of prayer within the Community, in the belief that God desires and accepts that offering. They are encouraged to persevere by some words of Abbé Paul Couturier with which he concluded one of his letters to the Community: "In Christ let us pray, pray, pray for Unity."

By simplicity of life-style, the Sisters try to identify with those for whom they share in Christ's work of intercession in the power of the Holy Spirit. The work of the Sisters includes giving hospitality for those seeking spiritual or physical refreshment and arranging retreats and quiet days. Some Sisters also give spiritual direction, lead quiet days and help in parishes. From time to time they are engaged in missions and cathedral chaplaincy work.

The Community motto is: 'Silentium et Spes' - In Quietness and Confidence - Let us pray to the Lord [Isaiah 30:15].

MOTHER GWENYTH SSB
*(Reverend Mother, assumed office 1 November 1994)*
SISTER MARY JOY SSB *(Assistant Superior)*
SISTER RITA-ELIZABETH SSB *(Novice Guardian)*

| | |
|---|---|
| Sister Margaret Faith | Sister Ann Patricia |
| Sister Christina Mary | Sister Constance Mary |
| Sister Katherine Maryel | Sister Joanna Elizabeth |
| Sister Ruth Etheldreda | *Postulants: 1* |
| Sister Florence May | |

### Associates

The Associates are a body of close friends who unite their life of prayer to that of the Community and who are accepted as members of an extended Community family. They live in their own homes and accept a simple rule of life which is the expression of a shared concern to love and serve God and one another after the example of Martha, Mary and Lazarus.

*Community Wares:* Cards.

*Community Publication:* Associates' magazine, July and December

*Guest and Retreat Facilities*: Four guest rooms (1 twin-bedded).
Individual retreatants can be accommodated.  Closed at Christmas.

*Most convenient time to telephone:* 9.30 am - 11.45 am, 1 pm - 4 pm, 6 pm - 7.45 pm

*Bishop Visitor:* Rt Revd Dr Kenneth Stevenson, Bishop of Portsmouth

*Registered Charity:* No. 226582

---

# *Some other Religious Communities in the Anglican Communion*

## AFRICA

**Community of the Blessed Lady Mary**        **(CBLM)**
  Shearly Cripps Children's Home, PB600E, Harare, ZIMBABWE

**Community of the Divine Compassion**        **(CDC)**
  Post Box 214, Nyanga, ZIMBABWE

**Community of St Paul**                       **(CSP)**
  Maciene, MOZAMBIQUE

**Little Sisters in Jesus**                    **(LSIJ)**
  PO Box 840119, Fiwila Mission Station, Mkushi, ZAMBIA    *Tel: 02 641125*

## ASIA

**Korean Franciscan Sisterhood**              **(KFS)**
  Box 1003, Gumi Post Office, Gumi, Gyeongbukdo 730-600,
  REPUBLIC OF KOREA    *Tel: (054) 451 2317*    *Email koreanfs@hotmail.com*

**Sisters of St Francis**                      **(SSF)**
  206 Eoamri, Miwonmyeon, Cheongwongun, Chungcheonbukdo 363-872,
  REPUBLIC OF KOREA    *Tel: (043) 225 6856*

## AUSTRALASIA AND THE PACIFIC

**Congregation of the Sisters of the Visitation of Our Lady (CVL)**
Convent of the Visitation, Hetune, Box 18 , Popondetta, Oro Province, PAPUA NEW GUINEA

## EUROPE

**Society of the Franciscan Servants of Jesus and Mary (FSJM)**
  Posbury St Francis, Crediton, Devon EX17 3QG, UK

**Society of Our Lady of the Isles**          **(SOLI)**
Lark's Hame, Aithness, Isle of Fetlar, Shetland ZE2 9DJ, UK    *Tel: 01957 733303*
St Mahri's Hame, Browland, Bridge of Walls, Shetland ZE2 9NR, UK

*Tel: 01595 809323*

## NORTH AMERICA & THE CARIBBEAN

**Community of St Mary** *(Southern Province)*           **(CSM)**
St Mary's Convent, 1100 St Mary's Lane, Sewanee, TN 37375 2614, USA
*Tel & Fax: 931 598 0059*      *Email: stmarys@sewanee.edu*
St Mary's Convent, 5608 Monte Vista, Los Angeles, CA 90042, USA
*Tel: 323 256 5337*

**Order of St Anne**                                      **(OSA)**
Convent of St Anne, 1125 North LaSalle Boulevard, Chicago, IL 60610-2601, USA
*Tel: 312 642 3638*

**Order of the Teachers of the Children of God**          **(TCG)**
5870 East 14th Street, Tucson, AZ 85711, USA
*Tel: 520 747 5280     Fax: 520 747 5236     Email: smltcg@aol.com*
Tuller School, Tuller Road, Fairfield, CT 06430, USA
*Tel: 203 374 3636*
Tuller School at Maycroft, PO Box 1991, Sag Harbor, NY 11963, USA
*Tel: 516 725 1121*

**Society of Our Lady St Mary**                           **(SLSM)**
Bethany Place, PO Box 762, Digby, Nova Scotia BOV 1AO, CANADA

---

## SINGLE CONSECRATED LIFE

O ne of the earliest ways of living the Religious life is for single people to take a vow of consecrated celibacy and to live in their own homes. This ancient form of commitment is also a contemporary one with people once again embracing this form of Religious life. Some may have an active ministry whilst others follow a contemplative lifestyle.

In 2002, the Advisory Council (for Religious communities in the Church of England) set up a Personal Vows group in response to enquiries from bishops and others to advise those who wish to take a vow of consecrated celibacy. The Sub Group now provides support for those who have professed this vow and arranges an annual gathering. In the Roman Catholic Church, this form of living the consecrated life was affirmed by Vatican II, which re-established the order of consecrated Virgins (OCV) and now an order of Widows is also emerging.

People exploring this call should be single, mature Christians (men or women) already committed to a life of prayer and willing to undertake a period of discernment before taking a temporary vow which may precede a life vow. An appropriate spiritual director and support from a Religious community or through the single consecrated life network is important to ensure adequate formation.

The vow is received by a person's bishop. The bishop (or his appointee) becomes the 'guardian of the vow' and the act of consecration is registered with the Advisory Council. Further information may be obtained from this address: *The Single Consecrated Life,* c/o St John's House, 652 Alum Rock Road, Birmingham B8 3NS.

# *Directory of dispersed Communities*

In this section are communities that from their foundation have lived as dispersed communities. In other words, their members do not necessarily live a common life in community, although they do come together for chapter meetings and other occasions each year.

Like traditional communities, they do take vows that include celibacy.

# Oratory of the Good Shepherd

## OGS

Founded *1913*

Website: www.ogs.net

*Bishop Visitor*
*Rt Revd Jack Nicholls,*
*Bishop of Sheffield*

The Oratory of the Good Shepherd is a society of priests and laymen founded at Cambridge (UK), which now has provinces in North America, Australia, Southern Africa and Europe.

Oratorians are bound together by a common Rule and discipline; members do not generally live together in community. The brethren are grouped in 'colleges' and meet regularly for prayer and support, and each province meets annually for retreat and chapter. Every three years, the General Chapter meets, presided over by the Superior of the whole Oratory, whose responsibility is to maintain the unity of the provinces.

Consecration of life in the Oratory has the twin purpose of fostering the individual brother's personal search for God in union with his brethren, and as a sign of the Kingdom. So through the apostolic work of the brethren, the Oratory seeks to make a contribution to the life and witness of the whole Church.

In common with traditional communities, the Oratory requires celibacy. Brothers are accountable to their brethren for their spending and are expected to live simply and with generosity. The ideal spiritual pattern includes daily Eucharist, Offices, and an hour of prayer. Study is also regarded as important in the life. During the time of probation which lasts one or two years, the new brother is cared for and nurtured in the Oratory life by another brother of his College. The brother may then, with the consent of the province, make his first profession, which is renewed annually for at least five years, though with the hope of intention and perseverance for life. After five years, profession can be made for a longer period, and after ten years a brother may, with the consent of the whole Oratory, make his profession for life.

### Companions and Associates
The Oratory has an extended family of Companions, with their own rule of life, and Associates. Companionship is open to men and women, lay or ordained, married or single.

### Community History
George Tibbatts, *The Oratory of the Good Shepherd: The First Seventy-five Years,* The Almoner OGS, Windsor, 1988.

### Obituaries
| | |
|---|---|
| 27 Apr 2006 | Brian Oman, aged 91, professed 67 years |
| 21 Oct 2006 | Henry Hill, *(bishop)*, aged 84, professed 15 years |

CARLSON GERDAU OGS
*(Superior, assumed office August 2005)*
Apt 19 A/N, 60 Sutton Place South, New York, NY 10022, USA
*Tel: 212 421 6942     Email: cgerdau@ogs.net*

*The Community in Australia*
TREVOR BULLED OGS   *(Provincial, assumed office 2002)*
Holy Trinity Rectory, Box 1220, Fortitude Valley, Brisbane,
Queensland 4006, AUSTRALIA
*Email: tbulled@ogs.net*

| | | |
|---|---|---|
| Michael Boyle | Barry Greaves | Kenneth Mason |
| Robert Braun | Charles Helms | Geoffrey Tisdall |
| Michael Chiplin | Ronald Henderson | Richard Waddell |
| Keith Dean-Jones | Roger Kelly | *Probationers: 0* |

*The Community in North America*
PHILIP HOBSON OGS   *(Provincial, assumed office August 2005)*
151 Glenlake Ave, Toronto, Ontario, M6P 1E8, CANADA
*Tel: 416 604 4438   Email: phobson@ogs.net*

| | | |
|---|---|---|
| David Brinton | Robert MacSwain | |
| Gregory Bufkin | Wally Raymond | *Probationers: 1* |
| William Derby | Edward Simonton | |

*The Community in Southern Africa*
THAMI SHANGI OGS   *(Provincial, assumed office 1999)*
Po Box 54890, Umlazi 4031, SOUTH AFRICA
*Tel: 031 908 1066   Email: tshange@ogs.net*

| | | |
|---|---|---|
| David Bailey | Thanda Ngcobo | John Salt |
| Siboniso Bhengu | Christopher Powell | Mark Vandeyar |
| Thami Masekani | Barry Roberts | *Probationers: 1* |

*The Community in Europe*
PETER FORD OGS   *(Provincial, assumed office April 2005)*
The Vicarage, Church Road, Warton, Preston PR4 1BD, UK
*Tel: 01772 632 227   Email: pford@ogs.net*

| | | |
|---|---|---|
| Peter Baldwin | Peter Hibbert | John Ruston |
| Michael Bartlett | David Johnson | John Thorold |
| Alexander Bennett | David Jowitt | Lindsay Urwin |
| Michael Bootes | Malcolm King | Dominic Walker |
| Michael Bullock | Brian Lee | |
| Nicholas Gandy | Michael Longstaffe | *Probationers: 1* |

# *Directory of*
## *(mainly non-celibate)*
# *acknowledged*
# *Communities*

In this section are communities that are 'acknowledged' by the Church as living out a valid Christian witness, but whose members do not all take traditional Religious vows. These communities include members who are married, and the specific vows they take will vary according to their own Rule.

Some are linked to communities listed in section 1, others were founded without ties to traditional celibate orders.

In the Episcopal Church of the USA, they are referred to in the canons as 'Religious communities' as distinct from those in section 1, which are referred to as 'Religious orders'. However, this distinction is not used in other parts of the Anglican Communion where 'communities' is also used for those who take traditional vows.

There are an estimated 3,500 members of acknowledged communities in the Anglican Communion.

# Brotherhood of Saint Gregory

## BSG

*Founded 1969*

*Brotherhood
of Saint Gregory
PO Box 57
White Plains
NY 10602
USA*

Email: Servant
@gregorians.org

Website:
www.gregorians.org

*Office Book
The Book of Common
Prayer (1979)*

The Brotherhood of Saint Gregory was founded on Holy Cross Day 1969, by Richard Thomas Biernacki, after consultation with many Episcopal and Roman Catholic Religious. The first brothers made their profession of vows in the New York monastery of the Visitation Sisters. Later that year, Bishop Horace Donegan of New York recognized the Brotherhood as a Religious Community of the Episcopal Church.

The community is open to clergy and laity, without regard to marital status. Gregorian Friars follow a common Rule, living individually, in small groups, or with their families, supporting themselves and the community through secular or church-related employment.

The Rule requires the Holy Eucharist, the four Offices of the Book of Common Prayer, meditation, theological study, Embertide reports, the tithe, and participation in Annual Convocation and Chapter.

The postulancy program takes a minimum of one year; novitiate at least two years, after which a novice may make first profession of annual vows. Members are eligible for life profession after five years in annual vows.

Gregorian Friars minister in parishes as liturgists, musicians, clergy, artists, visitors to the sick, administrators, sextons, and teachers. A number serve the diocesan and national church. For those in secular work the 'servant theme' continues, and many are teachers, nurses, or administrators.

### Community Publications
The Brotherhood produces a quarterly newsletter titled *The Servant*. Subscription is US$8.00 per year. An order blank is available by mail or via our website.

### Community Wares
There are a number of Brotherhood publications - please write or visit our website for further details regarding placing an order.

*Associates*
There are currently one hundred and fifty-two associates of the Brotherhood. Please write or visit our website for further information.

### Bishop Visitor
Rt Revd Rodney R Michel,
                    Suffragan Bishop of Long Island, retired

BROTHER RICHARD THOMAS BIERNACKI, BSG
*(Minister General and founder, assumed office 14 September 1969)*

Brother James Teets
Brother Luke Antony Nowicki
Brother William Francis Jones
Brother Stephen Storen
Brother Tobias Stanislas Haller *(priest)*
Brother Edward Munro *(deacon)*
Brother Donovan Aidan Bowley
Brother Christopher Stephen Jenks
Brother Ciarán Anthony DellaFera
Brother Damian-Curtis Kellum
Brother Richard John Lorino
Brother Ronald Augustine Fox
Brother Maurice John Grove
Brother Charles Edward LeClerc
*(deacon)*
Brother Virgilio Fortuna
Brother Gordon John Stanley *(deacon)*
Brother Karekin Madteos Yarian
Brother William David Everett

Brother Thomas Bushnell
Brother Thomas Mark Liotta *(deacon)*
Brother James Mahoney
Brother Robert James McLaughlin
Brother Peter Budde
Brother John Henry Ernestine
Brother Francis Sebastian Medina
Brother Aelred Bernard Dean
Brother Joseph Basil Gauss
Brother Mark Andrew Jones
Brother Emmanuel Williamson *(priest)*
Brother Richard Matthias
Brother William Henry Benefield
Brother Nathanael Deward Rahm
Brother Thomas Lawrence Greer
Brother Enoch John Valentine
Brother Ron Fender

*Novices: 3*
*Postulants: 2*

**Obituaries**

| | |
|---|---|
| 20 Jul 2005 | Brother Patrick Ignatius Dickson, aged 67, professed 6 years |
| 15 Sep 2006 | Brother Edward Riley, aged 65, professed 17 years |
| 23 Oct 2006 | Brother Charles Kramer, aged 71, professed 22 years |

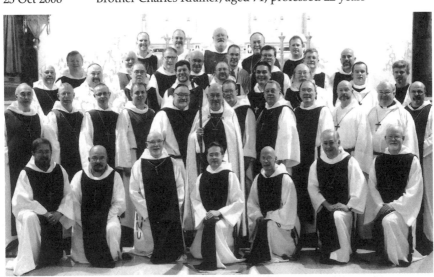

*Brotherhood of Saint Gregory*

## (Society of the) Community of Celebration

## SCC

*Founded 1973*

809 *Franklin Avenue*
*Aliquippa*
PA 15001-3302,
USA
Tel: 724 375 1510
Fax: 724 375 1138
Email: mail@
communityof
celebration.com
Website:
communityof
celebration.com

*Morning Prayer  8.00 am*

*Noonday Prayer  12.30 pm*

*Evening Prayer  5.30 pm*

*Compline  9.00 pm*

*Conventual Eucharist is
celebrated on Saturday
evenings, and saints' days
as applicable.  Monthly
service Taizé worship.*

*Office Book*
*Book of Common Prayer*

**Bishop Visitor:** *Rt Revd C.
Christopher Epting*

The Community of Celebration is a contemporary residential community whose roots stretch back to the renewal of the Church of the Redeemer, Houston, Texas, in the 1960s.  Today the Community resides in Aliquippa (near Pittsburgh), Pennsylvania.

Members are women and men, single and married, adults and children, lay and ordained.  Following the Rule of St Benedict, members live a rhythm of prayer, work, study, and recreation.

Our ministry is to be a Christian presence among the poor, responding to the needs around us by offering safe, afforsARCYBdable housing; wellness programs to women in the county jail; serving with neighborhood organizations concerned with the revitalization of Aliquippa, and providing hospitality, retreats, sabbaticals, and conferences.  We provide various chaplaincies, supply clergy, liturgical consultants, worship leadership and speakers for conferences.

BILL FARRA
*(Primary Guardian, assumed office 1995)*
MAY McKEOWN *(Guardian for Vocations)*

| | |
|---|---|
| Mimi Farra | Joe Beckey |
| Revd Steven McKeown | Revd Phil Bradshaw |
| James von Minden | Margaret Bradshaw |

*Associates*
Companions of the Community of Celebration follow the Rule of Life for companions.

*Other address:* Celebration UK Branch house, c/o Revd Phil Bradshaw, 35 Cavendish Road, Redhill, Surrey RH1 4AL, UK

*Community Publication*
*News from Celebration* - twice a year.  Contact Bill Farra for a free subscription.

*Community Wares:* Music and worship resources, psalms, anthems, books and recordings - see website store.

*Guest Facilities*
We offer a chapel, meeting and dining spaces, and overnight accommodation for 13-17 people (one guest-house can be self-catering for 4-5 people).  We welcome individual retreatants and groups, men and women.  For further information contact celebration's hospitality director by mail, telephone or email.
*Most convenient time to telephone:*
                9.00 am - 5.00 pm Eastern Time (Mon-Fri)

# Community of St Denys CSD

*Founded 1879*

St Denys Retreat Centre
2/3 Church Street
Warminster BA12 8PG
UK

Tel: 01985 214824
*(Warden of the Retreat House)*

Email:
stdenys.ivyhouse
@btopenworld.com

Website:
www.ivyhouse.org

*(Contact for Sisters only)*
Revd Sister Frances Anne
Flat 7
St Nicholas Hospital
St Nicholas Road
Salisbury SP1 2SW
UK
Tel: 01722 339761

**Office Book**
Celebrating Common Prayer
& Common Worship

**Bishop Visitor**
Rt Revd David Stancliffe,
Bishop of Salisbury

A Registered Charity.

The Community was founded in 1879 for mission work at home and overseas. We now fulfil our calling as a dispersed community engaged in parish work, spiritual guidance, retreat work, and hospital chaplaincy. CSD's members include Sisters, and men and women committed to a Rule of Life. The revised constitution has been recognised by the Advisory Council, and the community is now an 'acknowledged community' (10 June 2004).

The Sisters live in individual accommodation. All enquiries should be sent to the Leader c/o the Retreat House or the deputy leader at her Salisbury address.

REVD CANON ALAN GILL *(priest associate CSD)*
*(Leader, assumed office 9 October 2005)*
MRS JUNE WATT *(Oblate CSD) (Deputy Leader)*
57 Archers Court, Castle St, Salisbury SP1 3WE, UK

Committed members: 40
*among whom the celibate professed sisters are:*

Sister Carol Ham
Sister Gladys Henbest
Sister Margaret
Mary Powell

Sister Phyllis Urwin
Sister Frances Anne
Cocker *(priest)*
Sister Elizabeth Mary
Noller *(priest)*
Sister Theresa
*(temporary vows)*

## Fellowship
CSD has a fellowship (i.e. friends).

## Community Publication
Annual *Newsletter* and quarterly prayer leaflet. Write to the Secretary of the S. Denys Fellowship, 2/3 Church St, Warminster, Wiltshire BA12 8PG, UK. The suggested donation is £5.00 per annum.

## Community History
*CSD: The Life & Work of St Denys', Warminster to 1979*, published by CSD, 1979.

## Guest and Retreat Facilities
ST DENYS RETREAT CENTRE is available for various types of retreat and parish conferences. Guests are also welcome. It has twenty-two rooms, six of which are double. The Centre is closed at Christmas. The Members lead Quiet days, Individually-Guided Retreats and traditional preached Retreats, both in Warminster and elsewhere. Apply to the Retreat Secretary for further details.

# Companions of St Luke

-

# Benedictine

*Founded 1992*

*Abbey of St Benedict*
*2288 220th Street*
*Donnellson*
*Iowa 52625*
*USA*

Tel: 319 837 8421
Email:
AbMichael-John@
holythoughts.org

Website: www.
holythoughts.org

**Matins**
*7.00 am*

**Mass**
*11.00 am*

**Noonday Prayer**
*12 noon*

**Vespers**
*5.00 pm*

**Compline**
*8.00 pm*

**Bishop Visitor**
*Rt Revd Dean Wolfe,*
*Episcopal Diocesan*
*of Kansas*

The Companions of St Luke is a Benedictine community founded on the Rule of St Benedict incorporating both traditional and contemporary aspects of Religious life. The Companions of St Luke is a community who honours the rich tradition and wisdom that has been passed down to us through the ages, yet knows that if Religious life is to prosper into the 21st century that it must be open to the movement of the Holy Spirit and the windows of opportunity that it might bring. The Companions are a hybrid reflecting the best of what 'Orders and Christian communities' offer.

The Companions of St Luke is about making choices. Members are given choices of living at the Abbey or living their life in mission in the larger community. Members may choose to follow the traditional model of living as a single person or in a married state, both requiring a chaste life. The Community is a blend of male and female.

Vowed members take vows of: obedience, conversion of life, and stability; Oblates take corresponding promises of the same.

Michael-John Austin was consecrated Abbot at Conception Abbey (Roman), Missouri, in 2004. Since then, the Abbot Primate of the Roman Catholic Church has invited Michael-John to participate in the gathering of the Abbots of the Americas, representing Anglican tradition. Michael-John is also a member of the National Association of Episcopal Christian Communities.

MICHAEL-JOHN AUSTIN
*(Abbot, founder 1992)*

Br Thomas Ferrell          Sr Claire Benedicta Myers
Br Christopher-John        Br Nathan-Gregory Miller
                 Baumann   Br Paul of the Desert
Br Raymond Owens           Br Camillus Converse
Br Matthias Smith          Br Augustine Colvert
Br Gabriel Hale            Sr Vincent-Marie
Sr Monica-Ruth Mullen                 Rittenhouse
Br Chad-Anselm Gerns       Br David-Vincent Cotton
Br Anthony-Bernard         Sr Cecilia Lamoy
                 Campos    *Novices: 6*
Sr Anna-Grace Madden       *Postulants: 3*
Sr Catherine Unterseher

### Oblates and Companions
The Companions of St Luke has an Oblate program. Oblates are considered by this community to have a 'full and authentic' vocation deserving its own formation.

Oblates sit with their vowed counterparts in the Office, have voice and seat in Chapter.

The Companions of St Luke also offers a 'Companion Associate' affiliation. These are individuals who desire to be affiliated with the Community and grow in their own understanding of what it means to live an intentional life grounded in baptism.

### Office Book

The Office Prayer Book. This prayer book is unique to the charism of the community and incorporates part of the Rule of St Benedict, as well as antiphons taken from the Gospel of Luke and Acts. The prayer book also includes the Eucharist, Rite II setting from the BCP.

### Community Publication

The Community has a quarterly newsletter called 'The Bridge'. This may be mailed, or downloaded from the website: www.holythoughts.org.

### Guest and Retreat Facilities

The Abbey of St Benedict has a small guest house able to host five individuals, male and female. We are in the process of developing funding for a much larger facility.

### Most convenient time to telephone

The Abbey welcomes calls at all times. If someone is not near the phone, an answering system will take the message.

# Company of Mission Priests

## CMP

Founded 1940

**Website:**
www.
missionpriests.org

*Warden's address:*
*99 Hilfield Avenue*
*Crouch End*
*London N8 7DG*

*Email: fathertimpike*
*@hotmail.com*

**Office Book**
*The Divine Office*
*(Vincentian calendar)*

**Community Publication**
*Occasional Newsletter*

**Associates**
*Laymen closely associated*
*with the Company in life*
*and work may be*
*admitted as Associates of*
*the Company.*

**Bishop Visitor:**
*Rt Revd Lindsay Urwin*
*OGS,*
*Bishop of Horsham*

The Company of Mission Priests is a dispersed community of male priests of the Anglican Communion who, wishing to consecrate themselves wholly to the Church's mission, keep themselves free from the attachments of marriage and the family, and endeavour to strengthen and encourage each other by mutual prayer and fellowship, sharing the vision of Saint Vincent de Paul of a priesthood dedicated to service, and living in a manner prescribed by our Constitution, and with a Vincentian rule of life. For many years the company, although serving also in Guyana and Madagascar, was best known for its work in staffing 'needy' parishes in England with two, three, or more priests who lived together in a clergy house. Although this is rarely possible nowadays, because of the shortage of priests, we encourage our members who work in proximity to meet as often as practicable in order to maintain some elements of common life. The whole company meets in General Chapter once a year, and the Regional Chapters more frequently.

We were among the founding members, in AD 2000, of the Vincentian Millennium partnership, which works 'in accordance with the principles established by St Vincent de Paul, to support and empower those who are poor, oppressed, or excluded.

FATHER TIMOTHY PIKE CMP
*(Warden, assumed office 2005)*

| | |
|---|---|
| Michael Whitehead | Mark McIntyre |
| Anthony Yates | Alan Watson |
| Allan Buik | Simon Atkinson |
| Brian Godsell | Peter Bostock |
| John Cuthbert | Kevin Northover |
| Peter Brown | Peter Bolton |
| Beresford Skelton | Alan Parkinson |
| Michael Shields | Jonathan Kester |
| David Beater | Robert Martin |
| Michael Gobbett | Christopher Buckley |
| John Vile | Kevin Palmer |
| Ian Rutherford | Antony Homer |
| Andrew Collins Jones | Philip Meadows |
| James Geen | Andrew Welsby |
| Robert Page | Derek Lloyd |
| Colin Patterson | Anthony Moore |
| Philip North | |
| Mark Elliott Smith | *Probationers: 1* |
| | *Aspirants: 1* |

# Little Sisters of Saint Clare

## LSSC

Founded 2002

Mother Guardian
Dorothy-Anne Kiest,
LSSC
19412 - 48th Avenue
West #206
Lynnwood, WA 98036
USA
Tel: 425 775 5072
Email: dkiest
@eartlink.net

Website: www.
stclarelittlesisters.org

Tovi Andrews,
Comp/LSSC
25732 Pioneer Way NW
Poulsbo, WA 98370
USA
Secretary:
Tel: 360 779 2610

**Prayer Time**
First Saturday of the
month
12 noon - 4.30 pm

**Office Books**
BCP, CCP,
Lesser Feasts & Fasts

**Episcopal Visitor**
Rt Revd Sanford Z K
Hampton, retd

Our primary mission is the same as that of other Franciscan orders: To make our Lord known and loved through the land. Secondly, it is our desire to bring the contemplative spirituality of St Clare out of the cloister and into our churches, being grounded in the roots of the past, while finding wings for the future.

We take seriously the original call to St Francis as he was praying before the cross in the ruins of the little church of San Damiano in Italy. In that spirit and with the greater freedom and equality between men and women of this age, we encourage one another to work in our respective churches, according to our individual abilities. We strive always to be mindful of our vocation to contemplative life and intercessory prayer, carefully maintaining the difficult balance between secular and religious life.

SISTER DOROTHY-ANNE KIEST, LSSC
*(Mother Guardian, assumed office October 2006)*
ABBESS GLORIA-MARY GOLLER, PCLS

| LSSC Sisters: | |
|---|---|
| Jeanne-Marie Williamson | Mary-Agnes Staples |
| Marion-Hilda Lofgren | Mary-Frances Yanagihara |
| Marie-Elise Trailov | Mary-Louise Sulonen |

Tovi Andrews, Companion LSSC

| Associates LSSC: | |
|---|---|
| Joan Lindall | Patricia Roberts |
| Rev Dr Sandra Bochonok | Marie McAnally |
| Kathryn Little | Laura Carroll |

### Associates

The Ecumenical associate membership is open to women both clergy and laity, who seek an active affiliation with the little sisters of St Clare. They take their life of prayer seriously and feel the need to be helped in their commitment by an accountability which is one of the features of a rule as established by a religious order. They also desire to be associated with then life and work of the Sisters, whether through prayer or through active involvement. Associates will want to support the Little Sisters of St Clare through prayer and alms as they may be able. Associates may attend our meetings but if, for matters of health or distance, may be unable to attend regular meetings. If two or more Associates live in one area, they may be recognized as a fellowship, getting together to pray and observe whatever part of the rule is practical for them, at least monthly. The Sisters in turn pledge their support and hospitality whenever possible.

# Order of the Community of the Paraclete

## OCP

*Founded 1971*

PO Box 61399
*Seattle*
*WA 98141*
*USA*

*Website: www.
theparacletians.org*

*To contact the minister:*
*Br Marvin Taylor OCP*
206 467 0281
brmarvintaylor@
hotmail.com

*Monthly gathering at*
*St George's Episcopal*
*Church,*
*2212 NE 125th Street,*
*Seattle, WA*

*Eucharist, meal, study*
*and fellowship, every third*
*Saturday*
*5.30 pm - 9.00 pm*

The Community of the Paraclete is an apostolic community offering an authentic Religious life of prayer and service. We were recognized by the Episcopal Church in 1992. The Paracletians are self-supporting women and men, lay and ordained, who have committed themselves to live under the Paracletian Rule and constitution. Our vision: We are a network of Paracletian communities learning how to grow spiritually and exercising our gifts in ministry.

BROTHER MARVIN TAYLOR
*(Minister, assumed office May 2006)*
REVD SISTER JOAN ENG *(Vice-Minister)*

Sister Suzanne Chambers
Sister Suzanne Forbes
Revd Dr George Gray Jr
Brother Carle Griffin
Sister Barrie Gyllenswan
Sister Patricia Ann Harrison
Brother John Ryan
Sister Martha Simpson

*Novices: 3*

**Obituaries**
21 Jan 2006     Brother Maurice Poirier, aged 59,
                member since 2002,
                first annual vows June, 2005

**Associates**
FRIEND: any baptized Christian, with the approval of
                                            chapter
ASSOCIATE: confirmed Episcopalian, active member of an Episcopal parish, or church in communion with the Episcopal Church or the Episcopal See of Canterbury; six months' attendance at local chapter, and the approval of chapter.

**Community Publication**
*Paracletian Presence*, distributed free

**Office Book**
Book of Common Prayer

**Bishop Visitor**
Rt Revd Nedi Rivera, suffragan Bishop of Olympia

# The Third Order, Society of Saint Francis

## TSSF

The Third Order of the Society of Saint Francis consists of men and women, ordained and lay, married or single, who believe that God is calling them to live out their Franciscan vocation in the world, living in their own homes and doing their own jobs. Living under a rule of life, with the help of a spiritual director, members (called tertiaries) encourage one another in living and witnessing to Christ. The Third Order is worldwide, with a Minister General and five Ministers Provincial to cover the relevant Provinces.

THE REVEREND DOROTHY BROOKER TSSF
*(Minister General, assumed office September 2005)*
16 Downing Avenue, Pirimai, Napier,
Aoteoroa-New Zealand
*Tel: 7 345 6006      Email: dmbrook@clear.co.nz*

THE VENERABLE RICHARD BIRD TSSF
*(Assistant Minister General)*

*Founded*
*1920s (Americas)*
*1930s (Europe)*
*1975 (Africa)*
*1959 (Australia)*
*1962*
*(Aoteoroa-New Zealand)*

### Statistics for the whole community

|             | Professed | Novices |
|-------------|-----------|---------|
| Americas    | 433       | 40      |
| Europe      | 1769      | 260     |
| Australia   | 265       | 83      |
| Africa      | 105       | 18      |
| NZ-Aoteoroa | 164       | 44      |
| **Total**   | **2736**  | **445** |

## PROVINCE OF THE AMERICAS

*Office Book*
Third Order Manual
The Manual includes a
form of daily prayer called
'The Community Obedience'.
Members are encouraged to
use this in the context of
Morning or Evening Prayer.

KENNETH E NORIAN TSSF *(Minister Provincial)*
45 Malone Street, Hicksville, NY 11801, USA
*Tel: +1 917 416 9579      Email: ken@tssf.org*
*Website of Province:* www.tssf.org

### Statistics of Province
*Professed: 433; Novices: 40; Postulants: 22*
*Deaths since the last Year Book: 7*

**Associates of the Society of Saint Francis:** Welcomes men, women, lay, clergy, married, single, young and old, to join us as Associates in our diverse Franciscan family.

*Bishop Protector General*
Rt Revd George Connor,
Bishop of Dunedin,
Aoteoroa - New Zealand

**Bishop Protector:** Rt Revd Gordon P Scruton,
Bishop of Western Massachusetts

### Provincial Publication
*The Franciscan Times*; Subscription contact: Caroline Benjamin, 8417 Highway 16 N, Bandera, Texas 78003, USA No Subscription cost - free will offering appreciated.

# EUROPEAN PROVINCE

THE VENERABLE RICHARD BIRD TSSF *(Minister Provincial)*
32 Bristol Road, Bury St Edmunds, Suffolk IP33 2DL, UK
*Tel: +44 1284 723810      Email: ministertssf@franciscans.org.uk*

Alex Calverley TSSF *(Administrator)*
St Peter's Vicarage, St Peter's Road, Birkdale, Southport PR8 4BY, UK
*Email: calveley@btclick.com*
*Website of Province:* www.tssf.org.uk

*Statistics of Province: Professed:* 1760; *Novices:* 260

**Provincial Publication**
*The Chronicle (twice yearly)          Third Order News (quarterly)*
Both available on our website.   Contact: Alan Williams TSSF, Communications
Coordinator      *Email: williams.a.r@btopenworld.com*

**Bishop Protector:** Right Revd Michael Perham, Bishop of Gloucester

# AUSTRALIAN PROVINCE

REVD TED WITHAM TSSF *(Minister Provincial)*
30A Milroy Street, Willagee, WESTERN AUSTRALIA 6156
*Tel: +8 9337 7045     Email: provincial.minister@tssf.org.au*
*Website of Province:* www.tssf.org.au

*Statistics of Province*:     *Professed:* 265; *Novices:* 83
*Deaths since last Year Book:* Effie Fitzpatrick, professed 15 years

**Provincial Publication**
*Quarterly Newsletter -*
      Available on request from the editor: Bill Gates TSSF   *Email: wgates@ix.net.au*

**Bishop Protector:** Most Revd Roger Herft, Archbishop of Perth

# AFRICAN PROVINCE

REVD DAVID BERTRAM TSSF *(Minister Provincial)*
82 Biccard Street, Polokwane 0699, SOUTH AFRICA
*Tel: +27 15 297 4650   Email: polo.dave@yahoo.com*

***Statistics of Province***
*Professed:* 105
  Central Region: 17; Northern Region: 19; Southern Region: 62; Western Region: 7
*Novices:* 18
  Central Region: 2; Northern Region: 8; Southern Region: 5; Western Region: 3
*Postulants:* 24
            Northern Region: 18; Southern Region: 6

*Deaths since last Year Book:* Thabani Mthiyane

*Provincial Publication*
*Pax et Bonum* (published three times a year)
Available free of charge from the Provincial Publications Officer:
Alan Rogers TSSF    *Email: AlanR@mcgind.co.za*
or the Newsletter Editor:
Neil Heslip  *Email: nheslip@medunsa.ac.za*

*Associates*
The African Province includes a small number of Companions who are associated with, and pray for, the First Order, but are in the Third Order address list. The Secretary of the Companions is:
Mrs Joyce Gunston, 2 Swannack Gardens, Vonkehouse, Lourensford Road, Somerset West 7130, SOUTH AFRICA        *Tel: 021 21 852 1830*

*Bishop Protector:* The Right Reverend Merwyn Castle, Bishop of False Bay

# NEW ZEALAND PROVINCE

REVD JOHN HEBENTON TSSF *(Minister Provincial)*
15 Farm Street, Mt. Maunganui, NEW ZEALAND
*Tel: 07 575 9930 (home); 07 574 0079 (work); 021679202 (mobile)*
*Fax: 07 574 0079*
*Email: jbheb@clear.net.nz  or  aynf.tp@clear.net.nz*

*Website of Province:* www.franciscanthirdorder.godzone.net.nz

*Statistics of Province:*

| | | |
|---|---|---|
| *Professed:* | New Zealand: 93 | Melanesia: 71 |
| *Novices:* | New Zealand: 10 | Melanesia: 34 |
| *Postulants:* | New Zealand: 5 | Melanesia: 14 |

*Deaths since the last Year Book:* 8

*Provincial Publication:*
*TAU;* Available from the Provincial Secretary: Anne Moody *Email: anne@ix.net.nz*

*Community History*
Both these are booklets:
Chris Barfoot, *Beginnings of the Third Order in New Zealand 1956-74*
Chris Barfoot, *Peace and Joy,*
        *Part 2 of the History of the Third Order, Society of St Francis in New Zealand*

*Bishops Protector*
The Right Reverend George Connor, Bishop of Dunedin
The Right Reverend Richard Naramana, Bishop of Ysabel *(for Melanesia)*

# The Worker Sisters and Brothers of the Holy Spirit

# WSHS & WBHS

*Founded 1972 in the Diocese of West Missouri (Sisters) & 1979 Brothers, and the community expanded to Canada*

*Contact address:*
Sr Catherine Marie WSHS
Executive Director
1125 Prescott Lane
Crystal Lake
Illinois 60014
USA
Tel: 1 815 455 0347
Fax: 1 815 455 0796

Email:
sr.catherine.marie@
gmail.com

Website: www.
workersisters.org
&
www.
workerbrothers.org

*Office Book*
Book of Common Prayer

The Worker Sisters and Brothers of the Holy Spirit is a Covenant Community which seeks to respond to God's call through the power of the Holy Spirit, participate in Jesus Christ's vision of unity, become his holy people, show forth Fruit, and in obedience to his command, go forth into the world. It offers women and men, regardless of marital status, a path for individual spiritual growth through a life commitment to a Rule which provides an opportunity to experience prayer, worship, becoming, discovery, belonging, relating, commitment and mission. Membership is made up of:
First Order: Sisters - Lay Workers and Lay Sisters;
Second Order: Brothers - Lay Workers and Lay Brothers;
Third Order: Clergy Sisters and Clergy Brothers;
Companions: Lay and Clergy Persons;
Friends: Lay and Clergy Persons
The first three Orders are bound together under a Life Commitment to a common Rule which is Benedictine in orientation. Companions make a Life commitment to a Rule of Life. Friends share in the prayer and spiritual journey of the community. Members do not live together, yet are not separated by geographical boundaries.

SISTER CATHERINE MARIE WSHS
*(Executive Director, assumed office April 2006)*
SISTER HELEN JOSEPH WSHS *(Canadian Director)*
SISTER JOANNA WSHS *(American Director)*
*Members: 147*
*Postulants: 6*

**Other Address**
Sister Pam Raphael WSHS, Director of Admissions, PO Box 658, St Helena Island, South Carolina 29920, USA

**Obituaries**
29 Sep 2005  Brother William, professed 22 years
20 Oct 2005  Brother Walter Benedict, professed 23 years
28 Nov 2005 Sister Ruth Jonah, professed 23 years
11 Feb 2006  Sister Velma Francis, professed 29 years
28 Aug 2006 Sister Cyndy Ambrose, professed 23 years

*Community Ecclesiastical Visitors*
CANADA, AUSTRALIA: Rt Revd Ron Ferris, Friend WSHS/ WBHS - Diocese of Algoma, Ontario, Canada
UNITED STATES, HAITI: Rt Revd Barry Howe, Friend WSHS/ WBHS - Diocese of West Missouri, USA

# OBITUARIES

# Dame RoseMary Francis Breeze OSB
## (1913-2005)
## Abbess of Edgware 1981-1993

Harriet Elizabether Breeze was born on 28 April 1913 into a farming family in Montgomery. Brought up in a devout Welsh Presbyterian household, the Scriptures became the bedrock of her life. After working on the farm until she was twenty-three, Harriet achieved her ambition to be a nurse, adding midwifery, children's nursing and orthopedics to her general training. In her first awareness of God's call, she had a great longing to serve on the mission in India, but later, after being received into the Anglican Church, she realized that she wished to enter the Religious life and so entered Edgware Abbey in 1945.

Dame Rosemary's nursing expertise was put to good use in the care of the sick and disabled women and children, one of the Community's principal works. In particular, she will be remembered for her periods of office as Abbess, Prioress, Novice Guardian and Infirmarian. She had a down-to-earth spirituality, combined with a deep devotion to the Passion of Our Lord. She had a large heart, a broad mind, a pure vision and an adventurous spirit, which kept thinking ahead. Under her care and encouragement, ecumenical relations developed and participation in inter-religious dialogue increased, for she considered it to be a necessary part of the Benedictine ethos. Dame RoseMary was an astute business woman and a compassionate friend, mother and counsellor to many. Her lasting tribute is the building of Henry Nihill House in 1991 to further the care work of the Community and where she herself spent her last days. After a long, progressive illness, she died in the early evening of 29 April 2005. May she rest in peace and rise in glory.

# Sister Thirza CSM&AA
## (1902-2005)

Sister Thirza was born in England but went out to South Africa as a very small child with her parents. She had a non-Conformist background, but became an Anglican when she felt the call to be a Sister. Confirmed privately by the Bishop of Johannesburg, she became first a missionary in Nigeria and qualified as a midwife, before entering the Community of St Michael & All Angels, being finally professed on 14 June 1954.

Small in stature, she nevertheless had plenty of energy and courage. She loved children and animals, belonging to animal welfare societies. She was also a keen

gardener. So she spent her Religious life in helping out at the schoolchildren's hostels, supervising the garden boy in the grounds, and being busy with odd jobs. She was very outspoken, but people understood her and found her fun.

In her last years, she had to be cared for in an Old Age Home, as she lost both her sight and her hearing. The nurses there loved her for her concern for them and for her unexpected and funny remarks. She died peacefully one cold morning aged 103. One of the last photographs taken of her, when she was 101, shows her sitting as she preferred out-of-doors, wearing her cricket hat to ward off the sun.

## *Dame Teresa Mary Hastie OSB (1914-2006)*

A Christ's Hospital scholar, links with her old school were strong throughout Mavis Hastie's life, including hilarious reunions at the Convent. A civil servant in Kent during the Second World War, she became free to join the Community at Edgware Abbey at its conclusion, being professed in 1948.

One thing we can be sure of in Religious life is that we never know what jobs we will be given, the flip side being that we also acquire undreamed of skills. Sister Teresa certainly did that. She was a pianist, but learned to play the organ. She loved singing and it was her sorrow that she could not play the organ and sing at the same time. The Community, however, still sings the antiphons and psalm tones that she composed.

As a novice, Sister Teresa learned to be a good bedside nurse in the wards, sharing in the Community's work of caring for many physically disabled women and girls. She also did book-keeping and accounts, staff wages, and endless letter writing. There were not many jobs Sister did not do!

In later years, she suffered from arthritis and had to have three hip operations. A series of minor strokes reduced her mobility but she continued to take a full part in the Divine Office. Early in 2004, she was moved into the Community's Nursing Home for care. Would she be alright? We need not have worried. From the first day, she won all hearts, taking on a new lease of life. She had always been fun loving, with an engaging smile, a deep chortle and a naughty sense of humour. All this came to life again, and singing too: she joined in with any singing, her voice as tuneful as ever. Even in her last illness, through laboured breathing, she sang with us in hospital till the very day before she died at the age of ninety-two.

Preaching at her clothing, Dom Benedict Ley urged her to "seek first the kingdom of God; to co-operate fully with the holy will of God, in its continuous making and creating of us." In her total dedication and faithful living out of her long Religious life, Sister Teresa did simply this, failing at times as we all do, but persevering unto death. She was greatly loved and is sorely missed.

## *Sister Mary Ruth Brewster CSM&AA (1905-2006)    Reverend Mother 1965-87*

Born and educated in England, Mary Brewster taught classes to Arabic-speaking girls in Palestine for four years after her degree in history, before moving to South Africa in 1932. She taught in the school for a while before joining the Community of St Michael & All Angels, in which she was finally professed on 29 February 1936.

Sister Mary Ruth served as superior from 1965 to 1987. On her retirement, she began work on the archives of the Community and its school, and wrote five booklets and various aspects of the Sisters work over more than hundred years. As the number of sisters was reduced and the Community faced the end of its earthly ministry, Mary Ruth took over again in 2002 as 'sister-in-charge', following the death of her successor, Sister Doreen Mary.

She celebrated her hundredth birthday on 12 May 2005 with a helicopter ride over Bloemfontein. She claimed to have no 'secret' for her longevity, only that she kept herself 'interested in all that goes on in my surroundings.' In February 2006, she kept her Platinum Jubilee of profession. She died peacefully in the early hours of 10 August 2006.

# Brother Justus SSF
# (1948-2006)
## Minister Provincial 1993-2002

Born in Staunton, Virginia, on 6 October 1948, Justus graduated from West Virginia Wesleyan in 1970, majoring in Theater and Theatrical Lighting. He then served in Vietnam as an interpreter. In 1973, he went to test his vocation at Little Portion Friary at Mt Sinai on Long Island, NY, and was professed in SSF in 1976 as Brother Justus Richard and life professed three years later.

After studying at Union Theological Theological Seminary, he was ordained in May 1986 to the Vocational Diaconate. Subsequently, he served as a deacon in half a dozen parishes in New York and San Francisco, and offered a wide variety of ministries, including hospital and campus chaplaincies. Notably, he was a presence at Ground Zero every Tuesday from 3-11pm from 9/11 until it was declared closed.

He served as Assistant Minister from 1982 and Minister Provincial of the Province of the Americas from 1993 to 2002. Leadership was something he exercised with both efficiency and compassion, and in which he gave of himself generously. He was elected into such roles outside the Society too. For a decade he participated in the leadership of the North American Association for the Diaconate and was its President 1995-98. He also served a term as President of CORL (now CAROA), the organization representing Religious in the Episcopal Church and the Anglican

Church of Canada. At the time of his death SSF brothers worldwide were poised to elect him as their Minister General.

In his last three years, he served as a Missionary of the Domestic & Foreign Missionary Society in Papua New Guinea, and at the time of his death was the Principal (Dean) of Newton Anglican Theological College in Popondetta. On a trip into a remote part of the country, he developed respiratory problems. His companions heroically began to carry him through the bush to reach medical care. On the way, however, he tragically died of cardiac failure. He was only 58.

He will be much missed by his family, his Franciscan brothers and sisters, and by many who came to value his reassuring presence, his humour and his love.

# Brother Geoffrey SSF (1921-2007)
## Minister General 1970-85

Educated at Shaftesbury and then Christ's College, Cambridge, Brother Geoffrey first encountered the SSF brothers at university. Having served a curacy in Weymouth, he tried his vocation as a Franciscan in 1948. Professed in 1950, he led the project in Plaistow to rebuild St Philip's Church and was noted as an evangelist. A postcard in 1958 from the Minister saying simply 'You are for New Guinea' was how he learned he would lead SSF's first overseas foundation.

He led a team of four friars to the Pacific and was the driving force in establishing houses throughout the region. From New Guinea, he pioneered work in Australia, and later New Zealand and the Solomons. Made Deputy Minister in the Pacific region in 1965, he became its first Minister Provincial when it gained full autonomy. In 1970, he was elected Minister General of the whole Society, a post he held for fifteen years, travelling throughout the world to many cultures and encouraging friars in a host of ministries. On retirement, for twelve years he helped an emerging community in Zimbabwe, until the burden of years meant, to his dismay, that he had to return to Britain.

He was one of the most significant brothers in SSF's expansion and one of its outstanding leaders. He died on 11 April 2007, just short of his 86th birthday.

# *Organizations*

# AFRICA

# Council for the Religious Life
## (in Southern Africa)

All Religious communities in the Church of the Province of Southern Africa come under the Council for the Religious Life. The superiors of all communities are members. The officers of the executive are:

The Rt Revd Merwyn Castle
The Most Revd Njongonkulu Ndungane, Archbishop of Cape Town *(ex officio)*
Sister Thandi CJC *(Chair)*
Sister Erika OHP *(Vice-Chair)*
Father Mark Vandeyar OGS *(Bursar)*
Mrs V M Rogers TSSF *(Secretary)*

# AUSTRALIA

# Advisory Council for Anglican Religious Life in Australia

The Council consists of:

Rt Revd Graeme Rutherford, Assistant Bishop of Newcastle *(chair)*
Rt Revd Godfrey Fryar, Bishop of North Queensland
Revd Michael Jobling, Diocese of Melbourne
Ann Skamp, Diocese of Grafton

| | | |
|---|---|---|
| Brother Robin BSB | Sr Josephine Margaret CHN | Sister Patricia SI |
| Mother Rita Mary CCK | Brother Wayne LBF | Sister Eunice SSA |
| Sister Jean CSBC | Father Trevor OGS | Br Alfred Boonkong SSF |
| Sister Linda Mary CSC | Abbot Michael King OSB | Father Matthew SSM |

*Observers from New Zealand:*
Mother Keleni CSN
Sister Anne SLG
Most Revd David Moxon, Bishop of Waikato *(liaison bishop)*

*Secretary of the Council:* Sister Linda Mary CSC      *Email: lindacsc@ausnet.net.au*

# EUROPE

## Advisory Council on the Relations of Bishops & Religious Communities
### (commonly called 'The Advisory Council')

Rt Revd Jack Nicholls, Bishop of Sheffield (*Chair*)
Rt Revd Graham James, Bishop of Norwich
Rt Revd Michael Lewis, Bishop of Middleton
Rt Revd David Walker, Bishop of Dudley
Rt Revd Andrew Burnham, Bishop of Ebbsfleet (*co-opted*)
Rt Revd Dominic Walker OGS, Bishop of Monmouth (*co-opted*)

*Communities' elected representatives (elected November 2005 for five-year term):*

| | |
|---|---|
| Sister Anita CSC | Sister Mary Julian CHC |
| Mother Ann Verena CJGS | Sister Mary Stephen OSB |
| Sister Barbara Claire CSMV | Father Peter Allan CR |
| Father Colin CSWG | Sister Rosemary CHN |
| Brother Damian SSF | Abbot Stuart Burns OSB |

*ARC representative:* Sister Joyce CSF
*Roman Catholic Observer:* Sister Catherine McGovern OSF

*Pastoral Secretary:* Revd Preb Bill Scott          *Tel and fax: 020 7379 8088*
*Administrative Secretary:* Miss Jane Melrose,
      Central Secretariat, Church House, Great Smith Street, London  SW1P  3NZ
*Tel: 020 7898 1379       Fax: 020 7898 1369       Email: jane.melrose@c-of-e.org.uk*

## Conference of the Leaders of Anglican Religious Communities (CLARC)

The Conference meets in full once a year, usually in June.

### Steering Committee 2007
**(dates indicate the year that the member's elected term ends)**

| | |
|---|---|
| Sister Anita CSC (2008) | Father Jonathan Ewer SSM (2008) |
| Mother Ann Verena CJGS | Sister Joyce CSF (2009) |
| (*administrative assistant*) | Mother Monica Jane CHN (2008) |
| Sister Dorothy Stella OHP (2009) | Brother Stuart OSB (2009) |
| Mother Elizabeth CAH (2009) | |

# *Anglican Religious Communities* in England (*ARC*)

A RC supports members of Religious communities of the Church of England. Its membership is the entire body of professed members of communities recognised by the Advisory Council *(see above)*.

ARC holds an Annual Conference in the first week of September each year when members can come together both to hear speakers on topics relevant to their way of life and to meet and share experiences together. A news sheet is regularly circulated to all houses and ARC represents Anglican Religious Life on various bodies, including the Vocations Forum of the Ministry Division of the C of E, The Advisory Council and the *Year Book* editorial committee. Some limited support is also given to groups of common interest within ARC who may wish to meet. Its activities are co-ordinated by a committee with members elected from Leaders, Novice Guardians, General Synod representatives and the professed membership. The committee normally meets three times a year.

Mother Ann Verena CJGS, Father Jonathan Ewer SSM & Sister Joyce CSF
*(representing Leaders)*
Sister Elizabeth Anne CSMV *(representing General Synod representatives)*
Sister Catherine CSC *(representing Novice Guardians)*
Brother Colin Wilfred SSF, Sister Jane Louise SSM,
Sister Janet Elizabeth OHP, Sister Jocelyn OHP, Sister Pamela CAH
& Brother Steven CR
*(representing professed members)*
Sister Christine James CSF *(Administrative Secretary)*

More information about Anglican Religious Life (in England) or about ARC itself, may be obtained from: The Anglican Religious Communities Secretary, c/o Miss Jane Melrose, Church House, Great Smith Street, London SW1P 3NZ
*Email: arc@fish.co.uk*

# *General Synod of the Church of England*

*Representatives of Lay Religious*
Sister Elizabeth Anne CSMV          (Elected 2003, re-elected 2005)
Sister Anita OHP                    (Elected 2006)

*Representatives of Ordained Religious*
Revd Sister Rosemary CHN            (Elected 2002, re-elected 2005)
Revd Thomas Seville CR             (Elected 2005)

# NORTH AMERICA

# Conference of Anglican Religious Orders in the Americas (CAROA)

The purpose of CAROA is to provide opportunities for mutual support and sharing among its member communities and co-ordinate their common interests and activities, to engage in dialogue with other groups, to present a coherent understanding of the Religious Life to the Church and to speak as an advocate for the Religious Orders to the Church. CAROA is incorporated as a non-profit organization in both Canada and the USA.

Father David Bryan Hoopes OHC (*President*)
Father Gregory Fruehwirth OJN (*Vice-President*)
Mother Marguerite Mae Eamon CSC (*Secretary-Treasurer*)

The Revd Dr Donald Anderson (*General Secretary*)x
PO Box 99, Little Britain, Ontario K0M 2C0, CANADA
*Tel & Fax: 705 786 3330    Email: dwa@nexicom.net*

# House of Bishops Standing Committee on Religious Orders in the Anglican Church of Canada

The Committee usually meets twice a year, during the House of Bishops' meeting. Its rôle is consultative and supportive.

Most Revd A Bruce Stavert, Archbishop of Quebec, Metropolitan of the Ecclesiastical Province of Canada (*chair*)
Rt Revd James A J Cowan, Bishop of British Columbia
Rt Revd Ann E Tottenham, Suffragan Bishop (Credit Valley) of Toronto
Most Revd Andrew S. Hutchison, Archbishop and Primate of Canada
The Superiors of CSC, OHC, SSJD & SSJE
Revd Dr Donald W Anderson, General Secretary of CAROA
Revd Paul Feheley, Principal Secretary to the Primate (*Secretary*)

# General Synod of the Anglican Church of Canada

*Religious Synod members:*
Father Leonard Abbah OHC
Sister Elizabeth Ann Eckert SSJD

# National Association for Episcopal Christian Communities (NÆCC)

The NAECC is an inclusive association that shares and communicates the fruits of the Gospel, realized in community, with the church and the world.    It is primarily a forum for those who are living or exploring new or continuing models of religious commitment within the context of community.

Tobias Stanislas Haller BSG *(Chair)*
Masud I Syedullah TSSF *(Vice-Chair)*
Carle Griffin OCP *(Recorder)*
Bill Farra SCC *(Treasurer)*

Website: home.earthlink.net/~naecc/index.htm

# ECUMENICAL & INTER-DENOMINATIONAL

# Conference of Religious (CoR)

The Conference of Religious is open to all Roman Catholic Provincial leaders of Religious Congregations in England and Wales.    The leaders of Anglican communities may be Associate members, which, apart from voting rights, means they receive all the same benefits and information as the Roman Catholic leaders. CoR is run by an executive committee, elected from its members, which meets every two months.  It deals with matters affecting men and women Religious, and various matters of interest to them.  There is particular emphasis on peace and justice issues.

CoR Secretariat, P.O. Box 37602, The Ridgeway, London NW7 4XG
*Tel: 020 8201 1861        Fax: 020 8201 1988        Email: confrelig@aol.com*

# Association of British Contemplatives (ABC)

The Association of British Contemplatives (ABC) is constituted by the women's contemplative communities of England, Scotland and Wales, Roman Catholic and Anglican.

Mother Mary of the Holy Spirit ODC *(Chairperson)*
*Carmelite Monastery, 17 Helenslee Road, Dumbarton, Scotland G82 4AN*

# *Glossary and Indices*

# Glossary

**Aspirant**
A person who hopes to become a Religious and has been in touch with a particular community, but has not yet begun to live with them.

**Celibacy**
The commitment to remain unmarried and to refrain from sexual relationships. It is part of the vow of chastity traditionally taken by Religious. Chastity is a commitment to sexual integrity, a term applicable to fidelity in marriage as well as to celibacy in Religious Life.

**Chapter**
The council or meeting of Religious to deliberate and make decisions about the community. In some orders, this may consist of all the professed members of the community; in others, the Chapter is a group of members elected by the community as a whole to be their representatives.

**Clothing**
The ceremony in which a postulant of a community formally becomes a novice, and begins the period of formation in the mind, work and spirit of the community. It follows the initial stage of being a postulant when the prospective member first lives alongside the community. The clothing or novicing ceremony is characterised by the Religious 'receiving' the habit, or common attire, of the community.

**Contemplative**
A Religious whose life is concentrated on prayer inside the monastery or convent rather than on social work or ministry outside the house. Some communities were founded with the specific intention of leading a contemplative lifestyle together. Others may have a single member or small group living such a vocation within a larger community oriented to outside work.

**Enclosed**
This term is applied to Religious who stay within a particular convent or monastery - the 'enclosure' - to pursue more effectively a life of prayer. They would usually only leave the enclosure for medical treatment or other exceptional reasons. This rule is intended to help the enclosed Religious be more easily protected from the distractions and attentions of the outside world.

**Eremitic**
The eremitic Religious is one who lives the life of a hermit, that is, largely on his or her own. Hermits usually live singly, but may live in an eremitic community, where they meet together for prayer on some occasions during each day.

**Evangelical Counsels**
A collective name for the three vows of poverty, chastity and obedience.

**Habit**
The distinctive clothing of a community. In some communities, the habit is worn at all times, in others only at certain times or for certain activities. In some communities, the habit is rarely worn, except perhaps for formal occasions.

**Novice**
A member of a community who is in the formation stage of the Religious Life, when she or he learns the mind, work and spirit of the particular community whilst living among its members.

**Oblate**
Someone associated closely with a community, but who will be living a modified form of the Rule, which allows him or her to live outside the Religious house. Oblates are so-called because they make an oblation (or offering) of obedience to the community instead of taking the profession vows. In some communities, oblates remain celibate, in others they are allowed to be married. A few oblates live within a community house and then they are usually termed intern(al) oblates. The term oblate is more usually associated with Benedictine communities.

**Office/Daily Office/Divine Office**
The round of liturgical services of prayer and worship, which mark the rhythm of the daily routine in Religious Life. Religious communities may use the services laid down by the Church or may have their own particular Office book. The Offices may be called Morning, Midday, Evening and Night Prayer, or may be referred to by their more traditional names, such as Mattins, Lauds, Terce, Sext, None, Vespers and Compline.

**Postulant**
Someone who is in the first stage of living the Religious Life. The postulancy usually begins when the aspirant begins to live in community and ends when he or she becomes a novice and 'receives the habit'. Postulants sometimes wear a distinctive dress or else may wear secular clothes.

**Profession**
The ceremony at which a Religious makes promises (or vows) to live the Religious Life with integrity and fidelity to the Rule. The profession of these vows may be for a limited period or for life. The usual pattern is to make a 'first' or simple profession in which the vows are made to the community. After three or more years a Life Profession may be made, which is to the Church and so the vows are usually received by a bishop. In the Anglican Communion, Life Professed Religious can usually be secularized only by the Archbishop or Presiding Bishop of a Province.

**Religious**
The general term for a person living the Religious Life, whether monk, nun, friar, brother, sister etc.

**Rule**
The written text containing the principles and values by which the members of a community try to live. The Rule is not simply a set of regulations, although it may contain such, but is an attempt to capture the spirit and charism of a community in written form. Some communities follow traditional Rules, such as those of St Benedict or St Augustine, others have written their own.

**Tertiary/Third Order**
This term is usually associated with Franciscan communities, but is used by others

too. A Third Order is made up of tertiaries, people who take vows, but modified so that they are able to live in their own homes and have their own jobs. They may also marry and have children. They have a Rule of Life and are linked to other tertiaries through regular meetings. In the Franciscan family, the Third Order complements both the First Order of celibate friars and sisters and the Second Order of contemplative Religious.

**Vows**
The promises made by a Religious at profession. They may be poverty, chastity and obedience. In some communities, they are obedience, stability and conversion of life.

# *Index of Communities by Dedication or Patron Saint*

# Index by location

# Index of Community Wares & Services for Sale

# Index of Communities by Initials

# Notes and Amendments